Cambridge University Press is part of the
University of Cambridge. It is a charitable
enterprise dedicated to printing and
publishing for the advancement of knowledge
throughout the world. In recognition of the
fact that there are many parts of the world
where students have difficulty in purchasing
their own copies of the best international
textbooks, Cambridge University Press is
now publishing a series of Low Price
Editions. These are reprints of internationally
respected books from Cambridge University
Press, specially printed and priced for the
benefit of students and teachers in selected
countries.

The study of language

The study of language

An introduction

George Yule

Louisiana State University

CAMBRIDGE
UNIVERSITY PRESS

Published by the Press Syndicate of the University of Cambridge
The Pitt Building, Trumpington Street, Cambridge CB2 1RP
40 West 20th Street, New York, NY 10011–4211, USA
10 Stamford Road, Oakleigh, Victoria 3166, Australia

First published 1985
Reprinted 1986 (twice), 1987 (twice), 1988 (twice), 1989, 1990, 1991, 1993, 1994
Low price edition 1995

Printed in Great Britain at the University Press, Cambridge

Library of Congress catalogue card number: 85-5914

British Library cataloguing in publication data
Yule, George
The study of language: an introduction.
1. Language and languages
I. Title
400   P121

ISBN 0 521 49854 6 low price edition

THIS BOOK MUST NOT BE SOLD OUTSIDE
AFRICA, THE CARIBBEAN, BANGLADESH,
INDIA, NEPAL, PAKISTAN, AND SRI LANKA.

FAILURE TO OBSERVE THIS REQUIREMENT
WILL DISQUALIFY THE OFFENDING
SUPPLIER FROM FURTHER PARTICIPATION
IN THE SCHEME.

BS

Contents

Preface

In preparing this book, I have tried to present a survey of what is known about language and also of the methods employed by linguists in arriving at that knowledge. Many questions about the nature of language are still unanswered, and linguistics – often described as the scientific study of language – is a relatively new field. In fact, any individual speaker of a language has a more comprehensive 'unconscious' knowledge of how language works than any linguist has yet been able to describe. Consequently, as you read the following chapters, take a critical view of the effectiveness of the descriptions, the analyses, and the claims made, by measuring them against your own intuitions about how your language works. By the end of the book, you should feel that you do know quite a lot about both the internal structure of language (its form) and the varied uses of language in human life (its function), and also that you are ready to ask a lot of the kinds of questions that professional linguists ask.

To help you find out more about the issues covered in this book, each chapter ends with a set of further readings which will provide you with more detailed treatments than are possible in this introduction. Each chapter also has a set of Study questions and a set of Discussion topics/projects. The Study questions at the end of each chapter are presented simply as a way for you to check that you understood some of the main points or important terms introduced in that chapter. They should be answered without difficulty and an appendix of suggested answers for each Study question is provided at the end of the book. The set of Discussion topics/projects provides an opportunity to apply some of the analytic procedures presented, to consider some of the controversies which exist in the study of individual topics, and to try to focus your own opinions on different language-related issues.

The origins of this book can be traced to introductory courses on language taught at the University of Edinburgh and the University of Minnesota, and to the suggestions and criticisms of several hundred students who forced me to present what I had to say in a way they could understand. An early version of the written material was developed for Independent Study students at the University of Minnesota, whose reactions prompted other changes in the direction of what I hope is greater relevance and clarity.

Naturally, a book like this does not come about without a lot of help from friends and colleagues. I would especially like to acknowledge my debt, for suggestions and advice, to Gill and Keith Brown, Penny Carter, Feride Erkü, Diana Fritz, Kathleen Houlihan, Tom McArthur, Jim Miller, Rocky Miranda, Eric Nelson, Sandra Pinkerton, Rich Reardon, Gerald Sanders, Elaine Tarone, Michele Trufant and, for my own introductory course, Willie and Annie Yule.

Chapter 1
The origins of language

> The genesis of language is not to be sought in the prosaic, but in the poetic side of life; the source of speech is not gloomy seriousness, but merry play and youthful hilarity ... In primitive speech I hear the laughing cries of exultation when lads and lassies vied with one another to attract the attention of the other sex, when everybody sang his merriest and danced his bravest to lure a pair of eyes to throw admiring glances in his direction. Language was born in the courting days of mankind.
>
> Otto Jespersen (1921)

Jespersen's proposal that human language originated while humans were actually enjoying themselves is one of the more endearing speculations concerning the origins of language. It remains, however, a speculation. We simply do not know how language originated. We do know that spoken language developed well before written language. Yet, when we uncover traces of human life on earth dating back half a million years, we never find any direct evidence relating to the speech of our distant ancestors. There are no dusty cassette tape fragments among the ancient bones, for example, to tell us how language was back in the early stages. Perhaps because of this absence of physical evidence, there has been no shortage of speculation about the origins of human speech. In this chapter, we shall consider the merits of some of those speculations.

The divine source

According to one view, God created Adam and "whatsoever Adam called every living creature, that was the name thereof" (Genesis, 2:19). Alternatively, following a Hindu tradition, language came from the goddess Sarasvati, wife of Brahma, creator of the universe. In most religions, there appears to be a divine source who provides humans with language.

In an attempt to rediscover this original, divine language, a few experiments have been carried out, with rather conflicting results. The basic hypothesis seems to have been that, if infants were allowed to grow up without hearing any language, then they would spontaneously begin using the original God-given language. An Egyptian pharaoh named Psammetichus tried the experiment with two newborn infants around 600 B.C. After two years in the company of sheep and a mute shepherd, the children were reported to have spontaneously uttered, not an Egyptian word, but the Phrygian word *bekos*, meaning 'bread'. The children may not have picked up this 'word' from any human source, but, as several commentators have pointed out, they must have heard what the sheep were saying.

James IV of Scotland carried out a similar experiment around A.D. 1500 and the children were reported to have started speaking Hebrew. It is unfortunate that all other cases of children who have been discovered living in isolation, without coming into contact with human speech, tend not to confirm the results of either of these 'divine-source' experiments. Children living without access to human speech in their early years grow up with no language at all. (We shall consider the case of one such child later in Chapter 14.) If human language did emanate from a divine source, we have no way of reconstructing that original language, especially given the events in a city called Babel, "because the Lord did there confound the language of all the earth" (Genesis, 11:9).

The natural sounds source

A quite different view of the beginnings of human speech is based on the concept of 'natural sounds'. The suggestion is that primitive words could have been imitations of the natural sounds which early men and women heard around them. When an object flew by, making a CAW-CAW sound, the early human imitated the sound and used it to refer to the object associated with the sound. And when another flying object made a CUCKOO sound, that natural sound was adopted to refer to that object. The fact that all modern languages have some words with pronunciations which seem to 'echo' naturally occurring sounds could be used to support this theory. In English, in addition to *cuckoo*, we have *splash*, *bang*, *boom*, *rattle*, *buzz*, *hiss*, *screech*, and forms such as *bow-wow*. In fact, this type of view has been called the "bow-wow theory" of language origin. While it is true that a number of words in any language are **onomatopoeic** (echoing natural sounds), it is hard to see how most of the soundless, not to mention abstract, entities in our world could have been referred to in a language that simply echoed natural sounds. We might also be rather skeptical about a view which seems to assume that a language is only a set of words which are used as 'names' for entities.

It has also been suggested that the original sounds of language came from natural cries of emotion, such as pain, anger and joy. By this route, presumably, OUCH came to have its painful connotations. However, it has been noted that the expressive noises people make in emotional reactions contain sounds which are not otherwise used in their language, and, consequently, seem to be unlikely candidates as source-sounds.

One other 'natural sound' proposal has come to be known as the "yo-heave-ho theory". The sounds of a person involved in physical effort could be the source of our language, especially when that physical effort involved several people and had to be coordinated. So, a group of early humans might develop a set of grunts and groans and swear words which they used when lifting and carrying bits of trees or lifeless mammoths. The appeal of this theory is that it places the development of human language in some social context. Human sounds, however produced, may have had some principled use within the social life of the human group. This is an interesting idea, though still a speculation, which may relate to the use of humanly produced sounds. It does not, however, answer the question regarding the origins of the sounds produced. Apes and other primates have grunts and social calls, but they do not seem to have developed the capacity for speech.

The oral–gesture source

One suggestion regarding the origins of the sounds of language involves a link between physical gesture and orally produced sounds. It does seem reasonable that physical gesture, involving the whole body, could have been a means of indicating a wide range of emotional states and intentions. Indeed, many of our physical gestures, using body, hands and face, are a means of nonverbal communication still used by modern humans, even with their developed linguistic skills.

The "oral–gesture theory", however, proposes an extremely specific connection between physical and oral gesture. It is claimed that originally a set of physical gestures was developed as a means of communication. Then a set of oral gestures, specifically involving the mouth, developed, in which the movements of the tongue, lips and so on were recognized according to patterns of movement similar to physical gestures. You might think of the movement of the tongue (oral gesture) in a 'goodbye' message as representative of the waving of the hand or arm (physical gesture) for a similar message. This proposal, involving what was called "a specialized pantomime of the tongue and lips" by Sir Richard Paget (1930), does seem a bit outlandish now. We can, indeed, use mime or specific gestures for a variety of communicative purposes, but it is hard to visualize the actual 'oral' aspect which would mirror many such gestures. Moreover, there is an extremely large number of linguistic messages which would appear to defy transmission via this type of gesturing. As a simple experiment, try to communicate, using only gesture, the following message to another member of your species: *My uncle thinks he's invisible*. Be prepared for a certain amount of misunderstanding.

Physiological adaptation

One further speculative proposal about the origin of human speech concentrates on some of the physical aspects of humans which are not shared with other creatures, not even with other primates. These physical features are best thought of as partial adaptations which, by themselves, would not lead to speech production, but which are good clues that a creature possessing such features probably has the capacity for speech.

Human teeth are upright, not slanting outwards like those of apes, and they are roughly even in height. Such characteristics are not needed for eating, but they are extremely helpful in making sounds such as *f*, *v* and *th*. Human lips have much more intricate muscle interlacing than is found in other primates and their resulting flexibility certainly helps with sounds like *p*, *b* and *w*. The human mouth is relatively small, can be opened and closed rapidly, and contains a very flexible tongue which can be used to shape a wide variety of sounds.

The human larynx, or the 'voice box' (containing the vocal cords), differs significantly in position from that of monkeys. In the course of human physical development, the assumption of an upright posture by the human moved the head forward and the larynx lower. This created a longer cavity, called the pharynx, above the vocal cords, which can act as a resonator for any sounds produced via the larynx. One unfortunate consequence is that the position of the human larynx makes it much more possible for the human to choke on pieces of food. Monkeys may not be able to use the larynx to produce speech sounds, but they do not suffer from the problem of getting food stuck in the windpipe.

The human brain is **lateralized**, that is, it has specialized functions in each of the two hemispheres. Those functions which are analytic, such as tool-using and language, are largely confined to the left hemisphere of the brain for most humans. It may be that there is an evolutionary connection between the tool-using and language-using abilities of humans, and that both are related to the development of the human brain. Most of the other theories of the origin of speech have humans producing single noises or gestures to indicate objects in their environment. This activity may indeed have been a crucial stage in the development of language, but what it lacks is any 'manipulative' element. All languages, including sign language, require the organizing and combining of sounds or signs in specific constructions. This does seem to require a specialization of some part of the brain. (We shall return to this topic in Chapter 14.)

In the analogy with tool-using, it is not enough to be able to grasp one rock (make one sound); the human must also be able to bring another rock (other sounds) into proper contact with the first. In terms of linguistic structure, the human may have first developed the naming ability, producing a specific noise (e.g. *bEEr*) for a specific object. The crucial additional step which was then accomplished was to bring another specific noise (e.g. *gOOd*) into combination with the first to build a complex message (*bEEr gOOd*). A few hundred thousand years of evolution later, man has honed this message-building capacity to the point where, on Saturdays, watching a football game, he can drink a sustaining beverage and proclaim *This beer is good*. Other primates cannot do this.

Speech and writing

In developing speech, humans have obviously incorporated versions of naturally occurring sounds such as *cuckoo* and *ding-dong*. They have also incorporated cries of emotional reaction, such as *Wow*, *Ugh* and *Oops*, and accompany much of their speech with physical gestures such as pointing and raising of the outstretched forearm, bent at the elbow. All this noise-making and gesturing, however, seems to be characteristic of only one of the major functions of language use, which we may describe as the **interactional** function. It has to do with how humans use language to interact with each other, socially or emotionally; how they indicate friendliness, cooperation, or hostility, or annoyance, pain, or pleasure. But there is another major function of language, the **transactional** function, whereby humans use their linguistic abilities to communicate knowledge, skills and information. It is unfortunate that we tend to imagine our cave-dwelling ancestors solely as hairy, grunting, bone-chewing individuals who mugged their mates, when a lot of that grunting may actually have been in the form of messages informing the junior caveboys and girls on the best way to hold the bones while chewing. The transactional function must have developed, in part, for the transfer of knowledge from one generation to the next. This transfer function of language remains fairly restricted in time and space as long as it can only be realized in speech. By its nature, speech is transient. The desire for a more permanent record of what was known must have been the primary motivation for the development of markings and inscriptions and, eventually, of written language.

Study questions

1. What is the name given to the theory which holds that the origin of human speech comes from the sounds heard by humans in their environment?
2. What is the basic idea behind the "yo-heave-ho theory"?
3. What specific type of claim is made by the "oral–gesture theory"?
4. What special features of human teeth and lips make them useful in the production of speech sounds?
5. What are the two major functions of language, and how do they differ?

Discussion topics/projects

A. It has been claimed that the development of the young human child may offer insights into how language originally developed. Are there any parallels between the behavior of infants and the proposals presented in this chapter about the behavior of early humans which leads to language use? (If you want to do some background reading, Lenneberg, 1967, and Bickerton, 1983a, present some relevant arguments.)
B. The limitations of a purely gestural theory of language origin may be related to differences in the range of message types. Consider these two messages: *The dog is eating a chicken* and *My brother believes he's a chicken*. Which message would be easier to convey via gesture (plus primitive grunting, if required), and why?
C. Jeremy Campbell (1982:156) has written: "The idea that tool making, the technology of subsistence, was the driving force behind the evolution of intelligence and language is open to serious question." Do you too have doubts about the proposal that the evolution of language can be tied to

the evolution of tool-using skills? How does the concept of 'intelligence' fit into this discussion?
D. It has been suggested that speech is, in fact, an 'overlaid' function, employing physical attributes of the human which were developed for other, more basic, functions (e.g. breathing, eating). What evidence would you use to support or refute such a proposal?

Further reading

For a fuller introductory account of views on language origin, chapter 10 of Bolinger (1975) provides an accessible treatment. A full account of the natural sounds source can be found in Diamond (1965), and more technical accounts of physiological development are presented in Lenneberg (1967) and Lieberman (1975). On some of the more specific points, a collection of readings edited by Salus (1969) contains selections from Plato (on 'natural sounds'), Rousseau (on 'cries of emotion'), Herder (against the 'natural cries' approach), plus a translated extract from Herodotus, describing the experiment conducted by Psammetichus. The original arguments for a 'gesture theory of speech' are to be found in Paget (1930), and for the distinction between interactional and transactional functions, see Brown & Yule (1983a).

Chapter 2

The development of writing

> The writings of divines are nothing else but a preaching the gospel to the eye as the voice preacheth it to the ear. Vocal preaching hath the pre-eminence in moving the affections, and being diversified according to the state of the congregations which attend it. This way the milk cometh warmest from the breast. But books have the advantage in many other respects. You may be able to read an able preacher when you have but a mean one to hear. Preachers may be silenced or banished, when books may be at hand. Books may be kept at a smaller charge than preachers. Books are, if well chosen, domestic, present, constant, judicious, pertinent, yea and powerful sermons, and always of very great use to your salvation.
>
> Richard Baxter (1673)

When we consider the development of writing, we should bear in mind that a very large number of the languages found in the world today are only used in the spoken form. They do not have a written form. For those languages which do have writing systems, the development of writing, as we know it, is a relatively recent phenomenon. We may trace human attempts to represent information visually back to cave drawings which were made at least 20,000 years ago, or to clay tokens from about 10,000 years ago which appear to have been an early attempt at bookkeeping, but these artifacts are best described as ancient precursors of writing. Writing which is based on some type of alphabetic script can only be traced back to inscriptions dated around 3,000 years ago.

Much of the evidence used in the reconstruction of ancient writing systems comes from inscriptions on stone or tablets found in the rubble of ruined cities. Many of these inscriptions have never been deciphered. It may be that some of this evidence is not the significant documentation of great events, but is the remains of scribbles and the graffiti of the day. Yet, tracing the development of those inscriptions allows us to discover the roots of a writing tradition going back a few thousand years whereby the human has sought to create a more permanent record of what was thought and said.

Pictograms and ideograms

Cave drawings may serve to record some event (e.g. Humans 3, Buffaloes 1), but they are not usually thought of as any type of specifically linguistic message. They are normally considered as part of a tradition of pictorial art. When some of the 'pictures' came to represent particular images in a consistent way, we can begin to describe the product as a form of picture-writing, or **pictograms**. Thus, a form such as ⧻ might come to be used for the sun. An essential part of this use of a representative symbol is that everyone should use similar forms to convey roughly similar meaning. In time, this picture might take on a more fixed symbolic form, such as ⊙, and come to be used for 'heat' and 'daytime', as well as for 'sun'. This type of symbol is considered to be part of a system of idea-writing, or **ideograms**. The distinction between pictograms and ideograms is essentially a difference in the relationship between the symbol and the entity it represents. The more 'picture-like' forms are pictograms, the more abstract, derived forms are ideograms. A key property of both pictograms and ideograms is that they do not represent words or sounds in a particular language. Modern pictograms, such as those represented in the accompanying illustration, are language-independent.

It is generally thought that there are pictographic or ideographic origins for a large number of symbols which turn up in later writing systems. For example, in Egyptian hieroglyphics, the symbol ⌑ is used to refer to a house and derives from the diagrammatic representation of the floor-plan of a house. In Chinese writing, the character 川 is used for a river, and has its origins in the pictorial representation of a stream flowing between two banks. However, it should be noted that both these Egyptian and Chinese written symbols are not in fact pictures of a house or a river. There is an abstraction away from the form of the real-world entity in producing the symbol.

When the relationship between the symbol and the entity or idea becomes sufficiently abstract, we can be more confident that the symbol is being used to represent words in a language. In Egyptian writing, the ideogram for water was 〰️. Much later, the derived symbol ∿ came to be used for the actual word meaning 'water'. When symbols come to be used to represent words in a language, they are described as examples of word-writing, or **logograms**.

Logograms

A good example of logographic writing is that used by the Sumerians, in the southern part of modern Iraq, between 5,000 and 6,000 years ago. Because of the particular shapes used in their symbols, these inscriptions are more generally described as **cuneiform** writing. The term 'cuneiform' means 'wedge-shaped' and the inscriptions used by the Sumerians were produced by pressing a wedge-shaped implement into soft clay tablets, resulting in forms like ⸘⸘◁.

The form of this symbol really gives no clue to what type of entity is being referred to. The relationship between the written form and the object it represents has become arbitrary, and we have a clear example of word-writing, or a logogram. The form above can be compared with a typical pictographic representation of the same fishy entity: ⚡. We can also compare the ideogram for sun, presented earlier as ☉, with the logogram used to refer to the same entity found in cuneiform writing: ▷▷⊤.

So, by the time of the Sumerians, we have evidence that a writing system which was word-based had come into existence. In fact, it is Sumerian cuneiform inscriptions which are normally referred to when the expression "the earliest known writing system" is used.

A modern writing system which is based, to a large extent, on the use of logograms is Chinese. Many Chinese written symbols, or characters, are used as representations of the meaning of words and not of the sounds of the spoken language. One of the advantages of such a system is that two speakers of very different dialects of Chinese, who might have great difficulty understanding each other's spoken forms, can both read the same written text. The major disadvantage is that an extremely large number of different written symbols (well over 70,000) exists within this writing system. Apparently, a working knowledge of only about 5,000 characters is sufficient for reading the daily newspaper. Remembering large numbers of different word-symbols, however, does seem to present a substantial memory load, and the history of most other writing systems illustrates a development away from logographic writing. To accomplish this, some principled method is required to go from symbols which represent words to a set of symbols which represent sounds.

Rebus writing

One way of using existing symbols to represent the sounds of language is via a process known as **Rebus writing**. In this process, the symbol for one entity is taken over as the symbol for the sound of the spoken word used to refer to that entity. That symbol then comes to be used whenever that sound occurs in any words. We can create an example, working with the sound of the English word *eye*. We can imagine how the pictogram ⊕ could have developed into the logogram ○. This logogram is pronounced as *eye*, and with the Rebus principle at work, you should be able to refer to yourself as ○ ("I"), to one of your friends as + ○ ("Crosseye"), combine this form with the logogram for 'deaf' and produce "defy", with the logogram for 'boat' and produce "bow-tie", and so on. Take another, non-English, example, in which the ideogram ≋ becomes the logogram ⌣ for the word pronounced *ba* (meaning 'boat'). We can then produce a symbol for the word pronounced *baba* (meaning 'father') which would be ⌣ ⌣. What this process accomplishes is a sizeable reduction in the number of symbols needed in a writing system.

Syllabic writing

In the last example, the symbol which is used for the pronunciation of parts of a word represents a combination of a consonant and a vowel (e.g. *ba*). This combination is one type of syllable. When a writing system employs a set of symbols which represent the pronunciations of syllables, it is described as **syllabic writing**.

There are no purely syllabic writing systems in use today, but modern Japanese has a large range of single symbols which represent spoken syllables and is consequently often described as having a (partially) syllabic writing system. In the nineteenth century, an American Indian named Sequoyah invented a syllabic writing system which was used by the Cherokee Indians to produce written messages from the spoken language. In these Cherokee examples, ⊢ (*ho*), ⊔ (*sa*) and Γ (*ge*), note that the symbols do not correspond to single consonants or vowels, but to syllables.

Both the Egyptian and the Sumerian writing systems evolved to the point where some of the earlier logographic symbols were used to represent spoken syllables. However, the full use of a syllabic writing system does not appear until that used by the Phoenicians, inhabiting what is modern Lebanon, between 3,000 and 4,000 years ago. It is clear that many of the symbols which they used were taken from earlier Egyptian writing. The Egyptian form ⌷, meaning 'house', was adopted, in a slightly reoriented form, as ⊟. After being used logographically for the word pronounced *beth* (still meaning 'house'), it came to represent syllables beginning with a *b* sound. Similarly, the Egyptian form ∾, meaning 'water', turns up as ∿, and is used for syllables beginning with an *m* sound. So, a word which might be pronounced *muba* could be written as ⊟∿, and the pronunciation *bima* as ∿⊟. Note that the direction of writing is from right to left. By about 1000 B.C., the Phoenicians had stopped using logograms and had a fully developed syllabic writing system.

Alphabetic writing

If you have a set of symbols being used to represent syllables beginning with, for example, a *b* sound or an *m* sound, then you are actually very close to a situation in which the symbols can be used to represent single sound types in a language. This is, in effect, the basis of **alphabetic writing**. An alphabet is essentially a set of written symbols which each represent a single type of sound. The situation described above is generally what seems to have occurred in the origins of the writing systems of Semitic languages such as Arabic and Hebrew. The alphabets of these languages, even in their modern versions, largely consist of consonant symbols. This early form of alphabetic script, originating in the writing systems of the Phoenicians, is the general source of most other alphabets to be found in the world. A modified version can be traced to the East into Indian writing systems and to the West through Greek.

Significantly, the early Greeks took the alphabetizing process a stage further by also using separate symbols to represent the vowel sounds as distinct entities, and so a remodeled alphabet was created to include these. In fact, for many writers on the origins of the modern alphabet, it is the Greeks who should be given credit for taking the inherently syllabic system from the Phoenicians, and creating a writing system in

which the single symbol to single sound correspondence was fully realized.

From the Greeks, this revised alphabet passed to the rest of Western
Europe via the Romans and, of course, it underwent several modifica-
tions to fit the requirements of the spoken languages encountered.
Another line of development took the same Greek writing system into
Eastern Europe where Slavic languages were spoken. The modified version, called the **Cyrillic** alphabet (after St Cyril, a ninth century Christian
missionary), is the basis of the writing system used in Russia today.

The actual form of a number of the letters in modern European alphabets can be traced, as in the illustration, from their origins in Egyptian
hieroglyphics.

Egyptian	Phoenician	Early Greek	Roman
⨅	⅃	B	B
≋	⸗	⅂	M
⌣	W	⅀	S
☞	Ψ	Ж	K

Written English

If indeed the origins of the alphabetic writing system were based on
a correspondence between single symbol and single sound type, then
one might reasonably ask why there is such a frequent mismatch between
the forms of written English and the sounds of spoken English.

The answer to that question must be sought in a number of historical
influences on the form of written English. The spelling of written English

was very largely fixed in the form that was used when printing was introduced in fifteenth century England. At that time, a number of conventions regarding the written representation of words derived from forms
used in writing other languages, notably Latin and French. Moreover,
many of the early printers were native Dutch speakers and could not
make consistently accurate decisions about English pronunciations. Perhaps more important is the fact that, since the fifteenth century, the
pronunciation of spoken English has undergone substantial changes.
Thus, even if there had been a good, written-letter to speech-sound
correspondence at that time, and the printers had got it right, there
would still be major discrepancies for the present-day speakers of English. If one adds in the fact that a large number of older written English
words were actually 'recreated' by sixteenth century spelling reformers
to bring their written forms more into line with what were supposed,
sometimes erroneously, to be their Latin origins (e.g. *dette* became *debt*;
iland became *island*), then the sources of the mismatch begin to become
clear. How one goes about describing the sounds of English words in
a consistent way, when the written forms provide such unreliable clues,
is a problem we shall investigate in Chapter 5.

Study questions

1. What is the name given to the writing system used for Russian?
2. Which modern language uses a partially syllabic writing system?
3. What are the disadvantages of a logographic writing system?
4. What is the process known as Rebus writing?
5. What type of writing system would typically have the following symbols?
   - (a) ⌐ (*hu*)   (c) casa ('house')
   - (b) ⋀ ('mountain')   (d) ⫶ ('country')

Discussion topics/projects

A. It has been claimed that alphabetic writing is "the most efficient writing
   system possible" (Hughes, 1962: 124). Do you agree? What criteria are
   involved in decisions about 'efficiency'? What might Chinese and Japanese
   speakers think about this claim?
B. One point not dealt with in this chapter concerns the fact that not all the
   writing systems mentioned use the same linear direction for their scripts.
   Egyptian hieroglyphics are read in columns, for example. In Phoenician writing, like modern Arabic, the script has to be read from right to left. In
   Roman writing, like modern English, the script has to be read from left

to right. This means that there must have been a period during which the development of alphabetic writing underwent a shift from right-to-left to left-to-right. Are there any clues in the chapter as to when this probably occurred?

C. Archaeologists do not normally depend on graffiti for evidence of writing systems. Indeed, the problem with a lot of graffiti is that its interpretation is quite difficult because it depends on a great deal of specific knowledge about the immediate physical location, political issues of the time, special vocabulary, and much else. Find some examples of graffiti and consider what other knowledge, in addition to knowledge of language, is needed in order to interpret the examples.

D. An occasional outcry is heard that there should be a 'spelling reform' of the English language, and examples like *right, ocean, photograph, knock* are cited as forms which should be changed. Is spelling reform necessary? What recent changes in spelling have there been and should they be considered an improvement or not (e.g. American *color, summarize*; British *colour, summarise*)?

Further reading

An accessible introductory account of the development of writing is available in Chapter 7 of Hughes (1962). A standard textbook is Gelb (1963). Another accessible account is Ullman (1969), and a much more comprehensive work is Diringer (1968). A historical survey of the archaeological discoveries relevant to the study of writing is presented in Pedersen (1972). For an original account of the role of clay tokens in the development of writing, see Schmandt-Besserat (1978). A good facsimile edition of Egyptian writing can be found in Budge (1913). A reproduction of the full Cherokee syllabary can be found in Gleason (1961). For a discussion of spelling reform, see Robertson & Cassidy (1954). A very comprehensive, and consequently rather technical, account of the history and variety of writing systems is to be found in Jensen (1970).

Chapter 3

The properties of language

> It is a very remarkable fact that there are none so depraved and stupid, without even excepting idiots, that they cannot arrange different words together, forming of them a statement by which they make known their thoughts; while, on the other hand, there is no other animal, however perfect and fortunately circumstanced it may be, which can do the same ...
>
> René Descartes (1637)

In Chapter 1 we considered some physiological properties of the human species as prerequisites for the production of language. The physical aspects of human teeth, larynx and so on are not shared by other creatures and may explain why only the human creature has the capacity for speech. However, we did not suggest that the human was the only creature which was capable of communicating. All creatures, from apes, bees, cicadas, dolphins, through to zebras, are capable of communicating with other members of their species. The range and complexity of animal communication systems are staggering and we could not hope even to summarize their diverse properties here. What we can do, as part of an investigation of language, is concentrate on those properties which differentiate human language from all other forms of signaling and which make it a unique type of communication system.

Communicative versus informative

In order to describe those properties, we should first distinguish what are specifically **communicative** signals from those which may be unintentionally **informative** signals. A person listening to you may become informed about you via a number of signals which you have not intentionally sent. He may note that you have a cold (you sneezed), that you aren't at ease (you shifted around in your seat), that you are untidy (unbrushed hair, rumpled clothing), that you are disorganized (non-matching socks), and that you are from some other part of the country (you have a strange accent). However, when you use language to tell this person, "I would like to apply for the vacant position of senior brain surgeon at the hospital," you are normally considered to be intentionally communicating something. By the same token, the blackbird is not normally taken to be communicating anything by having black feathers, perching on a branch and eating a worm, but is considered to be sending a communicative signal with the loud squawking to be heard when a cat appears on the scene. So, when we consider the distinctions between human language and animal communication, we are considering both in terms of their potential as a means of intentional communication.

Unique properties

There have been a number of attempts to determine the defining properties of human language and different lists of features can be found. We shall take six of these features and describe how they are manifested in human language. We shall also try to describe in what ways these features are uniquely a part of human language and unlikely to be found in the communication systems of other creatures. We should remain aware, however, that our view of how other creatures communicate is essentially an outsider's view and may be inaccurate. It is possible that your pet has quite complex communication with other members of its species and frequently comments on how hard it is to get points across to the lumbering bipeds who act as if they know it all. Bearing that caveat in mind, we can now consider some of the properties which the bipeds believe are unique to their linguistic system.

Displacement

When your pet cat comes home after spending a night in the back alleys and stands at your feet calling *meow*, you are likely to understand this message as relating to that immediate time and place. If you ask the cat where it was the night before and what it was up to, you may get the same *meow* response. It seems that animal communication is almost exclusively designed for this moment, here and now. It cannot effectively be used to relate events which are far removed in time and place. When your dog says *GRRR*, it is likely to mean *GRRR, right now*, because it does not appear capable of communicating *GRRR, last night, over in the park*. Now, human language-users are perfectly capable of producing messages equivalent to *GRRR, last night, over in the park*, and going on to say *In fact, I'll be going back tomorrow for some more*. They can refer to past and future time, and to other locations. This property of human language is called **displacement**. It allows the users of language to talk about things and events not present in the immediate environment. Animal communication is generally considered to lack this property.

However, it has been proposed that bee communication does have the property of displacement. For example, when a worker bee finds a source of nectar and returns to the hive, it can perform a complex dance routine to communicate to the other bees the location of this nectar. Depending on the type of dance, round dance for nearby and tail-wagging dance, with variable tempo, for further away, and how far, the other bees can work out where this newly discovered feast can be found. This ability of the bee to indicate a location some distance away must mean that bee communication has, at least, some degree of displacement as a feature. The crucial consideration involved, of course, is that of degree. Bee communication has displacement in an extremely limited form. Certainly, the bee can direct other bees to a food source. However, it must be the most recent food source. It cannot be *that rose garden on the other side of town that we visited last weekend*, nor can it be, as far as we know, possible future nectar in bee heaven.

The factors involved in the property of displacement, as it is manifested in human language, are much more comprehensive than the communication of a single location. It enables us to talk about things and places whose existence we cannot even be sure of. We can refer to mythical creatures, demons, fairies, angels, Santa Claus, and recently invented characters such as Superman. It is the property of displacement which allows the human, unlike any other creature, to create fiction and to describe possible future worlds.

Arbitrariness

It is generally the case that there is no 'natural' connection between a linguistic form and its meaning. You cannot look at the Arabic word كلب, and from its shape, for example, determine that it has a natural meaning, any more than you can with its English translation form – *dog*. The linguistic form has no natural or 'iconic' relationship with that four-legged barking object out in the world. Recognizing this general fact about language leads us to conclude that a property of linguistic signs is their arbitrary relationship with the objects they are used to indicate. The forms of human language demonstrate a property called **arbitrariness** – they do not, in any way, 'fit' the objects they denote. Of course, you can play a game with words to make them 'fit', in some sense, the property or activity they indicate, as in these examples from a child's game:

Look   fall   tall   kick   my

However, such a game only emphasizes how arbitrary the connection normally is between the linguistic form and its meaning.

There are, of course, some words in language which have sounds which seem to 'echo' the sounds of objects or activities. English examples might be *cuckoo*, *crash* or *slurp*, which are onomatopoeic, and which we have already noted (Chapter 1) as part of the 'natural sounds' theory of language origin. In most languages, these onomatopoeic words are relatively rare, and the vast majority of linguistic expressions are in fact arbitrary. For the majority of animal signals, however, there appears to be a clear connection between the conveyed message and the signal used to convey it. This impression we have of the non-arbitrariness of animal signaling may be closely connected with the fact that, for any animal, the set of signals used in communication is finite. That is, each variety of animal communication consists of a fixed and limited set of (vocal or gestural) forms. Many of these forms are used only in specific situations (e.g. establishing territory) and at particular times (e.g. during the mating season). As far as mating is concerned, the human seems to behave as if it is always open season, and the range and frequent novelty of linguistic expressions used in connection with that activity may provide evidence for another property of human language, normally described as 'productivity'.

Productivity

It is a feature of all languages that novel utterances are continually being created. A child learning language is especially active in forming and producing utterances which he or she has never heard before. With adults, new situations arise or new objects have to be described, so the language-users manipulate their linguistic resources to produce new expressions and new sentences. This property of human language has been termed **productivity** (or 'creativity', or 'open-endedness'). It is an aspect of language which is linked to the fact that the potential number of utterances in any human language is infinite.

Non-human signaling, on the other hand, appears to have little flexibility. Cicadas have 4 signals to choose from and vervet monkeys have about 36 vocal calls (including the noises for vomiting and sneezing). Nor does it seem possible for animals to produce 'new' signals to communicate novel experiences or events. The worker bee, normally able to communicate the location of a nectar source, will fail to do so if the location is really 'new'. In one experiment, a hive of bees was placed at the foot of a radio tower and a food source at the top. Ten bees were taken to the top, shown the food source, and sent off to tell the rest of the hive about their find. The message was conveyed via a bee dance and the whole gang buzzed off to get the free food. They flew around in all directions, but couldn't locate the food. (It is probably one way to make bees really mad.) The problem may be that bee communication regarding location has a fixed set of signals, all of which relate to horizontal distance. The bee cannot manipulate its communication system to create a 'new' message indicating vertical distance. According to Karl von Frisch, who conducted the experiment, "the bees have no word for *up* in their language". Moreover, they cannot invent one.

The problem seems to be that animal signals have a feature called **fixed reference**. Each signal is fixed as relating to a particular object or occasion. Among the vervet monkey's repertoire, there is one danger signal *CHUTTER*, which is used when a snake is around, and another *RRAUP*, used when an eagle comes by. These signals are fixed in terms of their reference and cannot be manipulated. What would count as evidence of productivity in the monkey's communication system would be the utterance of something like a *CHUTT-RRAUP* type of signal when a flying creature that looked like a snake came by. That is, the monkey would be capable of manipulating its 'language' to cope with the new situation. Unfortunately, we have no evidence that the monkey could produce a new danger signal. The human, given similar circumstances, is quite capable of creating a new 'signal', after initial surprise, by uttering something along the lines of *Wow, I don't believe it, an eagle-snake!*

Cultural transmission

While you may inherit brown eyes and dark hair from your parents, you do not inherit their language. You acquire a language in a culture with other speakers and not from parental genes. An infant born to Chinese parents (who live in China and speak Cantonese), which is brought up from birth by English speakers in the United States, may have physical characteristics inherited from its natural parents, but it will inevitably speak English. A kitten, given comparable early experiences, will produce *meow* regardless.

This process whereby language is passed on from one generation to the next is described as **cultural transmission**. While it has been argued that humans are born with an innate predisposition to acquire language (discussed in more detail in Chapter 15), it is clear that they are not born with the ability to produce utterances in a specific language, such as English. The general pattern of animal communication is that the signals used are instinctive and not learned. There is, however, some experimental evidence which suggests that some birds do actively 'learn' the distinctive calls used by their species. If those birds are reared in isolation, they will instinctively produce songs or calls, but these songs will be abnormal in some way. Human infants, growing up in isolation, produce no 'instinctive' language. Cultural transmission of a specific language is crucial in the human acquisition process.

Discreteness

The sounds used in language are meaningfully distinct. For example, the difference between a *b* sound and a *p* sound is not actually very great, but when these sounds are used in a language, they are used in such a way that the occurrence of one rather than the other is meaningful. The fact that the pronunciation of the forms *pack* and *back* leads to a distinction in meaning can only be due to the difference between the *p* and *b* sound in English. This property of language is described as **discreteness**. Each sound in the language is treated as discrete. It is possible, in fact, to produce a range of sounds in a continuous stream which are all generally like the *p* and *b* sounds. These physically different sounds could be conceived of as the spoken counterpart of a written set such as:

$$\mathcal{P} \quad P \quad {}_{p} \quad \rho \quad \textit{b} \quad b \quad B \quad \mathcal{B}$$

However, that continuous stream will only be interpreted as being either a *p* sound, or a *b* sound (or, possibly, as a non-sound) in the language. We have a very discrete view of the sounds of our language and wherever a pronunciation falls within the physically possible range of sounds, it will be interpreted as a linguistically specific and meaningfully distinct sound.

Duality

Language is organized at two levels or layers simultaneously. This property is called **duality**, or 'double articulation'. In terms of speech production, we have the physical level at which we can produce individual sounds, like *n*, *b* and *i*. When we produce those sounds in a particular combination, as in *bin*, we have another level producing a meaning which is different from the meaning of the combination in *nib*. So, at one level, we have distinct sounds, and, at another level, we have distinct meanings. This duality of levels is, in fact, one of the most economical features of human language since, with a limited set of distinct sounds, we are capable of producing a very large number of sound combinations (e.g. words) which are distinct in meaning.

It is obvious that, although your dog may be able to produce *woof*, it does not seem to be a feature of the canine repertoire that the *w*, *oo* and *f* elements can be separated out as a distinct level of production. If your dog could operate with the double level (i.e. duality), then you might expect to hear *oowf* and even *foow*, each with different meanings.

Other properties

These six properties of displacement, arbitrariness, productivity, cultural transmission, discreteness and duality may be taken as the core features of human language. Human language does of course have many other properties, but generally they are not unique to it.

The use of the **vocal–auditory channel**, for example, is certainly a feature of human speech. Human linguistic communication is typically generated via the vocal organs and perceived via the ears. Linguistic communication, however, can also be transmitted without sound, via writing or via the sign languages of the deaf. Moreover, many other species (e.g. dolphins) use the vocal–auditory channel. Thus, this property is not a defining feature of human language. Similar points can be made about **reciprocity** (any speaker/sender of a linguistic signal can also be a listener/receiver); **specialization** (linguistic signals do not normally serve any other type of purpose, such as breathing or feeding); **non-directionality** (linguistic signals can be picked up by anyone within hearing, even unseen); and **rapid fade** (linguistic signals are produced and disappear quickly). Most of these are properties of the spoken language, but not of the written language. They are also not present in many animal communication systems which characteristically use the visual mode or involve frequent repetition of the same signal. Such properties are best treated as ways of describing human language, but not as a means of distinguishing it from other systems of communication.

Study questions

1. What is the property which relates to the fact that a language must be acquired or learned by each new generation?
2. Can you briefly explain what the term *arbitrariness* means as it is used to describe a property of human language?
3. Which term is used to describe the ability of human language-users to discuss topics which are remote in space and time?
4. Is the fact that linguistic signals do not normally serve any other type of purpose, such as feeding, a good reason to consider this a unique property of human language?
5. What is the term used to describe the fact that, in a language, we can have different meanings for the three words *tack*, *act* and *cat*, yet, in each case, use the same basic set of sounds?

Discussion topics/projects

A. A distinction is made, at the beginning of the chapter, between 'communicative' and 'informative' signals. No mention is made of the phenomenon known as 'body language'. Would 'body language', or other aspects of nonverbal signaling, be considered 'communicative' or 'informative', or both?
B. The properties of 'non-directionality' and 'reciprocity' are not considered unique to human language. In what other communication systems are they present and are they present in all forms of human communication via language?
C. Hockett (1963) proposed that 'prevarication' could be treated as a property of language. In discussing this property, he pointed out that "linguistic messages can be false" and that "lying seems extremely rare among animals". Can you give reasons for or against including prevarication (either deception or misinforming) among the properties of human language?
D. In this chapter the set of properties is simply enumerated and described. There was no discussion of whether a communication system having these properties would provide its users with advantages in terms of survival or development. Can a case be made for these unique properties of language being viewed as advantageous for the human creature? (For background reading, Hockett, 1963, has some speculations on this subject.)

Further reading

An introductory treatment of the properties of language and a discussion of the communication systems of bees, birds and primates can be found in Akmajian, Demers & Harnish (1984). The fullest treatment of the topic is to be found in the work of Hockett (1958; 1960; 1963). More specifically, on the distinction between communicative and informative signals, see Chapter 2 of Lyons (1977) which also has, in Chapter 3, a summary of views on the properties of language. For the original studies on bee communication, see von Frisch (1962; 1967). The source of the term 'double articulation', used sometimes in place of 'duality', is Martinet (1964). On the significance of 'productivity' and a discussion of what might be 'innate' about human language, consult Chomsky (1965; 1983) or Chapter 2 of Aitchison (1976), which also has extended discussion of human versus animal language.

Chapter 4

Animals and human language

My principal Endeavour was to learn the Language, which my Master
and his Children, and every Servant of his House were desirous to
teach me. For they looked upon it as a Prodigy, that a brutal Animal
should discover such Marks of a rational Creature. I pointed to
everything, and enquired the Name of it, which I wrote down in my
Journal Book when I was alone, and corrected my bad Accent, by
desiring those of the Family to pronounce it often. In this
Employment, a Sorrel Nag, one of the under Servants, was ready to
assist me.

Jonathan Swift, *Gulliver's Travels*, Book 4 (1726)

In the preceding chapter, we concentrated on the ways in which human
language is distinct from the 'languages' of other creatures. If human
language is indeed such a unique form of communication, then it would
seem inconceivable that other creatures would be able to develop an
understanding of this specialized human mode of expression. Some
humans, however, do not behave as if this is the case. There is, after
all, a lot of spoken language directed by humans to animals, apparently
under the impression that the animal follows what is being said. Riders
can say *Whoa* to horses and they stop (or so it seems), we can say
Heel to dogs and they will follow at heel (well, sometimes), and, in
circus rings, a variety of animals go *Up*, *Down* and *Roll over* in accordance with spoken commands. Would we wish to use these examples
as evidence that non-humans can understand human language? Surely
not. As far as animal behavior is concerned, the standard explanation
is that the animal produces a particular behavior in response to a particular sound-stimulus, but does not actually 'understand' the meaning of
the words uttered.

If it seems difficult to conceive of animals 'understanding' human language, then it appears to be even less likely that an animal would be
capable of 'producing' human language. After all, we do not generally
observe animals of one species learning to produce the signals of another

species. You could keep your horse in a field of cows for years, but it still won't say *Moo*. And, in many households, a new baby and a puppy may arrive at the same time (by different routes). Baby and puppy grow up in the same environment, hearing mostly the same things, but about three years later, the baby is making human noises and the puppy is not.

Teaching chimpanzees

The outcome of raising animal and child together may seem rather obvious, but this is basically the technique which was employed in early attempts to teach chimpanzees to use human language. In the 1930s, two scientists (Luella and Winthrop Kellogg) reported on their experiences of raising an infant chimpanzee together with their infant son. The chimpanzee, called Gua, was reported to be able to understand about a hundred words, but did not 'say' any of them. In the 1940s, a chimpanzee named Viki was reared by another scientist couple (Catherine and Keith Hayes) in their own home, exactly as if she were a human child. These foster parents attempted to get Viki to 'say' English words by trying to shape her mouth as she produced sounds. Viki eventually managed to produce some 'words', rather poorly articulated versions of *mama*, *papa* and *cup*. In retrospect, this was a remarkable achievement since it has become clear that non-human primates do not have a physically structured vocal tract which is suitable for producing human speech sounds.

Washoe

Recognizing that a chimpanzee was a poor candidate for spoken language learning, Beatrix and Allen Gardner set out to teach a female chimpanzee called Washoe to use a version of American Sign Language. This sign language, used by the deaf, has all the properties described earlier as basic features of human language and is learned by many congenitally deaf children as their natural first language. (It is discussed in greater detail in Chapter 17.)

Beginning in June 1966, the Gardners and their research assistants raised Washoe like a human child in a comfortable domestic environment. Sign language was always used when Washoe was around and she was encouraged to use signs, even her own incomplete 'baby-versions' of the signs used by adults. In a period of three and a half years, Washoe came to use signs for more than a hundred words, ranging from *airplane*, *baby* and *banana* through to *window*, *woman* and *you*. Even more impressive was Washoe's ability to take these forms and combine them to produce 'sentences' of the type *gimme tickle*, *more fruit* and *open food drink* (to get the refrigerator opened). Some of the forms used appear to have been inventions by Washoe, as in her novel sign for *bib* and in the combination *water bird* (referring to a swan), which would seem to indicate that her linguistic system had the potential for productivity. Moreover, Washoe demonstrated understanding of a much larger number of signs than she actually produced. She also seemed capable of holding rudimentary conversations, mainly in the form of question–answer sequences.

Sarah and Lana

At the same time as Washoe was learning sign language, another chimpanzee named Sarah was being taught (by Ann and David Premack) to use a set of plastic shapes for the purposes of communicating with humans. These plastic shapes represented 'words' which could be arranged (Sarah preferred a vertical order) in sequence to build 'sentences'. The basic approach was quite different from that of the Gardners. Sarah was systematically trained to associate these shapes with objects or actions. She remained an animal in a cage, being trained with food rewards to manipulate a set of symbols. Once she had learned

(Mary)

(give)

(chocolate)

(Sarah)

to use a large number of these plastic shapes, Sarah was capable of getting an apple by selecting the correct plastic shape (a blue triangle) from a large array. Notice that this symbol is arbitrary, since it would be hard to argue for any natural connection between an apple and a blue plastic triangle. Sarah was also capable of producing 'sentences' such as *Mary give chocolate Sarah*, and had the impressive capacity to understand complex structures such as *If Sarah put red on green, Mary give Sarah chocolate*. Sarah got the chocolate.

A similar training technique with a similar artificial language was used (by Duane Rumbaugh) to train a chimpanzee called Lana. The language she learned was called Yerkish and consisted of a set of symbols on a large keyboard linked to a computer. When Lana wanted some water, she had to press four symbols, in the correct sequence, to produce the message *please machine give water*.

| (please) | (machine) | (give) | (water) |

Both Sarah and Lana demonstrated an ability to use what look like logographic codes in ways which superficially resemble the use of language. There was, however, a lot of skepticism regarding these apparent linguistic skills. It was pointed out that when Lana used the symbol for 'please', she did not have to understand the meaning of the English word *please*. There was no choice involved, as, for example, in omitting *please*, as we often do, in order to produce a different, but nevertheless meaningful, 'utterance'. The symbol for 'please' on the computer keyboard was the equivalent of a button on a vending machine and, so the argument goes, we can learn to operate vending machines without necessarily knowing language. The strongest arguments against accepting the achievements of Washoe, Sarah and Lana as evidence of linguistic abilities have been put forward by the psychologist Herbert Terrace, who worked with a chimpanzee called Nim.

Nim Chimpsky

The name given to this chimpanzee, Nim Chimpsky, was a deliberate play on the name of the linguist Noam Chomsky who had claimed that language is an innate ability and unique to the human species. Perhaps Nim would show that Noam was mistaken. Beginning in 1973, a concentrated effort was made to teach Nim American Sign Language under controlled conditions, with careful records and videotaping of Nim's classroom activities. Over a two-year period, Nim produced a large number of single-word signs, developed two-word combinations such as *more drink* and *give banana*, and used them in appropriate circumstances. The initial impression was that Nim, like Washoe, was developing an ability to use language in much the same way as human children. However, this impression did not survive some close inspection of the videotaped record. The structure of Nim's longer 'utterances' was simply a repetition of simpler structures, not an expansion into more complex structures, as produced by human children. Moreover, in contrast to the human child, Nim only rarely used sign language to initiate interaction with his teachers. In general, he produced signs in response to their signing and tended to repeat signs they used.

This type of finding prompted Terrace to reinvestigate the filmed record of Washoe's use of sign language and led him to argue that both Nim and Washoe only appeared to use signs as language. In fact, he argued, they were simply producing prompted repetitions of their teachers' signs, yet being interpreted as if they were taking part in 'conversations'. His conclusion was that chimpanzees are clever creatures who learn to produce a certain type of behavior (signing) in order to get rewards, and who are essentially performing sophisticated 'tricks'. Consequently, their signing is not linguistic behavior at all.

Hans, Buzz and Doris

The arguments presented by Terrace are very similar to those which have been used in the past to discredit claims that any animal was capable of understanding and using any form of linguistic communication. At the turn of the century, a German horse called Clever Hans astounded many with the use of his hoofbeats to answer arithmetical questions and to tap out the letters of the alphabet. However, it was demonstrated that Hans was actually responding to subtle visual cues provided by those asking him questions. If the questioner didn't know the answer to the question, he couldn't unconsciously indicate that Hans had tapped the correct number of hoofbeats and consequently Hans got the answers wrong.

In the 1960s, two dolphins called Buzz and Doris were reported to have developed a means of signaling, across an opaque barrier, which enabled one of them to 'tell' the other how they could both get a fish snack. When Doris saw a flashing light, she had to press a paddle on the left-hand side and 'tell' Buzz (who couldn't see the light or Doris) to press his left-hand paddle. When the light was kept steady, Doris had to press the right-hand paddle and 'tell' Buzz to press his right-hand paddle. Over thousands of trials, these dolphins inevitably got the fish. However, it turned out that Doris would continue to 'tell' Buzz when Buzz could see the light himself and even when Buzz was taken out of the tank. The conclusion was that Doris' behavior consisted of conditioned responses to the different light signals and Buzz's behavior was conditioned to responding to Doris' calls.

The controversy

These two phenomena, the unwitting cues provided by human trainers and the conditioned response behavior of animals, are usually cited as the explanation of language-like behavior in animals generally, and of chimpanzees in particular. However, those foster parents of Washoe, the Gardners, have argued that they were neither 'animal trainers', nor were they inculcating and then eliciting conditioned responses from Washoe. In a complex experiment, designed to eliminate any possible provision of cues, they showed that, in the absence of any human, Washoe could produce correct signs to identify objects in pictures. They also emphasize what they consider to be a major advantage of their approach over most other work with chimpanzees. They note that Terrace carefully instructed his research assistants to remember that Nim was a research animal and not a child. Most of Nim's training took place in a bare windowless cell and the majority of research assistants involved were not fluent in American Sign Language. The Gardners point out that a deaf human child might not develop into a fully interactive and sociable user of sign language under comparable circumstances.

In sharp contrast, the Gardners have stressed the need for a domestic environment, without cages, in which the chimpanzee has a lot of opportunity for imaginative play and interaction with fluent sign language users who use the language normally with each other. Their most recent project involves a number of chimpanzees, Moja, Pili, Tatu and Dar, being raised together from birth in a domestic environment with a number of human companions who naturally use sign language. They report that these chimpanzees, beginning earlier than Washoe, are acquiring sign language much faster. The hope is, of course, that these chimpanzees will come to use sign language naturally to communicate with each other and there have been some indications that this is not a forlorn hope.

There are important lessons which have been learned from attempts to teach chimpanzees to use some forms of language. We have answered some questions. Was Washoe capable of taking part in interaction by using a symbol system which was chosen by humans and not chimpanzees? The answer is clearly "Yes". Did Washoe perform linguistically on a level comparable to a human child at the same stage of development? The answer is just as clearly "No". In addition, one of the most important lessons for those who study the nature of language is the realization that we clearly do not have a totally objective and non-controversial definition of what counts as 'using language'. We assume that when young human children make 'language-like' noises we are witnessing language development, but when young chimpanzees produce 'language-like' signs in interaction with humans, we are very unwilling to classify this as language use. Yet, the criteria we use in each case do not seem to be the same. This problem remains, as does the controversy among different psychologists over the reported abilities of chimpanzees to use language. However, given the mass of evidence from the studies described here, we might suggest that the linguist Noam Chomsky should revise his claim that "acquisition of even the barest rudiments of language is quite beyond the capacities of an otherwise intelligent ape". We may not have had reports on the chimpanzee view of nuclear disarmament, but on "the barest rudiments of language" we have.

Study questions

1. Have any chimpanzees ever been taught to produce human speech sounds? What's been the problem?
2. Did Washoe's use of American Sign Language provide any evidence of the feature called 'productivity'?
3. In Sarah's vocabulary, the color 'red' was represented by a grey plastic shape. If Sarah could use this plastic shape to convey the meaning 'red', which property does her 'language' have?
4. What was the basis of Terrace's conclusion that the chimpanzee's use of sign language is not true language?
5. How did the Gardners try to show that Washoe was not necessarily repeating signs made by interacting humans?

Discussion topics/projects

A. What do you think is meant by "the Clever Hans phenomenon" and how could it be avoided in studies of linguistic behavior in animals?

B. No mention was made in this chapter of the abilities of parrots to produce English sentences like "Close the door, you idiot." Why is this, and similar 'speech' by mynah birds, not considered to be genuine linguistic behavior?

C. What are the advantages and disadvantages of the different symbol systems (plastic shapes, keys on a computer console, sign language) which have been used with chimpanzees? Which system (one of these or one of your own invention) would you use if you were given the opportunity to try to teach language to a chimpanzee?

D. Here are some examples of (i) the earliest two-word combinations of a typical child and some examples of (ii) the two-sign combinations from Washoe. On the basis of this evidence, do you think that the child and Washoe are doing essentially the same linguistic thing?

(i) red book	(ii) baby mine
mommy lunch	go flower
go store	drink red
hit ball	tickle Washoe
book table	more fruit

Further reading

For a general overview, there is Linden (1976), or the more comprehensive volume edited by Sebeok & Sebeok (1980). More specifically, life with Gua is described in Kellogg & Kellogg (1933), with Viki in Hayes (1951). On the original Washoe project, see Gardner & Gardner (1969), or more recently, Gardner & Gardner (1978). On Sarah, see Premack & Premack (1972), and on Lana, see Rumbaugh (1977). For Nim's experiences, see Terrace (1979) which is reviewed very critically by Gardner (1981). On Hans, see Pfungst (1911), and on Buzz and Doris, check Evans & Bastain (1969). The quotation from Chomsky, and a fuller version of his ideas on the matter, can be found in Chomsky (1972).

Chapter 5

The sounds of language

I take it you already know
Of tough and bough and cough and dough?
Others may stumble but not you
On hiccough, thorough, lough and through.
Well done! And now you wish, perhaps,
To learn of less familiar traps?
Beware of heard, a dreadful word,
That looks like beard and sounds like bird.
And dead: it's said like bed, not bead –
For goodness sake don't call it 'deed'.
Watch out for meat and great and threat
(They rhyme with suite and straight and debt).

From *Hints on Pronunciation for Foreigners* by T. S. W.

Imagine that a restaurant manager who has always had trouble with the spelling of English words places an advertisement for a new *SEAGH*. You see the advertisement and your confusion leads you to ask how he came to form this unfamiliar word. It's very simple, he says. Take the first sound of the word *SURE*, the middle sound of the word *DEAD*, and the final sound of the word *LAUGH*. You will, of course, recognize that this form conveys the pronunciation usually associated with the word *chef*.

This tale, however unlikely, may serve as a reminder that the sounds of spoken English do not match up, a lot of the time, with letters of written English. If we cannot use the letters of the alphabet in a consistent way to represent the sounds we make, how do we go about describing the sounds of a language like English? One solution is to produce a separate alphabet with symbols which represent sounds. Such a set of symbols does exist and is called the 'phonetic alphabet'. We will consider how these symbols are used to represent both the consonant and vowel sounds of English words and what physical aspects of the human vocal tract are involved in the production of those sounds.

Phonetics

The general study of the characteristics of speech sounds is called **pho-netics**. Our primary interest will be in **articulatory phonetics**, which is the study of how speech sounds are made, or 'articulated'. Other areas of study within phonetics are **acoustic phonetics**, which deals with the physical properties of speech as sound waves 'in the air', and **auditory** (or perceptual) **phonetics**, which deals with the perception, via the ear, of speech sounds.

Voiced and voiceless sounds

In articulatory phonetics, we investigate how speech sounds are produced using the fairly complex oral equipment we have. We start with the air pushed out by the lungs up through the trachea (the 'windpipe') to the larynx. Inside the larynx are your vocal cords which take two basic positions.

(1) When the vocal cords are spread apart, the air from the lungs passes between them unimpeded. Sounds produced in this way are described as **voiceless**.

(2) When the vocal cords are drawn together, the air from the lungs repeatedly pushes them apart as it passes through, creating a vibration. Sounds produced in this way are described as **voiced**.

As examples of this distinction, you can try saying the words *pick* and *fish*, which have voiceless sounds at the beginning and end. Then say the words *big* and *viz*, which have voiced sounds at the beginning and end. The distinction can also be felt physically if you place a fingertip gently on the top of your 'Adam's apple' (i.e. part of your larynx) and produce sounds like Z-Z-Z-Z or V-V-V-V. Since these are voiced sounds, you should be able to feel some vibration. Keeping your fingertip in the same position, make the sounds S-S-S-S or F-F-F-F. Since these are voiceless sounds, there should be no vibration. Another trick is to put a finger in each ear, not too far, and produce the voiced sounds (e.g. Z-Z-Z-Z) to hear some vibration, whereas no vibration will be heard if the voiceless sounds (e.g. S-S-S-S) are produced in the same manner.

Place of articulation

Once the air has passed through the larynx, it comes up and out through the mouth and/or the nose. Most consonant sounds are produced by using the tongue and other parts of the mouth to constrict, in some way, the shape of the oral cavity through which the air is passing. The terms used to describe many sounds are those which denote the place of articulation of the sound, that is, the location, inside the mouth, at which the constriction takes place.

What we need is a slice of head. If you crack a head right down the middle, you will be able to see which parts of the oral cavity are crucially involved in speech production.

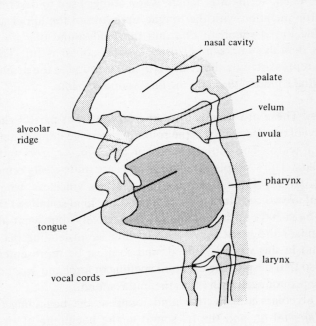

To describe the place of articulation of most consonant sounds, we can start at the front of the mouth and work back. We can also keep the voiced–voiceless distinction in mind and begin using the symbols of the phonetic alphabet to denote specific sounds. These symbols will be enclosed within square brackets [ ].

Bilabials. These are sounds formed using both lips. The initial sounds in the words *pat*, *bat* and *mat* are all bilabials. They are represented by the symbols [p], which is voiceless, and [b] and [m], which are voiced. The [w] sound found at the beginning of *way*, *walk* and *world* is also a bilabial.

Labiodentals. These are sounds formed with the upper teeth and the lower lip. The initial sounds of the words *fat* and *vat* and the final sounds in the words *safe* and *save* are labiodentals. They are represented by the symbols [f], which is voiceless, and [v], which is voiced. Notice that the final sounds of *laugh* and *cough*, and the initial sound of *photo*, despite the spelling differences, are all pronounced as [f].

Dentals. These sounds are formed with the tongue tip behind the upper front teeth. The term 'interdental' is sometimes used to describe a manner of pronunciation with the tongue tip between the upper and lower teeth. The initial sound of *thin* and the final sound of *bath* are both voiceless dentals. The symbol used for this sound is [θ]. The voiced dental is represented by the symbol [ð] and is found in the pronunciation of the initial sound of *thus* and the final sound of *bathe*.

Alveolars. These are sounds formed with the front part of the tongue on the alveolar ridge, which is the rough, bony ridge immediately behind the upper teeth. The initial sounds in *top*, *dip*, *sit*, *zoo* and *nut* are all alveolars. The symbols for these sounds are quite easily remembered – [t], [d], [s], [z], [n]. Of these, [t] and [s] are voiceless, whereas [d], [z] and [n] are voiced. It may be clear that the final sounds of the words *bus* and *buzz* have to be [s] and [z] respectively, but what about the final sound of the word *raise*? The spelling is misleading because the final sound in this word is voiced, and so must be represented by [z]. Notice also that despite the different spelling of *knot* and *not*, both these words are pronounced with [n] as the initial sound.

Other alveolars are the [l] sound found at the beginning of words such as *lap* and *lit*, and the [r] sound at the beginning of *right*, *write* and *rip*.

Alveo-palatals. If you feel back behind the alveolar ridge, you should find a hard part in the roof of your mouth. This is called the palate. Sounds which are produced with the tongue at the very front of the palate, near the alveolar ridge, are called alveo-palatals. Examples are the initial sounds in the words *shoot* and *child*, which are voiceless. Although there are two letters in the spelling of 'sh' and 'ch', the sounds are represented by the single phonetic symbols [š] and [č] respectively. So, the word *shoe-brush* begins and ends with the voiceless alveo-palatal sound [š], and the word *church* begins and ends with the voiceless alveo-palatal sound [č].

One of the voiced alveo-palatal sounds, represented by the symbol [ž], is not very common in English, but can be found as the middle consonant sound in words like *treasure* and *pleasure*, or the final sound in *rouge*. The other voiced alveo-palatal sound is represented as [ǰ] and is the initial sound in words like *joke* and *gem*. The word *judge* and the name *George* both begin and end with the sound [ǰ], despite the obvious differences in spelling.

One sound which is produced with the tongue in the middle of the palate is the [y] sound to be found at the beginning of words like *you* and *yet*. This sound is usually described as a **palatal**.

Velars. Even further back in the roof of the mouth, beyond the hard palate, you will find a soft area which is called the soft palate, or the velum. Sounds produced with the back of the tongue against the velum are called velars. There is a voiceless velar sound, represented by the symbol [k], which occurs not only in *kid* and *kill*, but is also the initial sound in *car* and *cold*. Despite the variety in spelling, this [k] sound is both the initial and final sound in the words *cook*, *kick* and *coke*. The voiced velar sound to be heard at the beginning of words like *go*, *gun* and *give* is represented by [g]. This is also the final sound in words like *bag*, *mug* and, despite the spelling, *plague*.

One other voiced velar is represented by the symbol [ŋ]. In English, this sound is normally written as the two letters 'ng'. So, the [ŋ] sound is at the end of *sing*, *sang* and, despite the spelling, *tongue*. It would occur twice in the form *ringing*. Be careful not to be misled by the spelling – the word *bang* ends with the [ŋ] sound only. There is no [g] sound in this word.

Glottals. There are two other sounds which are produced without the active use of the tongue and other parts of the mouth. One is the sound [h] which occurs at the beginning of *have* and *house*, and, for most speakers, as the first sound in *who* and *whose*. This sound is usually described as a voiceless glottal. The 'glottis' is the space between the vocal cords in the larynx. When the glottis is open, as in the production of other voiceless sounds, but there is no manipulation of the air passing out through the mouth, the sound produced is that represented by [h].

When the glottis is closed completely, very briefly, and then released, the resulting sound is called a **glottal stop**. This sound occurs in many dialects of English, but does not have a written form in the Roman alphabet. The symbol used in phonetic transcription is [ʔ]. You can produce this sound if you try to say the words *butter* or *bottle* without pronouncing the *-tt-* sound in the middle. In Britain, this sound is considered to be a characteristic aspect of Cockney speech and, in the United States, of the speech of many New Yorkers.

Charting consonant sounds

Having described in some detail the place of articulation of English consonant sounds, we can summarize the basic information in the following chart. Along the top of the chart are the different labels for places of articulation and, under each, the labels −V (= voiceless) and +V (= voiced). Also included in this chart, on the left-hand side, is a set of terms used to describe 'manner of articulation' which we will discuss in a later section.

	Bilabial	Labio-dental	Dental	Alveolar	Alveo-palatäl	Velar	Glottal
	−V +V	−V +V	−V +V	−V +V	−V +V	−V +V	−V +V
Stops	p b			t d		k g	ʔ
Fricatives		f v	θ ð	s z	š ž		
Affricates					č ǰ		
Nasals	m			n		ŋ	
Liquids				l,r			
Glides	w					y	h

A note on the chart. This chart is far from complete. It does contain the majority of consonant sounds used in the description of English pronunciation. There are, however, several differences between this basic set of symbols and the much more comprehensive chart produced by the International Phonetic Association (IPA). The most obvious difference is in the range of sounds covered. The IPA aims to describe the sounds of all languages and includes, for example, symbols for the velar fricative sound you may have heard in the German pronunciation of the "ch" part of *Bach* or *Achtung*. It also includes sounds made with the back of the tongue and the uvula (below the velum) which represents the "r" parts of the French pronunciation of *rouge* and *lettre*. Uvular sounds also occur in many American Indian languages. Other, non-English, sounds such as pharyngeals (produced in the pharynx) occur in Semitic languages like Arabic. Another shortcoming of the chart above is the single entry covering *r* sounds in English. There can be a lot of variation across speakers in the pronunciation of the initial sound in *raw* and *red*, the medial sound in *very*, and the final sound in *hour* and *air*. Different symbols (e.g. [ɹ], [r]) may be encountered in transcriptions where the different *r* sounds are distinguished. Finally, the IPA uses different symbols for a few of the sounds represented here. These alternatives are [ʃ] = [š]; [ʒ] = [ž]; [tʃ] = [č]; [dʒ] = [ǰ] and [j] = [y]. For a fuller discussion of the use of IPA symbols, see Ladefoged (1982).

Manner of articulation

So far, we have concentrated on describing consonant sounds in terms of where they are articulated. We can, of course, describe the same sounds in terms of how they are articulated. Such a description is necessary if we wish to be able to differentiate between some sounds which, in the preceding discussion, we have placed in the same category. For example, we can say that [t] and [s] are both voiceless alveolar sounds. How do they differ? They differ in their manner of articulation, that is, in the way they are pronounced. The [t] sound is one of a set of sounds called stops and the [s] sound is one of a set called fricatives.

Stops. Of the sounds we have already mentioned, the set [p], [b], [t], [d], [k], [g], [ʔ] are all produced by some form of complete 'stopping' of the airstream (very briefly) and then letting it go abruptly. This type of consonant sound resulting from a blocking or stopping effect on the airstream is called a stop. A full description of the [t] sound at the beginning of a word like *ten* is as a 'voiceless alveolar stop'. On occasion, only the manner of articulation is mentioned, as when it is said that the word *bed*, for example, begins and ends with 'voiced stops'.

Fricatives. The manner of articulation used in producing the set of sounds [f], [v], [θ], [ð], [s], [z], [š], [ž] involves almost blocking the airstream, and having the air push through the narrow opening. As the air is pushed through, a type of friction is produced and the resulting sounds are called fricatives. If you put your open hand in front of your mouth when making these sounds, [f] and [s] in particular, you should be able to feel the stream of air being pushed out. A word like *fish* will begin and end with 'voiceless fricatives'. The word *those* will begin and end with the 'voiced fricatives' [ð] and [z].

Affricates. If you combine a brief stopping of the airstream with an obstructed release which causes some friction, you will be able to produce the sounds [č] and [ǰ]. These are called affricates and occur at the beginning of the words *cheap* and *jeep*. In the first of these, there is a 'voiceless affricate', and in the second a 'voiced affricate'.

Nasals. Most sounds are produced orally, with the velum raised, preventing airflow from entering the nasal cavity. However, when the velum is lowered and the airflow is allowed to flow out through the nose to produce [m], [n] and [ŋ], the sounds are described as nasals. These three sounds are all voiced. Words like *morning*, *knitting* and *name* begin and end with nasals.

Liquids. The initial sounds in the words *led* and *red* are generally described as liquids. The [l] sound is formed by letting the airstream flow around the sides of the tongue as it makes contact with the alveolar ridge. The [r] sound is formed with the tongue tip raised and curled back behind the alveolar ridge.

Glides. The sounds [w] and [y] are produced very much as transition sounds. They are called glides, or 'semi-vowels'. In pronunciation, they are usually produced with the tongue moving, or 'gliding', to or from a position associated with a neighboring vowel sound. They are both voiced. Glides occur at the beginning of *we*, *wet*, *you* and *yes*.

This rather lengthy list of the phonetic features of English consonant sounds is not presented as a challenge to your ability to memorize a lot of terminology and symbols. It is presented as an illustration of how a thorough description of the physical aspects of speech production will allow us to characterize the sounds of spoken English, independently of the vagaries of spelling found in written English. There are, however, some sounds which we have not yet investigated. These are the types of sounds known as vowels and diphthongs.

Vowels

While the consonant sounds are mostly articulated via closure or obstruction in the vocal tract, vowel sounds are produced with a relatively free flow of air. To describe vowel sounds, we consider the way in which the tongue influences the 'shape' through which the airflow must pass. Because these sounds are not so easily defined in terms of place and manner of articulation, we use labels which serve to indicate how each vowel sounds in relation to the others. Thus, we talk of there being

a 'high, front vowel' in the pronunciation of *heat* because the sound
is made with the front part of the tongue in a raised position, whereas
the vowel sound in *hot* is produced with the back of the tongue in a
relatively lower position and is described as a 'low, back vowel'. These
labels are usually presented in the form of a chart, as shown below,
which provides a means of identifying the most common vowel sounds
of English.

	Front	Central	Back
High	i		u
	ɪ		ʊ
	e	ə	o
Mid	ɛ		ɔ
		ʌ	
Low	æ		a

The easiest way to become familiar with the distinctions within the set
of vowel sounds is to have some examples of familiar words which for
a lot of American English speakers, most of the time, contain those
sounds. The following list goes from the high front vowels through to
the low back vowel and ends with three diphthongs:

[i]	*see, eat, key*		[ʊ]	*put, could, foot*
[ɪ]	*hit, myth*		[o]	*no, know, though*
[e]	*tail, great, weight*		[ɔ]	*raw, fall, caught*
[ɛ]	*pet, said, dead*		[a]	*cot, father, body*
[æ]	*sat, laugh*		[ay]	*my, buy, eye*
[ə]	*the, above*		[aw]	*cow, loud*
[ʌ]	*putt, blood, tough*		[ɔy]	*boy, void*
[u]	*move, two, glue*			

Diphthongs. The last three symbols in the list above contain two sounds.
These 'combined' vowel sounds are called diphthongs. Note that in each
case they begin with a vowel sound and end with a glide. With the
majority of single vowel sounds, the vocal organs remain relatively
steady, but in pronouncing diphthongs, we move from one vocalic position to another. If you try to pronounce the consonants and diphthongs
in the following transcription, you should recognize a traditional speech-
training exercise: [haw naw brawn kaw].

A note on the vowel chart. Vowel sounds are notorious for varying
between one English dialect and the next, so you may find that some

of the sounds listed here are not commonly used in your dialect. It may be, for example, that you make no distinction between the vowels in the words *caught* and *cot*. Some transcriptions only use [a] for this back vowel sound. Or, you may not make a significant distinction between the central vowels [ə] and [ʌ]. If not, then just use the symbol [ə]. Remember that the point of this investigation is not to make your speech 'fit' the symbols used, but to try to use the available symbols to describe the sounds you make. The exercise is aimed at describing what you do and not at prescribing what you should do.

Study questions

1. What are the general terms used to describe the sounds produced (a) when the vocal cords are drawn together and (b) when the vocal cords are spread apart?
2. Try pronouncing the initial sounds of the following words and then determine the place of articulation (e.g. bilabial, alveolar, etc.) of each:
   - (a) foot
   - (b) tooth
   - (c) box
   - (d) chips
   - (e) think
   - (f) cup
3. Which of the following words end with voiceless sounds and which end with voiced sounds?
   - (a) touch
   - (b) pig
   - (c) maze
   - (d) lip
   - (e) lathe
   - (f) sit
4. Produce a phonetic transcription of your own pronunciation of the following words:
   - (a) bee
   - (b) tape
   - (c) fell
   - (d) dope
   - (e) walk
   - (f) sigh
5. Which written English words are usually pronounced as transcribed here?
   - (a) [fes]
   - (b) [šip]
   - (c) [ðə]
   - (d) [hu]
   - (e) [etθ]
   - (f) [bæk]
   - (g) [bɔt]
   - (h) [haw]
   - (i) [ǰɔy]
   - (j) [šɛf]

Discussion topics/projects

A. Below is a set of English words with different written forms representing the same sounds in a number of ways. Can you identify the alternative spellings of the sounds [i], [f] and [e]?

elephant, rare, marines, pear, hay, feet, quay, air, suite, weigh, giraffe, pier, tough, keys, meat, Sikh.

How many different ways of spelling the sounds [s], [k], [š] and [ɛ] can you discover?

B. Below are two transcriptions of the author's way of pronouncing two English sentences. First, can you work out what was said, and then, do you think that you pronounce those expressions in the same way? What differences do you think would be present in your transcribed speech?

(a) ðætsɪnkənsivəbəl   (b) hinozfayvlæŋwɪjəz

C. Using the first two examples as a guide, can you provide a description, in terms of manner of articulation, of your pronunciation of the initial consonants of the following English words?

(a) mist (NASAL)   (g) thin
(b) bat (VOICED STOP)   (h) near
(c) far   (i) tall
(d) wall   (j) joke
(e) rope   (k) shop
(f) zoo   (l) gun

D. Consider the following set of transcribed 'words'. Can you divide the set into those forms which are English words, those which could not possibly be English words, and those which are not English words at this time, but might possibly become English words? How do you make the decision regarding what goes in the second or third group?

(1) flem   (5) ksɪn   (9)   črɪs
(2) θrɪnz   (6) šlop   (10) blʌnk
(3) θiətər   (7) kwɪk   (11) fɛrtəm
(4) sɔng   (8) zun   (12) bɔylɪŋ

Further reading

Introductory treatments of phonetics can be found in any basic linguistics textbook, for example, Fromkin & Rodman (1983), Chapter 2 or Lehmann (1983), Chapter 3. The standard textbook is Ladefoged (1982). Alternatives are Roach (1983) or Abercrombie (1967). A programmed introduction, designed for independent study, was produced by Buchanan (1963) and an introduction to the more general area of speech science can be found in Borden & Harris (1980). Another simple and practical text, based on British English, is O'Connor (1973). Prator & Robinett (1985) is a basic introduction to the pronunciation of American English, designed for those learning English as a second language. For an overview of aspects of acoustic and auditory phonetics, try Denes & Pinson (1973) or Fry (1979).

Chapter 6

The sound patterns of language

In the preceding chapter, we investigated the physical production of speech sounds in terms of the articulatory mechanisms of the human vocal tract. That investigation was possible because of some rather amazing facts about the nature of language. When we considered the human vocal tract, we did not have to specify whether we were talking about a fairly large male, over 6 feet tall, weighing over 200 pounds, or about a rather small female, about 5 feet tall, weighing 100 pounds. Yet those two physically different individuals would inevitably have physically different vocal tracts, in terms of size and shape. In a sense, every individual has a physically different vocal tract. Consequently, in purely physical terms, every individual will pronounce sounds differently. There are, then, potentially thousands of physically different ways of saying the simple word *me*. Moreover, each individual will not pronounce the word *me* in a physically identical manner on every occasion. Obvious differences occur when the individual is shouting, is asking for a sixth martini, or is suffering from a cold. Given this vast range of potential differences in the actual physical production of a speech sound, how do we manage consistently to recognize all those versions of *me* as the phonetic form [mi], and not [ni], or [si], or [ma], or [mo], or something else entirely? The answer to that question is provided to a large extent by the study of phonology.

Phonology

Phonology is essentially the description of the systems and patterns of speech sounds in a language. It is, in effect, based on a theory of what

44

every speaker of a language unconsciously knows about the sound patterns of that language. Because of this theoretical status, phonology is concerned with the abstract or mental aspect of the sounds in language rather than with the actual physical articulation of speech sounds. Thus, when we say that the [t] sounds in the pronunciation of *satin* and *eighth* are the same, we are actually saying that in the phonology of English they would be represented in the same way. In actual speech, these [t] sounds may be very different. In the first word, the influence of a following nasal sound could result in some form of nasal release, while, in the second word, the influence of the following [θ] sound would result in a dental articulation of the [t] sound. This distinction between one [t] sound and another [t] sound can be captured in a detailed, or narrow, phonetic transcription.

However, in the phonology of English, this distinction is less important than the distinction between the [t] sounds in general and, for example, the [d] sounds or the [b] sounds, because there are meaningful consequences related to the use of one rather than the others. These sounds must be distinct meaningful sounds, regardless of which individual vocal tract is being used to pronounce them, since they are what make the words *tie*, *die* and *buy* meaningfully distinct. Considered from this point of view, we can see that phonology is concerned with the abstract set of sounds in a language which allows us to distinguish meaning in the actual physical sounds we say and hear.

Phonemes

Each one of these meaning-distinguishing sounds in a language is described as a **phoneme**. When we considered the basis of alphabetic writing in Chapter 2, we were actually working with the concept of the phoneme as the single sound type which came to be represented by a single symbol. It is in this sense that the phoneme /t/ is described as a sound type, of which all the different spoken versions of [t] are tokens. Note that slash marks are conventionally used to indicate a phoneme, /t/, an abstract segment, as opposed to the square brackets, [t], used for each phonetic, or physically produced, segment.

An essential property of a phoneme is that it functions contrastively. We know that there are two phonemes /f/ and /v/ in English because they are the only basis of the contrast in meaning between the forms *fat* and *vat*, or *fine* and *vine*. This contrastive property is the basic operational test for determining the phonemes which exist in a language. If we substitute one sound for another in a word and there is a change of meaning, then the two sounds represent different phonemes. The consonant and vowel charts presented in Chapter 5 can now be seen as essentially a mapping out of the phonemes of English.

The terms which were used in creating that chart can be considered 'features' which distinguish each phoneme from the next. Thus, /p/ can be characterized as [−voice, +bilabial, +stop] and /k/ as [−voice, +velar, +stop]. Since these two sounds share some features, they are sometimes described as members of a natural class of sounds. The prediction would be that sounds which have features in common would behave phonologically in some similar ways. A sound which does not share those features would be expected to behave differently. For example, /v/ has the features [+voice, +labiodental, +fricative] and so cannot be in the same 'natural class' as /p/ and /k/. Although other factors will be involved, this feature-analysis could lead us to suspect that there may be a good phonological reason why words beginning with /pl-/ and /kl-/ are common in English, but words beginning /vl-/ are not. Could it be that there are some definite sets of features required in a sound in order for it to occur word-initially before /l/? If so, then we will be on our way to producing a phonological account of permissible sound sequences in the language.

Minimal pairs and sets

When two words such as *pat* and *bat* are identical in form except for a contrast in one phoneme, occurring in the same position, the two words are described as a **minimal pair**. More accurately, they would be classified as a minimal pair in the phonology of English since Arabic, for example, does not have this contrast between the two sounds. Other examples of English minimal pairs are *fan – van*, *bet – bat*, *site – side*. Such pairs have been used frequently in tests of English as a second language to determine non-native speakers' ability to understand the contrast in meaning resulting from the minimal sound contrast.

When a group of words are differentiated, each one from the others, by changing one phoneme (always in the same position), then we have a **minimal set**. Thus, a minimal set based on the vowel phonemes of English would include *feat, fit, fat, fate, fought, foot,* and one based on consonants could have *big, pig, rig, fig, dig, wig.*

One insight provided by this type of exercise with phonemes is that we can see that there are indeed definite patterns to the types of sound combinations permitted in a language. In English, the minimal set we have just listed does not include forms such as *lig* or *vig*. As far as I know, these are not English words, but they can be viewed as possible English words. That is, your phonological knowledge of the pattern of sounds in English words would allow you to treat these forms as acceptable if, at some future time, they came into use. They represent 'accidental' gaps in the vocabulary of English. It is, however, no accident that forms such as [fsɪg] or [ŋɪg] do not exist or are unlikely ever to exist, since they break what must be phonological rules about the sequence or position of English phonemes.

Phones and allophones

We have already established that, while a phoneme is an abstract unit of sound, there can be different phonetic realizations of any phoneme. These phonetic units are technically described as **phones**. It has been noted by phoneticians that, in English, there is a difference in pronunciation of the /i/ sound in words like *seed* and *seen*. In the second word, the effect of the nasal consonant [n] makes the [i] sound nasalized. This nasalization can be represented by a diacritic over the symbol, [ĩ] in narrow phonetic transcription. So, there are at least two phones, [i] and [ĩ], used in English to realize a single phoneme. These phonetic variants are technically known as **allophones**. The crucial distinction between phonemes and allophones is that substituting one phoneme for another will result in a word with a different meaning (as well as a different pronunciation), but substituting allophones only results in a different pronunciation of the same word.

It is possible, of course, for two languages to have the same phones, or phonetic segments, but to treat them differently. In English, the effect of nasalization on a vowel is treated as allophonic variation because the nasalized version is not meaningfully contrastive. In French, however, the pronunciation [mɛ] is used for one word *mets*, meaning 'dish', and [mɛ̃] for a different word *main*, meaning 'hand', and [so] for *seau*, meaning 'pail', contrasts with [sõ] for *son*, meaning 'sound'. Clearly, in these cases, the distinction is phonemic.

Assimilation

The example of vowel nasalization in English which we have just noted is a good illustration of another regular process involving phonemes.

When two phonemes occur in sequence and some aspect of one phoneme is taken or 'copied' by the other, the process is known as **assimilation**. In terms of the physical production of speech, one might assume that this regular process is occasioned by ease of articulation in everyday speech. In isolation, you would probably pronounce /ɪ/ and /æ/ without any nasal quality at all. However, in saying words like *pin* and *pan*, the anticipation of forming the final nasal consonant will make it 'easier' to go into the nasalized articulation in advance and consequently the vowel sounds in these words will be, in precise transcription, [ĩ] and [æ̃]. This is a very regular feature of English speakers' pronunciation. So regular, in fact, that a phonological rule can be stated in the following way: 'Any vowel becomes nasal whenever it immediately precedes a nasal.'

This type of assimilation process occurs in a variety of different contexts. It is particularly noticeable in ordinary conversational speech. By itself, you may pronounce the word *can* as [kæn], but, if you tell someone *I can go*, the influence of the following velar [g] will almost certainly make the preceding nasal sound come out as [ŋ] (a velar) rather than [n] (an alveolar). The most commonly observed 'conversational' version of the phrase is [aykəŋgo]. Notice that the vowel in *can* has also changed to [ə] from the isolated-word version [æ]. The vowel sound [ə], called 'schwa', is very commonly used in conversational speech when a different vowel would occur in words spoken in isolation. In many words spoken carefully, the vowel receives stress, but in the course of ordinary talk, that vowel may no longer receive any stress. For example, you may pronounce *and* as [ænd] in isolation, but in the casual use of the phrase *you and me*, you almost certainly say [ən], as in [yuənmi].

Elision

Note that in the last example, in the environment of preceding and following nasals, the [d] sound of *and* has simply disappeared. The [d] sound is also commonly 'omitted' in the pronunciation of a word like *friendship*, [frɛnšɪp]. This 'omission' of a sound segment which would be present in the deliberate pronunciation of a word in isolation is technically described as **elision**. Word-final /t/ is a common casualty in this process, as in the typical pronunciation [æspɛks] for *aspects*, or in [hɪmʌsbi] for *he must be*. You can, of course, slowly and deliberately pronounce the phrase *we asked him*, but the process of elision in casual speech is likely to produce [wiæstɪm]. Vowels also disappear, as in the middle of [ɪntrɪst] for interest, or [kæbnɪt] for *cabinet*.

These two processes of assimilation and elision occur in everyone's speech and should not be treated as a form of sloppiness or laziness in speaking. In fact, consistently avoiding the regular patterns of assimilation and elision used in a language would result in extremely artificial sounding talk. The point of investigating phonological processes (only a very small number of which have been explored here) is not to arrive at a set of rules about how a language should be pronounced, but to try to come to an understanding of the regularities and patterns which underlie the actual use of sounds in language.

Study questions

1. Broadly speaking, how does phonology differ from phonetics?
2. What is the test used for determining phonemes in a language?
3. Which of the following words would be treated as minimal pairs?
   pat, pen, more, heat, tape, bun, fat, ban, chain, tale, bell, far, meal, vote, bet, pit, heel.
4. How does an allophone differ from a phoneme?
5. What processes are involved in the relationships between:
   (a) [grænd] *grand* and [græmpa] *grandpa*
   (b) [post] *post* and [posmən] *postman*

Discussion topics/projects

A. The use of plural -*s* in English has three different, but very regular, phonemic alternatives. You add:
   /s/ to words like *ship, bat, book* and *cough*
   /z/ to words like *cab, lad, cave, rag* and *thing*
   /əz/ to words like *bus, bush, judge, church* and *maze*
   Can you work out the set of sounds which regularly precedes each of these alternatives? What features do each of these sets have in common?
B. In the following pairs, the first word was pronounced carefully in isolation and the second was produced in the middle of conversational speech. Identify which sounds have 'changed', what type of change has occurred, and try to offer a possible explanation for the direction of change.
   | [nɔrθ] | [hænd] | [fayv] | [wet] |
   | [nɔrðərn] | [hæŋkərčif] | [fɪfθ] | [wedɪŋ] |
C. The word-initial sequences of /pl-/, /bl-/, /kl-/, /gl-/, /sl-/, /fl-/ are permissible in English, but other sequences involving /l/ are not. Can you produce a description of the required features a consonant must have in order to precede /l/?

D. It is possible to simulate electronically all the phonemes of English and have machines produce individual English sounds. However, there have been quite a number of problems getting the machines to produce non-artificial sounding phrases and sentences. Why do you think this is?

Further reading

Most of the works listed in the Further reading section of Chapter 5 also contain some treatments of phonology, with Ladefoged (1982) as a particularly useful introduction. Additional introductory treatments can be found in Callary (1981) and in Chapter 4 of Akmajian, Demers & Harnish (1984). The standard textbook on the subject is Hyman (1975). All these introductions provide some account of specific systems of rules for associating a phonological with a phonetic level of representation. If you wish to tackle one of the major original (but rather technical) works on this aspect of phonology, try Chomsky & Halle (1968). For an illuminating account of assimilation and elision in spoken English, see Brown (1977).

Chapter 7
Words and word-formation processes

Chemists, manufacturers of quack medicines, inventors of new explosives etc., supported by the freemasonry of their respective classes and the acquiescent public, float their *-ites* and *-ates*, *-ides* and *-ades*, with dire intent: *terrorite* and *americanite* have been invented recently to match *dynamite*, and one feels like drawing the curtain over the indecently profuse offspring of *vaseline* – the *rosalines*, the *bloomines*, the *fragelines* and the *nosulines*. The banality of these processes is offset by the startling subtleness of the categories which are accentuated by an adapted suffix: they are often the very stuff that dreams are made of. The sinister *electrocution* reminds us that the toddling onward steps of our civilization may yield us further a *hydrocution*, if perchance the theory that drowning is rather pleasant than otherwise should prevail.

Maurice Bloomfield (1895)

Imagine that a new word came into use as a general term to refer to anyone who worked as a technical assistant on projects. Say that the new word was *somp*, and that, if you asked a friend what she was doing these days, she might say *Oh, I'm a somp at a local radio station*. You might even hear variations of the term in conversation: *Are somps well paid? Oh, it's not bad. But I can't imagine somping for the rest of my life*. The term may turn up in headlines or advertisements such as *The Sompist Role in Broadcasting* or *Sompism as a Vocation*.

The point of considering these examples is that, although you had never heard the term *somp* before, you probably had no difficulty understanding the meaning of the other new words, *somps, somping, sompist* and *sompism*. That is, you can very quickly understand a new word in your language and cope with the use of different forms of that new word. This ability must derive in part from the fact that there is a lot of regularity in the word-formation processes in your language. In this chapter, we shall explore some of those basic processes by which new terms are created.

Word-formation processes

In some respects, the study of the processes whereby new words come into being in a language like English seems relatively straightforward. This apparent simplicity, however, masks a number of controversial issues, some of which we shall consider in the following chapter. Despite the disagreements among scholars in this area, there do seem to be some regular processes involved and, in the following sections, we shall cover the technical terms used to describe those processes and identify examples currently in use which are the result of those processes. It should be remembered that these processes have been at work in the language for some time and many words in daily use today were, at one time, considered barbaric misuses of the language. It is difficult now to understand the views expressed in the early nineteenth century over the "tasteless innovation" of a word like *handbook*, or the horror expressed by a London newspaper in 1909 over the use of the newly coined word *aviation*. Yet many terms of recent currency cause similar outcries. Rather than heed such protests that the language is being debased, we might prefer to view the constant evolution of new terms and new uses of old terms as a reassuring sign of vitality and creativeness in the way a language is shaped by the needs of its users. Let us consider the ways.

Coinage

One of the least common processes of word-formation in English is **coinage**, that is, the invention of totally new terms. Our fanciful creation of *somp* would be one example. Words like *aspirin* and *nylon*, originally invented trade names, are others. Familiar recent examples are *kleenex* and *xerox*, which also began as invented trade names, and which have quickly become everyday words in the language.

Borrowing

One of the most common sources of new words in English is the process simply labeled **borrowing**, that is, the taking over of words from other languages. Throughout its history, the English language has adopted a vast number of loan-words from other languages, including *alcohol* (Arabic), *boss* (Dutch), *croissant* (French), *lilac* (Persian), *piano* (Italian), *pretzel* (German), *robot* (Czech), *tycoon* (Japanese), *yogurt* (Turkish) and *zebra* (Bantu). Other languages, of course, borrow terms from English, as can be observed in the Japanese use of *suupaamaaketto* ('supermarket') and *rajio* ('radio'), or Hungarians talking about *sport*, *klub* and *futbal*, or the French discussing problems of *le parking*, over a glass of *le whisky*, during *le weekend*.

A special type of borrowing is described as **loan-translation**, or **calque**. In this process, there is a direct translation of the elements of a word into the borrowing language. An interesting example is the French term *un gratte-ciel*, which literally translates as 'a scrape-sky', and is used for what, in English, is normally referred to as a *skyscraper*. The English word *superman* is thought to be a loan-translation of the German *Übermensch*, and the term *loan-word* itself is believed to have come from the German *Lehnwort*. Nowadays, some Spanish speakers eat *perros calientes* (literally 'dogs hot'), or *hot dogs*.

Compounding

In some of those examples we have just considered, there is a joining of two separate words to produce a single form. Thus, *Lehn* and *Wort* are combined to produce *Lehnwort* in German. This combining process, technically known as **compounding**, is very common in languages like German and English, but much less common in languages like French and Spanish. Obvious English examples would be *bookcase*, *fingerprint*, *sunburn*, *wallpaper*, *doorknob*, *textbook*, *wastebasket* and *waterbed*.

This very productive source of new terms has been well-documented in English and German, but can also be found in totally unrelated languages, such as Hmong, in South East Asia, which combines *hwj* ('pot') and *kais* ('spout') to produce *hwjkais* ('kettle'). The forms *pajkws* ('flower' + 'corn' = 'popcorn') and *hnab looj tes* ('bag' + 'cover' + 'hand' = 'glove') are recent creations.

Blending

This combining of two separate forms to produce a single new term is also present in the process called **blending**. However, blending is typically accomplished by taking only the beginning of one word and joining it to the end of the other word. In some parts of the United States, there's a product which is used like *gasoline*, but is made from *alcohol*, so the 'blended' term for referring to this product is *gasohol*. If you wish to refer to the combined effects of *smoke* and *fog*, there's the term *smog*. Some other commonly used examples of blending are *brunch* (breakfast/lunch), *motel* (motor/hotel) and *telecast* (television/broadcast). The British have, for a number of years, considered the feasibility of constructing a tunnel under the English Channel to France, and newspapers inevitably refer to this project by using the blended expression *Chunnel*. A fairly recent invention, based on the blending process, was President Reagan's version of economic policy, that is, *Reaganomics*.

Clipping

The element of reduction which is noticeable in blending is even more apparent in the process described as **clipping**. This occurs when a word of more than one syllable is reduced to a shorter form, often in casual speech. The term *gasoline* is still in use, but occurs much less frequently than *gas*, the clipped form. Common examples are *ad* ('advertisement'), *fan* ('fanatic'), *bus*, *plane*, *prof*, *lab* and *flu*.

Backformation

A very specialized type of reduction process is known as **backformation**. Typically, a word of one type (usually a noun) is reduced to form another word of a different type (usually a verb). A good example of backformation is the process whereby the noun *television* first came into use and then the verb *televise* was created from it. Other examples of words created by this process are: *edit* (from 'editor'), *donate* (from 'donation'), *opt* (from 'option'), *emote* (from 'emotion') and *enthuse* (from 'enthusiasm').

Conversion

A change in the function of a word, as, for example, when a noun comes to be used as a verb (without any reduction) is generally known as **conversion**. Other labels for this very common process are 'category change' and 'functional shift'. A number of nouns, such as *paper*, *butter*, *bottle*, *vacation*, can, via the process of conversion, come to be used as verbs, as in the following sentences: *He's papering the bedroom walls*; *Have you buttered the toast?*; *We bottled the home-brew last night*; *They're vacationing in France*.

This process is particularly productive in modern English, with new uses occurring frequently. The conversion can involve verbs becoming nouns, with *guess*, *must* and *spy* as the sources of *a guess*, *a must* and *a spy*. Or adjectives, such as *dirty*, *empty*, *total*, *crazy* and *nasty*, can become the verbs *to dirty*, *to empty*, *to total*, or the nouns *a crazy* and *a nasty*. Other forms, such as *up* and *down*, can also become verbs, as in *They up the prices* or *We down a few beers*.

Acronyms

Some new words are formed from the initial letters of a set of other words. These **acronyms** often consist of capital letters, as in *NATO*, *NASA* or *UNESCO*, but can lose their capitals to become everyday terms such as *laser* ('light amplification by stimulated emission of radiation'), *radar* ('radio detecting and ranging') and *scuba* ('self contained underwater breathing apparatus'). You might even hear talk of a *snafu* which is reputed to have its origins in 'situation normal, all fouled up'.

Derivation

In our list so far, we have not dealt with what is by far the most common word-formation process to be found in the production of new English words. This process is called **derivation**, and it is accomplished by means of a large number of small 'bits' of the English language which are not usually given separate listings in dictionaries. These small 'bits' are called **affixes** and a few examples are the elements *un-*, *mis-*, *pre-*, *-ful*, *-less*, *-ish*, *-ism*, *-ness* which appear in words like *unhappy*, *misrepresent*, *prejudge*, *joyful*, *careless*, *boyish*, *terrorism* and *sadness*.

Prefixes and suffixes

In the preceding group of words, it should be obvious that some affixes have to be added to the beginning of a word (e.g. *un-*). These are called **prefixes**. The other affix forms are added to the end of the word (e.g. *-ish*) and are called **suffixes**. All English words formed by this derivational process use either prefixes or suffixes, or both. Thus, *mislead* has a prefix, *disrespectful* has both a prefix and a suffix, and *foolishness* has two suffixes.

Infixes

There is a third type of affix, not normally to be found in English, but fairly common in some other languages. This is called an **infix** and, as the term suggests, it is an affix which is incorporated inside another word. It is possible to see the general principle at work in certain expressions, occasionally used in fortuitous or aggravating circumstances by emotionally aroused English speakers: *Hallebloodylujah!*, *Absogoddamlutely!* and *Unfuckingbelievable!* We could view these 'inserted' forms as a special version of infixing. However, a much better set of examples can be provided from Kamhmu, a language spoken in South East Asia. These examples are taken from Merrifield *et al.* (1962):

('to drill')	*see – srnee*	('a drill')
('to chisel')	*toh – trnoh*	('a chisel')
('to eat with a spoon')	*hiip – hrniip*	('a spoon')
('to tie')	*hoom – hrnoom*	('a thing with which to tie')

It can be seen that there is a regular pattern whereby the infix *-rn-* is added to verbs to form corresponding nouns. If this pattern is generally found in the language and you know that the form *krnap* is the Kamhmu word for 'tongs', then you should be able to work out what the corresponding verb 'to grasp with tongs' would be. It is *kap*.

Multiple processes

Although we have concentrated on each of these word-formation processes in isolation, it is possible to trace the operation of more than one process at work in the creation of a particular word. For example, the term *deli* seems to have become a common American English expression via a process of first 'borrowing' *delicatessen* (from German) and then 'clipping' that borrowed form. If you hear someone complain that *problems with the project have snowballed*, the final term can be noted as an example of 'compounding', whereby *snow* and *ball* have been combined to form the noun *snowball*, which has then undergone 'conversion' to be used as a verb. Forms which begin as 'acronyms' can also undergo other processes, as in the use of *lase* as a verb, the result of 'backformation' from *laser*. In the expression, *waspish attitudes*, the form *WASP* ('white Anglo-Saxon Protestant') has lost its capital letters and gained a suffix in the 'derivation' process.

Many such forms can, of course, have a very brief life-span. Perhaps the generally accepted test of the 'arrival' of recently formed words in a language is their published appearance in a dictionary. However, even this may not occur without protests from some, as Noah Webster found when his first dictionary, published in 1806, was criticized for citing words like *advocate* and *test* as verbs, and for including such 'vulgar' words as *advisory* and *presidential*. It would seem that Noah had a keener sense than his critics of which new word-forms in the language were going to last.

Study questions

1. Which of the following expressions is an example of 'calque'? How would you describe the others?
    (a) *luna de miel* (Spanish) – *honeymoon* (English)
    (b) *mishin* (Japanese) – *machine* (English)
    (c) *tréning* (Hungarian) – *training* (English)
2. The term *vaseline* was originally a trade name for a product, but has become an ordinary English word. What is the technical term used to describe this process?
3. Identify the affixes used in the words *unfaithful*, *carelessness*, *refillable* and *disagree*, and decide whether they are prefixes or suffixes.
4. Can you identify the word-formation processes involved in producing the italicized forms in these sentences?
    (a) Laura *parties* every Saturday night.
    (b) Tom was worried that he might have *AIDS*.
    (c) Zee described the new toy as *fantabulous*.
    (d) Eliza exclaimed, "*Absobloominglutely!*"
5. More than one process was involved in the creation of each of the indicated forms below. Can you identify them?
    (a) I just got a new *car-phone*.
    (b) Shiel wants to be a *footballer*.
    (c) The negotiators *blueprinted* a new peace proposal.
    (d) Another *skyjacking* has just been reported.

Discussion topics/projects

A. The compound word *birdcage* is formed from a noun *bird* plus another noun *cage*, while the word *widespread* is formed from an adjective *wide* and a verb *spread*. So, compounds differ in terms of the types of elements which are combined. Can you identify the different elements involved in each of the following compounds?
    bedroom, blackbird, brainwash, catfish, clean-shaven, crybaby, haircut, heartbeat, hothouse, hovercraft, leadfree, madman, ready-made, seasick, sunflower, sunrise, telltale, threadbare, watchdog, well-dressed.

B. The work of Bruce Downing and Judy Fuller (at the University of Minnesota) in a study of the language of Hmong refugees now living in the United States has produced some interesting examples of new word-formations designed to cope with new objects and experiences. If you are given the translation equivalents of some Hmong terms, can you work out the English equivalents of the Hmong compounds which follow?

kws ('artisan'); *kev* ('way'); *ntaus* ('hit', 'mark'); *ntoo* ('tree'); *nqaj* ('rail'); *ntawv* ('paper'); *niam* ('mother'); *hlau* ('iron'); *tshuaj* ('medicine'); *tsheb* ('vehicle'); *kho* ('fix'); *hniav* ('teeth'); *mob* ('sick'); *cai* ('right', 'law'); *dav* ('bird', 'hawk'); *daim* ('flat'); *muas* ('buy').

dav hlau ('airplane')	*kws ntoo*	*kev kho mob*
kws ntawv	*kws ntaus ntawv*	*kws kho tsheb*
kws tshuaj	*kws hlau*	*kev cai*
kev nqaj hlau	*tsheb nqaj hlau*	*niam hlau*
kws kho hniav	*daim ntawv muas tshuaj*	

C. A number of interesting word-formation processes can be discerned in some of the following examples. Can you identify what is going on in these, and have you come across any comparable examples?

When I'm ill, I want to see a doc, not a vet.
I was a deejay before, but now I emcee in a nightclub.
That's a-whole-nother problem.
The deceased's cremains were scattered over the hill.
He's always taking pills, either uppers or downers.

D. Only a handful of the English words borrowed from other languages were presented in this chapter. Can you find out, by consulting a dictionary (an etymological dictionary if possible), which of the following words are borrowings and from which languages they came?

advantage, assassin, caravan, cash, child, clinic, cobalt, cockroach, crime, have, laundry, measles, physics, pony, ranch, scatter, slogan, violent, wagon, yacht, zero.

Further reading

There are a number of general treatments of word-formation in English, with the textbooks of Adams (1973) and, more recently, Bauer (1983) as good examples. A more technical treatment is offered by Aronoff (1976). Comprehensive reference works are Marchand (1969) or Quirk *et al.* (1972), Appendix 1, which is mainly based on British English. For American English, the journal *American Speech* regularly carries articles on word-formation. For an exhaustive survey of contemporary examples of conversion, see Clark & Clark (1979) and on infixing in English, see McMillan (1980). A good survey of attitudes toward 'good' and 'bad' English usage can be found in Finnegan (1980). A comprehensive bibliography of works dealing with word-formation can be found in Stein (1973).

Chapter 8
Morphology

To our language may be with great justness applied the observation
of Quintilian, that speech was not formed by an analogy sent from
heaven. It did not descend to us in a state of uniformity and perfection,
but was produced by necessity and enlarged by accident, and is
therefore composed of dissimilar parts, thrown together by negligence,
by affectation, by learning, or by ignorance.

Samuel Johnson (1747)

Throughout the preceding chapter, we approached the description of
processes involved in word-formation as if the unit called the 'word'
was a regular and easily identifiable form. This doesn't seem unreason-
able when we look at a text of written English, since the 'words' in
the text are, quite obviously, those sets of things marked in black with
the bigger spaces separating them. Unfortunately, there are a number
of problems with using this observation as the basis of an attempt to
describe language in general, and individual linguistic forms in particular.

Morphology

In many languages, what appear to be single forms actually turn out
to contain a large number of 'word-like' elements. For example, in
Swahili (spoken throughout East Africa), the form *nitakupenda* conveys
what, in English, would have to be represented as something like *I
will love you*. Now, is the Swahili form a single word? If it is a 'word',
then it seems to consist of a number of elements which, in English,
turn up as separate 'words'. A very rough correspondence can be presented in the following way:

    ni – ta   – ku   – penda
    'I'   'will' 'you' 'love'

It seems as if this Swahili 'word' is rather different from what we think
of as an English 'word'. Yet, there clearly is some similarity between
the languages, in that similar elements of the whole message can be

found in both. Perhaps a better way of looking at linguistic forms in different languages would be to use this notion of 'elements' in the message, rather than to depend on identifying 'words'. The type of exercise we have just performed is an example of investigating forms in language, generally known as **morphology**. This term, which literally means 'the study of forms', was originally used in biology, but, since the mid nineteenth century, has also been used to describe that type of investigation which analyzes all those basic 'elements' which are used in a language. What we have been describing as 'elements' in the form of a linguistic message are more technically known as **morphemes**.

Morphemes

We do not actually have to go to other languages such as Swahili to discover that 'word-forms' may consist of a number of elements. We can recognize that English word-forms such as *talks*, *talker*, *talked* and *talking* must consist of one element *talk*, and a number of other elements such as *-s*, *-er*, *-ed*, *-ing*. All these elements are described as morphemes. The definition of a morpheme is "a minimal unit of meaning or grammatical function". Let's clarify this definition with some examples. We would say that the word *reopened* in the sentence *The police reopened the investigation* consists of three morphemes. One minimal unit of meaning is *open*, another minimal unit of meaning is *re-* (meaning 'again'), and a minimal unit of grammatical function is *-ed* (indicating past tense). The word *tourists* also contains three morphemes. There is one minimal unit of meaning, *tour*, another minimal unit of meaning *-ist* (meaning 'person who does something'), and a minimal unit of grammatical function *-s* (indicating plural).

Free and bound morphemes

From these two examples, we can make a broad distinction between two types of morphemes. There are **free morphemes**, that is, morphemes which can stand by themselves as single words, e.g. *open* and *tour*. There are also **bound morphemes**, that is, those which cannot normally stand alone, but which are typically attached to another form, e.g. *re-*, *-ist*, *-ed*, *-s*. You will recognize this last set as a group of what we have already described in Chapter 7 as affixes. So, all affixes in English are bound morphemes. The free morphemes can be generally considered as the set of separate English word-forms. When they are used with bound morphemes, the basic word-form involved is technically known as the **stem**. For example:

undressed			*carelessness*		
un-	*dress*	*-ed*	*care*	*-less*	*-ness*
prefix	stem	suffix	stem	suffix	suffix
(bound)	(free)	(bound)	(free)	(bound)	(bound)

It should be noted that this type of description is a partial simplification of the morphological facts of English. There are a number of English words in which the element which seems to be the 'stem' is not, in fact, a free morpheme. In words like *receive, reduce, repeat* we can recognize the bound morpheme *re-*, but the elements *-ceive, -duce* and *-peat* are clearly not free morphemes. There is still some disagreement over the proper characterization of these elements and you may encounter a variety of technical terms used to describe them. It may help to work with a simple distinction between forms like *-ceive* and *-duce* as 'bound stems' and forms like *dress* and *care* as 'free stems'.

Free morphemes

What we have described as free morphemes fall into two categories. The first category is that set of ordinary nouns, adjectives and verbs which we think of as the words which carry the 'content' of messages we convey. These free morphemes are called **lexical morphemes** and some examples are: *boy, man, house, tiger, sad, long, yellow, sincere, open, look, follow, break*.

The other group of free morphemes are called **functional morphemes**. Examples are: *and, but, when, because, on, near, above, in, the, that, it*. This set consists largely of the functional words in the language such as conjunctions, prepositions, articles and pronouns.

Bound morphemes

The set of affixes which fall into the 'bound' category can also be divided into two types. One type we have already considered in Chapter 7 are the **derivational morphemes**. These are used to make new words in the language and are often used to make words of a different grammatical category from the stem. Thus, the addition of the derivational morpheme

-ness changes the adjective *good* to the noun *goodness*. A list of derivational morphemes will include suffixes such as the *-ish* in *foolish*, the *-ly* in *badly* and the *-ment* in *payment*. It will also include prefixes such as *re-*, *pre-*, *ex-*, *dis-*, *co-*, *un-* and many more.

The second set of bound morphemes contains what are called **inflectional morphemes**. These are not used to produce new words in the English language, but rather to indicate aspects of the grammatical function of a word. Inflectional morphemes are used to show if a word is plural or singular, if it is past tense or not, and if it is a comparative or possessive form. Examples of inflectional morphemes at work can be seen in the use of *-ed* to make *jump* into the past tense form *jumped*, and the use of *-s* to make the word *boy* into the plural *boys*. Other examples are the *-ing*, *-s*, *-er*, *-est* and *-'s* inflections in the phrases *Myrna is singing*, *she sings*, *she is smaller*, *the smallest* and *Myrna's horse*. Note that, in English, all inflectional morphemes are suffixes.

Morphological description

Armed with all these terms for the different types of morphemes, you can now take most sentences of English apart and list the 'elements'. As an example, the English sentence *The boy's wildness shocked the teachers* contains the following elements:

The	*boy*	*-'s*	*wild*	*-ness*
(functional)	(lexical)	(inflectional)	(lexical)	(derivational)
shock	*-ed*	*the*	*teach*	*-er*	*-s*
(lexical)	(inflectional)	(functional)	(lexical)	(derivational)	(inflectional)

As a useful way to remember the different categories of morphemes, the following chart can be used:

Problems in morphological description

The rather neat chart presented above conceals a number of outstanding problems in the analysis of English morphology. So far, we have only considered examples of English words in which the different morphemes are easily identifiable as separate elements. Thus, the inflectional morpheme -*s* is added to *cat* and we get the plural *cats*. What is the inflectional morpheme which makes *sheep* the plural of *sheep*, or *men* the plural of *man*? A related question concerns the inflection which makes *went* the past tense of *go*. And yet another question concerns the derivation of an adjective like *legal*. If -*al* is the derivational suffix, as it is in forms like *institutional*, then what is the stem? No, it isn't *leg*.

These problematic issues, and many others which arise in the analysis of different languages, have not been fully resolved by linguists. The solutions to these problems are clearer in some cases than in others. The relationship between *law* and *legal* is a reflection of the historical influence of other languages on English word-forms. The modern form *law* is a result of a borrowing into Old English from Old Norse, over 1,000 years ago. The modern form *legal* is a borrowing from the Latin form *legalis* ('of the law'). Consequently, there is no derivational relationship between the two forms in English, nor between the noun *mouth* (an Old English form) and the adjective *oral* (a Latin borrowing). It has been pointed out that an extremely large number of English forms owe their morphological patterning to languages like Latin and Greek. Consequently, a full description of English morphology will have to take account of both historical influences and the effect of borrowed elements.

Morphs and allomorphs

The solution to other problems remains controversial. One way to treat differences in inflectional morphemes is by proposing variation in morphological realization rules. In order to do this, we draw an analogy with some processes already noted in phonology (Chapter 6). If we consider 'phones' as the actual phonetic realization of 'phonemes', then we can propose **morphs** as the actual forms used to realize morphemes. Thus, the form *cat* is a single morph realizing a lexical morpheme. The form *cats* consists of two morphs, realizing a lexical morpheme and an inflectional morpheme ('plural'). Just as we noted that there were 'allophones' of a particular phoneme, then we can recognize **allomorphs** of a particular morpheme. Take the morpheme 'plural'. Note that it can be attached to a number of lexical morphemes to produce structures like 'cat + plural', 'sheep + plural', and 'man + plural'. Now, the actual forms of the morphs which result from the single morpheme 'plural' turn out to be different. Yet they are all allomorphs of the one morpheme. It has been suggested, for example, that one allomorph of 'plural' is a zero-morph, and the plural form of *sheep* is actually 'sheep + $\emptyset$'. Otherwise, those so-called 'irregular' forms of plurals and past tenses in English are described as having individual morphological realization rules. Thus, 'man + plural' or 'go + past', as analyses at the morpheme-level, are realized as *men* and *went* at the morph-level.

Other languages

This type of analytic approach is not without its critics, particularly when applied to other languages. Yet, the absence of a comprehensive analytic system should not discourage us from exploring and describing some of the morphological features of other languages. Some patterns appear to be describable in terms of the basic categories we listed earlier. The first example below is from English and the second is from Aztec:

Stem	Derivational	Inflectional		
DARK	+ -*EN* ('make')	+ -*ED* ('past')	=	*DARKENED*
MIC ('die') +	*TIA* ('cause to') +	-*S* ('future')	=	*MICTIAS* ('will kill')

Different patterns occur in other languages. Let's look at some sample data, adapted from examples originally presented in Gleason (1955), and try to work out which morphological features can be identified. The first is from Kanuri, a language spoken in Nigeria.

Kanuri

('excellent')	*karite*– *nəmkarite*	('excellence')
('big')	*kura* – *nəmkura*	('bigness')
('small')	*gana* – *nəmgana*	('smallness')
('bad')	*dibi* – *nəmdibi*	('badness')

From this set, we can propose that the prefix *nəm-* is a derivational morpheme which can be used to derive nouns from adjectives. Discovering a regular morphological feature of this type will enable us to make certain predictions when we encounter other forms in the language. For example, if the Kanuri word for 'length' is *nəmkurugu*, then we can be reasonably sure that 'long' is *kurugu*.

Different languages also employ different means to produce inflectional marking on forms. Here are some examples from Ganda, a language spoken in Uganda:

Ganda

('doctor')	*omusawo – abasawo*	('doctors')
('woman')	*omukazi – abakazi*	('women')
('girl')	*omuwala – abawala*	('girls')
('heir')	*omusika – abasika*	('heirs')

From this small sample, we can observe that there is an inflectional prefix *omu-*, used with singular nouns, and a different inflectional prefix *aba-*, used with the plural of those nouns. If you are told that *abalenzi* is a Ganda plural, meaning 'boys', you should be able to determine the singular form, meaning 'boy'. It is, of course, *omulenzi*.

The following data from Ilocano, a language of the Philippines, will serve to illustrate a quite different method for marking plurals:

Ilocano

('head')	*úlo – ulúlo*	('heads')
('road')	*dálan – daldálan*	('roads')
('life')	*bíag – bibíag*	('lives')
('plant')	*múla – mulmúla*	('plants')

In these examples, there seems to be repetition of the first part of the singular form. When the first part is *bi-* in the singular, the plural begins with this form repeated, *bibi-*. The process involved here is technically known as **reduplication** and several languages use this repetition device as a means of inflectional marking. Having seen how plurals differ from singular forms in Ilocano, you should be able to take this plural form *taltálon* ('fields') and work out what the singular ('field') would be. If you follow the pattern observed, you should get *tálon*.

Finally, here are some intriguing data provided by Lisa Miguel, who speaks Tagalog, another language of the Philippines:

Tagalog

basa ('read')	*tawag* ('call')	*sulat* ('write')
bumasa ('Read!')	*tumawag* ('Call!')	*sumulat* ('Write!')
babasa ('will read')	*tatawag* ('will call')	*susulat* ('will write')

If we assume that the first form in each set is some type of stem, then it appears that in the second member of each set an element *-um-* has been inserted after the first consonant. It must be an example of an infix. In the third member of each set, note that the change in form involves, in each case, a repetition of the first syllable. So, the marking of future reference in Tagalog appears to be accomplished via reduplication. If you know that *lapit* is the verb meaning 'come here' in Tagalog, how would you expect the expressions 'Come here!' and 'will come here' to be realized? How about *lumapit* and *lalapit*?

Study questions

1. (a) List the 'bound' morphemes to be found in these words: *misleads, previewer, shortened, unhappier, fearlessly*.
   (b) In which of the following examples should the 'a' be treated as a bound morpheme: *a boy, apple, atypical, AWOL*?
2. What are the functional morphemes in the following sentence:
   The old man sat on a chair and told them tales of woe.
3. What are the inflectional morphemes in the following phrases:
   (a) *the teacher's books*   (c) *the newest model*
   (b) *it's snowing*   (d) *the cow jumped over the moon*
4. What would we list as allomorphs of the morpheme 'plural' from this set of English words: *dogs, oxen, deer, judges, curricula*?
5. Provide the equivalent forms, in the languages listed, for the English translations shown on the right below.

Tagalog	'buy'	*bili*	'will buy'
Kanuri	'sweetness'	*nəmkəji*	'sweet'
Kamhmu	'an ear ornament'	*srnal*	'to place in earlobe'
Ganda	'twin'	*omuloŋgo*	'twins'
Ilocano	'windows'	*tawtáwa*	'window'
Kamhmu	'a small package'	*trniap*	'to fold a small package'
Tagalog	'eat'	*kain*	'Eat!'

Discussion topics/projects

A. There are often regular meanings associated with particular English derivational affixes (e.g. *-en* added to *dark* or *sharp* gives the meaning 'make dark' or 'make sharp'). Is there regularity of meaning in the derivational affixes used in the following sets of words? Can you think of others which do, or do not, have consistent meanings?
   shorten, blacken, golden, deepen, soften, wooden
   laughable, readable, breakable, reasonable, perishable, enjoyable
   rewrite, rebuild, refine, remiss, relax, refuse
B. Here are some data from Turkish, provided by Feride Erkü.
   (a) Can you provide the missing forms in the table?

('man')	*adam*	– *adamlar*	('men')
('secret')	_____	– *sɪrlar*	('secrets')
('place')	*yer*	– *yerler*	('places')
('road')	_____	– *yollar*	('roads')
('lock')	_____	– *kilitler*	('locks')

('hand')	*el*	_ _____	('hands')
('arm')	*kol*	_ _____	('arms')
('bell')	_____	– *ziller*	('bells')
('friend')	_____	– *dostlar*	('friends')

(b) In Turkish, consider *a*, *o* and *ı* as representing back vowels, and *e* and *i* as representing front vowels. Given this information, can you state the conditions under which the two different plural morphs (*-ler* and *-lar*) are used?

C. Here are some further examples of Swahili sentences. Can you work out the forms which correspond to the elements in the English translations?

alipita	('she passed by')	*alikupiga*	('she beat you')
waliondoka	('they left')	*nilimlipa*	('I paid him')
niliwapika	('I cooked them')	*nitakupenda*	('I will love you')
utawauza	('you will sell them')	*utanipiga*	('you will beat me')
nitaondoka	('I will leave')	*tuliwapenda*	('we loved them')
tutapita	('we will pass by')	*watamlipa*	('they will pay him')

D. Remembering the morphological processes identified in Tagalog, can you extend the analysis to describe the elements and processes involved in the following examples, also from Tagalog?

hanap	('look for')	*sulat*	('write')
hinanap	('was looked for')	*sinulat*	('was written')
humahanap	('is looking for')	*sumusulat*	('is writing')
hinahanap	('is being looked for')	*sinusulat*	('is being written')

basag	('break')	*tawag*	('call')
binasag	('was broken')	*tinawag*	('was called')
bumabasag	('is breaking')	*tumatawag*	('is calling')
binabasag	('is being broken')	*tinatawag*	('is being called')

Further reading

Most introductory linguistic texts have a section on morphology, for example, Chapter 4 of Fromkin & Rodman (1983) or Chapter 3 of Akmajian, Demers & Harnish (1984). An array of interesting exercises involving a wide variety of different languages can be found in Gleason (1955). A particularly clear presentation of the relationship between morphemes and morphs is in part 2 of Brown & Miller (1980) and why the distinction is necessary is covered in Chapter 5 of Lyons (1968). A comprehensive textbook on the subject is Matthews (1974). Interest in morphology was much greater in earlier works on language and you might like to go back to Bloomfield (1933) for one approach and then try Hockett (1954; 1958) for another. If your interest in Swahili has been aroused, a relatively brief and very clear introduction to the language can be found in Hinnebusch (1979).

Chapter 9

Phrases and sentences: grammar

O what a midnight Curse has he, whose side
Is pester'd with a Mood and Figure Bride.
Let mine, ye Gods, (if such must be my Fate)
No Logick Learn, nor History Translate:
But rather be a quiet, humble Fool;
I hate a Wife, to whom I go to School.
Who climbs the Grammar-Tree; distinctly knows
Where Noun, and Verb, and Participle grows.

John Dryden, *The Sixth Satyr of Juvenal* (1693)

We have already considered two levels of description used in the study of language. We have described linguistic expressions as sequences of sounds which can be represented phonetically. For example:

We can take the same linguistic expression and describe it as a sequence of morphemes. For example:

With these descriptions, we could characterize all the words of a language in terms of their phonetic and morphological make-up.

Grammar

However, we have not yet accounted for the fact that these words can only be combined in a limited number of patterns. We recognize that the phrase *the lucky boys* is a well-formed piece of English, but that the following two 'phrases' are not at all well-formed:

     * *boys the lucky*   **lucky boys the*

> (Beside each of these ill-formed structures there is an asterisk, which is a conventional way of indicating that a structure is ill-formed, or ungrammatical.)

So, we need a way of describing the structure of phrases and sentences which will account for all of the grammatical sequences and rule out all the ungrammatical sequences. Providing such an account involves us in the study of **grammar**. We should note that this term is frequently used to cover a number of different phenomena.

Types of grammar

Each adult speaker of a language clearly has some type of 'mental grammar', that is, a form of internal linguistic knowledge which operates in the production and recognition of appropriately structured expressions in that language. This 'grammar' is subconscious and is not the result of any teaching. A second, and quite different, concept of 'grammar' involves what might be considered 'linguistic etiquette', that is, the identification of the 'proper' or 'best' structures to be used in a language. A third view of 'grammar' involves the study and analysis of the structures found in a language, usually with the aim of establishing a description of the grammar of English, for example, as distinct from the grammar of Russian or French or any other language. There are, in fact, other ways in which the term 'grammar' may be used. However, given these three concepts, we can say that, in general, the first may be of most interest to a psychologist, since it deals with what goes on in people's minds, the second may be of interest to a sociologist, since it has to do with people's social attitudes and values, while the third is what occupies many linguists, since the concern is with the nature of language, often independently of the users of the language. The study of grammar, in this narrow sense of the study of the structure of expressions in a language, has a very long tradition.

The parts of speech

You may already be familiar with many of the terms used in a grammatical description, particularly the terms for the parts of speech, as illustrated in this sentence:

The	*lucky*	*boys*	*saw*	*the*	*clowns*	*at*
article	adjective	noun	verb	article	noun	preposition

the	*circus*	*and*	*they*	*cheered*	*loudly*
article	noun	conjunction	pronoun	verb	adverb

Traditional grammar

Terms like these, used to label the grammatical categories of words in sentences, come from traditional grammar, which has its origins in the description of languages like Classical Latin and Greek. Since there were well-established grammatical descriptions of these older languages, it seemed appropriate to adopt the existing categories from these descriptions and apply them in the analysis of languages like English. After all, Latin and Greek were the languages of scholarship, religion, philosophy and 'knowledge', so the grammar of these languages was taken to be the best grammar.

Traditional categories

In addition to the terms used for the parts of speech, traditional grammatical analysis also uses a number of other categories, including 'number', 'person', 'tense', 'voice' and 'gender'. These categories can be discussed in isolation, but their role in describing language structure becomes clearer when we consider them in terms of **concord** or **agreement**. For example, we say that the verb *likes* 'agrees with' the noun *boy* in the sentence *The boy likes his dog*. This agreement is partially based on the category of **number**, that is, whether the noun is singular or plural. It is also based on the category of **person**, which covers the distinctions of first person (involving the speaker), second person (involving the hearer) and third person (involving any others). The different forms of English pronouns are usually described in terms of person and number, in that we have first person singular (*I*), second person singular (*you*), third person singular (*he, she, it*) and so on. So, in the sentence *The boy likes his dog*, we have a noun *boy* which is third person singular and the verb *likes* 'agrees with' the noun.

In addition, the form of the verb must also be described in terms of another category, that of **tense**. In this case, the verb is in the present tense, which results in a different form from the past tense (e.g. *liked*). And, the sentence is in the **active voice**, rather than the **passive voice**, which would have produced the form *The boy is liked by his dog*.

Our final category is that of **gender**, which is used to describe the agreement between *boy* and *his* in our example sentence. In English, we have to describe this relationship in terms of **natural gender**, mainly derived from a biological distinction between male and female. The 'agreement' between *boy* and *his* is based on a distinction English makes between reference to male entities (*he, his*), female entities (*she, her*), and sexless entities, or animals, when the sex of the animal is irrelevant (*it, its*).

This type of biological distinction is quite different from the more common distinction found in languages which use **grammatical gender**. In this latter sense, nouns are classified according to their gender class and, typically, articles and adjectives take different forms to 'agree with' the gender of the noun. Spanish, for example, has two grammatical genders, masculine and feminine, illustrated by the expressions *el sol* ('the sun') and *la luna* ('the moon') respectively. German uses three genders, masculine *der Mond* ('the moon'), feminine *die Sonne* ('the sun') and neuter *das Feuer* ('the fire'). Note the different forms of the articles in both the Spanish and German examples, corresponding to differences in the gender class of the nouns. Also note that the gender distinction is not based on a distinction in sex. A young girl is biologically 'female', but the German noun *das Mädchen* is grammatically 'neuter'. The French word *le livre* ('the book') is grammatically masculine, but we would not consider books to be biologically male. So, the grammatical category of gender is very usefully applied in describing a number of languages (including Latin), but may not be particularly appropriate for English.

Traditional analysis

The notion of 'appropriateness' of analytic categories has not always been a consideration. In traditional grammar books, tables such as the following were often presented for English, constructed by analogy with similar tables of forms in Latin grammars. The forms for the Latin verb *amare* ('to love') are listed on the right.

	First person, singular	*I love*	amo
Present	Second person, singular	*you love*	amas
tense,	Third person, singular	*he loves*	amat
active	First person, plural	*we love*	amamus
voice	Second person, plural	*you love*	amatis
	Third person, plural	*they love*	amant

Note that each of the Latin verb forms is different, according to the categories of person and number, yet the English forms are, with one exception, the same. Thus it makes some sense, in describing a language like Latin, to have all those descriptive categories to characterize verb forms, yet it seems a rather extravagant descriptive system for English. The influence of Latin, however, goes beyond the descriptive labels.

The prescriptive approach

It is one thing to adopt the grammatical labels (e.g. 'noun', 'verb') to categorize words in English sentences; it is quite another thing to go on to claim that the structure of English sentences should be like the structure of sentences in Latin. Yet this was an approach taken by some grammarians, mainly in eighteenth century England, who set out rules for the correct or 'proper' use of English. This view of grammar as a set of rules for the 'proper' use of a language is still to be found today and may be best characterized as the **prescriptive approach**. Some familiar examples of prescriptive rules for English sentences are as follows:

(1) You must not split an infinitive.
(2) You must not end a sentence with a preposition.

There are, of course, many such rules which generations of English teachers have attempted to instill in their pupils via corrections such as the following:

It may, in fact, be a valuable part of one's education to be made aware of this 'linguistic etiquette', or the 'proper' use of the language. If it is a social expectation that someone who writes well should obey these prescriptive rules, then social judgments such as "poorly educated" may be made about someone who does not follow these rules.

However, it is worth considering the probable origins of these rules and asking whether they are appropriately applied to the English language. Let us take one example: "You must not split an infinitive."

Captain Kirk's infinitive

The infinitive in English has the form *to* + the verb, e.g. *to go*, and can be used with an adverb such as *boldly*. So, at the beginning of each televised 'Star Trek' episode, Captain Kirk uses the expression *To boldly go . . .* This is an example of a split infinitive. Captain Kirk's English teacher should have taught him to say *To go boldly*. If Captain Kirk had been a Roman astronaut, speaking Latin, he would have used the expressions *ire* ('to go') and *audacter* ('boldly'). Now, in saying *Ire audacter . . .* in Latin, Captain Kirkus would not even have the opportunity to split his infinitive (*ire*), because Latin infinitives are single words and just do not split.

So, it would be very appropriate in Latin grammar to say that you cannot split an infinitive. But is it appropriate to carry this idea over into English, where the infinitive does not consist of a single word, but of two words, *to* and *go*? If it is a typical feature of the use of English that speakers and writers do produce forms such as *to boldly go* or *to solemnly swear*, then we may wish to say that there are structures in English which differ from those found in Latin, rather than to say that the English forms are "bad" because they are breaking a supposed rule of Latin grammar.

The descriptive approach

It may be that using a well-established grammatical description of Latin is a useful guide for studying some languages (e.g. Italian or Spanish), is less useful for others (e.g. English), and may be absolutely misleading if you want to describe some non-European languages. This last point became clear to those linguists who wanted to describe the structure of North American Indian languages at the end of the nineteenth century. The categories and rules which were appropriate for Latin grammar just did not seem to fit the Indian languages encountered. As a consequence, throughout the present century, a rather different approach has been taken. The analyst collects samples of the language he or she is interested in and attempts to describe the regular structures of the language as it is used, not according to some view of how it should be used. This is called the **descriptive approach** and it is the basis of most modern attempts to characterize the structure of different languages.

Structural analysis

One type of descriptive approach is called **structural analysis** and its main concern is to investigate the distribution of forms (e.g. morphemes) in a language. The method employed involves the use of 'test-frames' which can be sentences with empty slots in them. For example:

> The _____ *makes a lot of noise.*
> *I heard a* _____ *yesterday.*

There are a lot of forms which can fit into these slots to produce good grammatical sentences of English (e.g. *donkey, car, dog, radio, child,* etc.). Consequently, we can suggest that because all of these forms fit in the same test-frame, they are likely to be examples of the same grammatical category. The label we give to this grammatical category is, of course, 'noun'. However, there are many forms which do not fit the test-frames above. Examples would be *Kathy, it, the dog, a car,* and so on. For these forms, we require different test-frames, which could be like this:

> _____ *makes a lot of noise.*
> *I heard* _____ *yesterday.*

Among the forms which fit these test-frames are *Kathy, Margaret Thatcher, it, the dog, an old car, the professor with the Scottish accent,* and many more. Once again, we can suggest that these forms are likely to be examples of the same grammatical category. The common label for this category is 'noun phrase'. By developing a set of test-frames of this type and discovering what forms fit the slots in the test-frames, you can produce a description of (at least some) aspects of the sentence structures of a language.

Immediate constituent analysis

An approach with the same descriptive aims is called **immediate constituent analysis**. The technique employed in this approach is designed to show how small constituents (or components) in sentences go together to form larger constituents. In the following sentence, we can identify eight constituents (at the word level): *Her father brought a shotgun to the wedding*.

How do those eight constituents go together to form constituents at the phrase level? Does it seem appropriate to put the words together as follows: *brought a, father brought, shotgun to, to the*? We don't normally think of these combinations as phrases in English. We are more likely to say that the phrase-like constituents here are combinations of the following types: *Her father, a shotgun, the wedding*, which are noun phrases; *to the wedding*, which is a prepositional phrase; *brought a shotgun*, which is a verb phrase.

This analysis of the constituent structure of the sentence can be represented in different types of diagrams. One type of diagram simply shows the distribution of the constituents at different levels.

Her	father	brought	a	shotgun	to	the	wedding

This type of diagram can be used to show the types of forms which substitute for each other at different levels of constituent structure.

Her	father	brought	a	shotgun	to	the	wedding
The	man	saw	the	thief	in	a	car
Sam		took		Anne	to		Paris
He		came					here

Labeled and bracketed sentences

An alternative type of diagram is designed to show how the constituents in sentence structure can be marked off via labeled brackets. The first step is to put brackets (one on each side) around each constituent, and then more brackets around each combination of constituents. For example:

$$\Big[\big[[\text{The}]\ [\text{dog}]\big]\ \big[[\text{followed}]\ \big[[\text{the}]\ [\text{boy}]\big]\big]\Big]$$

With this procedure, the different constituents of the sentence are shown at the word level – [*the*]; at the phrase level – [*the boy*]; and at the sentence level – [*The dog followed the boy*].

We can, of course, label each constituent with grammatical terms such as 'Art' (= article), 'N' (= noun), 'NP' (= noun phrase), 'V' (= verb), 'VP' (= verb phrase) and 'S' (= sentence). In the following diagram, these labels are placed beside each bracket which marks the beginning of a constituent. The result is a labeled and bracketed analysis of the constituent structure of the sentence.

$$\left[\left[\left[\text{The}\right]_{\text{Art}} \left[\text{dog}\right]_{\text{N}}\right]_{\text{NP}} \left[\left[\text{followed}\right]_{\text{V}} \left[\left[\text{the}\right]_{\text{Art}} \left[\text{boy}\right]_{\text{N}}\right]_{\text{NP}}\right]_{\text{VP}}\right]_{\text{S}}$$

This type of analysis is not restricted to the description of English sentences. We can take a sample sentence from a language with a structure quite different from English and apply the same type of analysis.

A Gaelic sentence. Here is a sentence from Scottish Gaelic which would be translated as *The boy saw the black dog*:

Chunnaic	*an*	*gille*	*an*	*cu*	*dubh*
'saw'	'the'	'boy'	'the'	'dog'	'black'

One very obvious difference between the structure of this Gaelic sentence and its English counterpart is the fact that the verb comes first in the sentence. Another noticeable feature is that, when an adjective is used, it follows rather than precedes the noun. We can represent these structural observations in our diagram.

$$\left[\left[\text{Chunnaic}\right]_{\text{V}} \left[\left[\text{an}\right]_{\text{Art}} \left[\text{gille}\right]_{\text{N}}\right]_{\text{NP}} \left[\left[\text{an}\right]_{\text{Art}} \left[\text{cu}\right]_{\text{N}} \left[\text{dubh}\right]_{\text{Adj}}\right]_{\text{NP}}\right]_{\text{S}}$$

It is not, of course, the aim of this type of analysis that we should be able to draw complicated-looking diagrams in order to impress our friends. The aim is to make explicit, via the diagram, what we believe to be the structure of grammatical sentences in a language. It also enables us to describe clearly how English sentences are put together as combinations of phrases which, in turn, are combinations of words. We can then look at similar descriptions of sentences in other languages, Gaelic, French, Spanish, or whatever, and see clearly what structural differences exist. At a very practical level, it may help us understand why a Spanish learner of English produces phrases like *the wine white (instead of *the white wine*), using a structural organization of constituents which is possible in Spanish, but not in English.

Study questions

1. Give the traditional terms for the grammatical categories of words used in the following sentence (e.g. *boy* = noun): *The boy rubbed the magic lamp and suddenly a genie appeared beside him*.
2. What prescriptive rules for the 'proper' use of English are not obeyed in the following sentences?
    (a) *That's the girl I gave my roller skates to.*
    (b) *He wanted to simply borrow your car for an hour.*
3. Most modern attempts to characterize the structure of sentences are based on a particular approach. What is this approach called, and what general principle is adhered to in such an approach?
4. Present a labeled and bracketed analysis of this sentence:
    The policeman chased a robber.
5. Given the following English translations of some other Gaelic words, can you translate the sentences which follow: *mor* ('big'), *beag* ('small'), *bhuail* ('hit'), *duine* ('man').
    (a) *Bhuail an gille beag an cu dubh.*
    (b) *Chunnaic an cu an duine mor.*

Discussion topics/projects

A. The grammatical category of 'tense' was mentioned briefly in this chapter and a distinction between present and past tense in English was noted. It has been claimed (Palmer, 1971: 193) that English has no future tense form, although it does have many ways of referring to future time. Consider the following sentences and decide what kind of time-reference is involved. Then, consider whether the labels 'past', 'present' and 'future' are appropriate for describing the verb forms used.
Water will freeze at zero degrees Centigrade. I'll leave if you want.

If John phones, tell him I am asleep. I wish I had a million dollars.
Your plane leaves at noon tomorrow. You always listen to the same songs.
We're going to visit Rome next year. He said Sandra was leaving next week.
Shall we dance? They were about to leave when I arrived.

B. The types of grammatical descriptions we have considered would simply treat the following examples as English sentences and present a description of their form and structural organization. Is this what everyone considers as 'grammar', and might there be more to say about sentences like these?

 (i) *I don't know nothing about that*
 (ii) *You wasn't here when he come looking for you*
 (iii) *There's hundreds of students in there*
 (iv) *Do you wanna go? Are you gonna go?*
 (v) *Are y'all coming to see us soon?*
 (vi) *That chair's broke, you shouldn't ought to sit on it*
 (vii) *I never seen them when they was doing that*
 (viii) *If you would have come with, we would have had more fun*

C. Can you produce a single diagram, following the format of an immediate constituent analysis, which would incorporate all the constituents of the following sentences? What problems have to be resolved in an exercise like this?

A friend borrowed my car in June. They arrived yesterday.
My parents bought two tickets at Christmas. Tom left.
We saw that film during the summer. The thief stole it last year.

D. Here are some sample sentences from two different languages. The first set is from Latin and the second set is from Amuzgo, a language of Mexico. (The examples used are adapted from data in Merrifield *et al.*, 1962.) Work out the basic constituent structure of the sentences from each language, and then describe them in terms of the phrase level constituents.

(1) *puellae aquilas portant*   'The girls carry the eagles'
     feminae columbas amant   'The women love the doves'
     puella aquilam salvat   'The girl saves the eagle'
     aquila columbam pugnat   'The eagle fights the dove'
     femina aquilam liberat   'The woman frees the eagle'
(2) *macei'na tyocho kwi com*   'The boy is reading a book'
     kwil'a yonom kwi w'aa   'The men are building a house'
     nnceihnda yusku kwi com we   'The woman will buy a red book'
     kwil'a yonom ndee meisa   'The men are making three tables'
     macei'na kwi tyocho com t'ma   'A boy is reading the big book'

Further reading

A clear introductory survey of grammar is presented in Palmer (1971). For more extended, and more technical, discussions of grammatical categories, try Chapters 5 and 6 of Robins (1964) or Chapter 7 of Lyons (1968). A really clear treatment of constituent structure is available in Brown & Miller (1980), which can also be consulted on Gaelic sentence structure. One attempt to modify the traditional concept of the 'parts of speech' can be found in Jespersen (1924), and for a more recent attempt, try Chapter 11 of Lyons (1977). A good reference grammar for contemporary English is the comprehensive work by Quirk *et al.* (1972), or in a shorter version, by Quirk & Greenbaum (1973). There is also a textbook by Huddleston (1984). An interesting recent grammar book for teachers of English as a second language is that of Celce-Murcia & Larsen-Freeman (1983). For some insight into early approaches to the description of American Indian languages, go back to the introduction to Boas (1911).

Chapter 10

Syntax

After a lecture on cosmology and the structure of the solar system,
William James was accosted by a little old lady who told him that
his view of the earth rotating round the sun was wrong.
"I've got a better theory," said the little old lady.
"And what is that, madam?" inquired James politely.
"That we live on a crust of earth which is on the back of a giant turtle."
"If your theory is correct, madam," he asked, "what does this turtle
stand on?"
"You're a very clever man, Mr. James, and that's a very good
question," replied the little old lady, "but I have an answer to it.
And it's this: the first turtle stands on the back of a second, far larger,
turtle, who stands directly under him."
"But what does this second turtle stand on?" persisted James patiently.
To this, the little old lady crowed triumphantly, "It's no use, Mr.
James, it's turtles all the way down."

Adapted from J. R. Ross (1967)

In the course of the preceding chapter, we moved from a consideration
of general grammatical categories and relations to specific methods of
describing the structure of phrases and sentences. If we concentrate
on the structure and ordering of components within a sentence, we are
studying what is technically known as the **syntax** of a language. The
word *syntax* came originally from Greek and literally meant 'a setting
out together' or 'arrangement'. In earlier approaches to the description
of syntax, as we have seen in Chapter 9, there was an attempt to produce
an accurate analysis of the sequence or the ordering 'arrangement' of
elements in the linear structure of the sentence. While this remains a
major goal of syntactic description, more recent work in syntax has taken
a rather different approach in accounting for the 'arrangements' we
observe in the structure of sentences.

Generative grammar

Since the 1950s, particularly developing from the work of the American linguist Noam Chomsky, there have been attempts to produce a particular type of grammar which would have a very explicit system of rules specifying what combinations of basic elements would result in well-formed sentences. (Let us emphasize the word "attempts" here, since no fully worked-out grammar of this or any other type yet exists.) This explicit system of rules, it was proposed, would have much in common with the types of rules found in mathematics. Indeed, a definitive early statement in Chomsky's first major work betrays this essentially mathematical view of language: "I will consider a language to be a set (finite or infinite) of sentences" (Chomsky, 1957: 13).

This mathematical point of view helps to explain the meaning of the term **generative**, which is used to describe this type of grammar. If you have an algebraic expression like $3x + 2y$, and you can give x and y the value of any whole number, then that simple algebraic expression can **generate** an endless set of values, by following the simple rules of arithmetic. When $x = 5$ and $y = 10$, the result is 35. When $x = 2$ and $y = 1$, the result is 8. These results will follow directly from applying the explicit rules. The endless set of such results is 'generated' by the operation of the explicitly formalized rules. If the sentences of a language can be seen as a comparable set, then there must be a set of explicit rules which yield those sentences. Such a set of explicit rules is a generative grammar.

Some properties of the grammar

A grammar of this type must have a number of properties, which can be described in the following terms. The grammar will generate all the well-formed syntactic structures (e.g. sentences) of the language and fail to generate any ill-formed structures. This grammar will have a finite (i.e. limited) number of rules, but will be capable of generating an infinite number of well-formed structures. In this way, the productivity of language (i.e. the creation of totally novel, yet grammatical, sentences) would be captured within the grammar.

The rules of this grammar will also need the crucial property of **recursiveness**, that is, the capacity to be applied more than once in generating a structure. For example, whatever rule yields the component *that chased the cat* in the sentence *This is the dog that chased the cat*, will have to be applied again to get *that killed the rat* and any other similar structure which could continue the sentence *This is the dog that chased the cat that killed the rat* ... There is, in principle, no end to the recursion which would yield ever-longer versions of this sentence, and the grammar must provide for this fact. (Recursiveness is not only to be found in descriptions of sentence structure. It is an essential part of the little old lady's view of the role of turtles in cosmic structure, as quoted at the beginning of this chapter.)

This grammar should also be capable of revealing the basis of two other phenomena: first, how some superficially distinct sentences are closely related, and second, how some superficially similar sentences are in fact distinct. We need some exemplification for these points.

Deep and surface structure

Two superficially distinct sentence structures would be, for example, *Charlie broke the window* and *The window was broken by Charlie*. In traditional terminology, the first is an active sentence and the second is passive. The distinction between them, it can be claimed, is a difference in their **surface structure**, that is, the syntactic form they take as actual English sentences. However, this difference in superficial form disguises the fact that the two sentences are very closely related, even identical, at some less 'superficial' level. This other 'underlying' level, where the basic components shared by the two sentences would be represented, has been called their **deep structure**. The deep structure is an abstract level of structural organization in which all the elements determining structural interpretation are represented. So, the grammar must be capable of showing how a single underlying, abstract representation can become different surface structures.

Structural ambiguity

On the second point noted above, let us say that we had two distinct deep structures expressing, on the one hand, the fact that 'Annie had an umbrella and she whacked a man with it'; and, on the other hand, that 'Annie whacked a man and the man happened to be carrying an umbrella.' Now, these two different concepts can, in fact, be expressed in the same surface structure form: *Annie whacked a man with an umbrella*. This sentence is structurally ambiguous. It has two different underlying interpretations which would be represented differently in the deep structure.

Phrases can also be structurally ambiguous, as in expressions like *the hatred of the killers*. Now, either 'someone hated the killers', or 'the

killers hated someone' could be the underlying interpretation. The grammar will have to be capable of showing the structural distinction between
these underlying representations.

Different approaches

We have considered some of the requirements which would have to
be met by a complete syntactic description of a language. However,
this area of linguistic investigation is notorious for giving rise to very
different approaches to producing that description. For some, the only
relevant issues are syntactic ones, that is, how to describe structure,
independently of 'meaning' considerations. For others, the 'meaning
component' is primary. In some later versions of generative grammar,
the level of deep structure is essentially taken over by a 'meaning' or
semantic interpretation which is assigned a structural or syntactic form
in its surface realization. (We shall explore semantic issues in detail
in Chapter 11.) Unfortunately, almost everything involved in the analysis
of generative grammar remains controversial. There continue to be many
different approaches among those who claim to analyze language in terms
of generative grammar, and many more among those who are critical
of the whole system. Rather than explore controversies, let us look at
some of the really basic features of the original analytic approach and
see how it is all supposed to work. First, we need to get the symbols
straightened out.

Symbols used in syntactic description

We have already introduced some symbols (in Chapter 9) which are
quite easily understood as abbreviations for the grammatical categories
involved. Examples are 'S' (= sentence), 'N' (= noun), 'Art' (= article)
and so on. We need to introduce three more symbols which are commonly used.

The first of these is in the form of an arrow → , and it can be interpreted
as 'consists of'. It will typically occur in the following format:

NP→ Art N

This is simply a shorthand way of saying that a noun phrase (e.g. *the
book*) consists of an article (e.g. *the*) and a noun (e.g. *book*).

The second symbol used is in the form of parentheses, or round brackets – ( ). Whatever occurs inside these brackets will be treated as an
optional constituent. Perhaps an example will make this clear. You can

describe an object as *the book*, or as *the green book*. We can say that both *the book* and *the green book* are examples of the category, noun phrase. In order for a noun phrase to occur in English, you may require an article (*the*) and a noun (*book*), but the inclusion of an adjective (*green*) is optional. You can include an adjective, but it isn't obligatory. We can capture this aspect of English syntax in the following way:

$$NP \rightarrow Art (Adj) N$$

This shorthand notation expresses the idea that a noun phrase consists of an obligatory article and an obligatory noun, but may also include an adjective in a specific position. The adjective is optional.

The third symbol used is in the form of braces, or curly brackets – { }. These indicate that only one of the elements enclosed within the brackets must be selected. They are used when there is a choice from two or more constituents. For example, we have already noted, in Chapter 9, that a noun phrase can consist of an expression like *the woman* (Art N), or *she* (pronoun), or *Kathy* (proper noun). We can, of course, write three single rules, as shown on the left below, but it is more succinct to write one rule, as shown on the right below, which incorporates exactly the same information:

$$
\begin{array}{ll}
NP \rightarrow Art\ N & \\
NP \rightarrow pronoun & NP \rightarrow \begin{Bmatrix} Art\ N \\ pronoun \\ proper\ noun \end{Bmatrix} \\
NP \rightarrow proper\ noun &
\end{array}
$$

It is important to remember that, although there are three constituents in these curly brackets, only one of them can be selected on any occasion.

We can now present a list of symbols and abbreviations commonly found in syntactic descriptions:

S	sentence	N	noun	Pro	pronoun
PN	proper noun	V	verb	Adj	adjective
Art	article	Adv	adverb	Prep	preposition
NP	noun phrase	VP	verb phrase	PP	prepositional phrase

   * = 'ungrammatical sequence'
$\rightarrow$ = 'consists of'
( ) = 'optional constituent'
{ } = 'one and only one of these constituents must be selected'

Labeled tree diagrams

In Chapter 9, we considered ways of describing the structure of sentences that (basically) concentrated on the linear sequence of constituents. It is, of course, possible to show the same sequence as, in a more explicit way, 'hierarchically' organized. So, instead of labeling and bracketing the constituents as shown on the left below, we can show the same information in the form of a **tree diagram**, as on the right below:

This type of tree diagram representation contains all the grammatical information found in the other analyses, but also shows more explicitly the fact that there are different levels in the analysis. That is, there is a level of analysis at which a constituent such as NP is represented and a different, lower level at which a constituent such as N is represented. Here's how a whole sentence would look in a tree diagram:

If you start at the top of this tree diagram, you are starting with a sentence (S) and then dividing the sentence into two constituents (NP and VP). In turn, the NP constituent is divided into two constituents (Art and N). Finally, one word is selected which fits the label Art (*the*), and another which fits N (*monkey*).

Phrase structure rules

We can view this tree diagram format in two different ways. In one way, we can simply treat it as a static representation of the structure of the sentence at the bottom of the diagram. We could propose that, for every single sentence in English, a tree diagram of this type could be drawn. The alternative view is to treat the diagram as a 'dynamic' format, in the sense that it represents a way of 'generating' not only that one sentence, but a very large number of sentences with similar structures. This alternative view is very appealing since it should enable us to generate a large number of sentences with only a small number of rules. These 'rules' are usually called **phrase structure rules**, and they present the information of the tree diagram in an alternative format. So, instead of the diagram form on the left below, we can use the notation shown on the right below:

The rule is then read as – "a sentence consists of a noun phrase followed by a verb phrase". In addition to rules of this type which generate structures, we can also have **lexical rules** which indicate the words to be used for constituents such as N. For example:

N→ {*boy, girl, dog, . . .*}

This means that N is rewritten as *boy*, or *girl*, or *dog*. We can create a set of extremely simple (and necessarily incomplete) phrase structure rules which can be used to generate a large number of English sentences:

$$S \rightarrow NP\ VP$$
$$NP \rightarrow \begin{cases} Art\ (Adj)\ N \\ PN \end{cases}$$
$$VP \rightarrow V\ NP\ (PP)\ (Adv)$$
$$PP \rightarrow Prep\ NP$$

N→ {*boy, girl, horse*}   V→ {*saw, followed, helped*}
PN→ {*George, Myrna*}   Prep→ {*with, near*}
Art→ {*a, the*}   Adv→ {*yesterday, recently*}
Adj→ {*small, crazy*}

These rules will generate the grammatical sentences shown below as (1) to (7), but will not yield the ungrammatical sentences shown as (8) to (10):

1. *The girl followed the boy.*
2. *A boy helped the horse.*
3. *The horse saw a girl.*
4. *Myrna helped George recently.*
5. *George saw a horse yesterday.*
6. *A small horse followed Myrna.*
7. *The small boy saw George with a crazy horse recently.*
8. **Boy the Myrna saw.*
9. **Helped a girl.*
10. **Small horse with girl.*

Transformational rules

One problem with these phrase structure rules is that they will generate all sentences with fairly fixed word order to the constituents. For example, adverbs will always come at the end of their sentences, if we follow the rules we have just illustrated. That is fine for generating the first sentence below, but how would we get the second sentence?

(i) *George helped Myrna yesterday.*
(ii) *Yesterday George helped Myrna.*

In order to accomplish this 'movement' of constituents, we need a set of rules which will change or move constituents in the structures which derive from the phrase structure rules. These are called **transformational rules**. Essentially what they do is take a 'branch' of the 'tree' away from one part of the tree diagram, and attach it to a different part. Here is an example of a movement transformation:

(George helped Myrna yesterday)   (Yesterday George helped Myrna)

We would, of course, specify which constituents can be moved, from where and to where.

One of the best arguments for having transformational rules involves what seems to be the movement of a very small element in English sentence structure. We recognize that the following two sentences have a great deal in common:

(i) *Doris picked up the magazine.*
(ii) *Doris picked the magazine up.*

These sentences contain a verb-particle construction (verb – *pick*; particle – *up*), and it is clear that the particle can be separated from the verb. A constituent structure analysis, as described in Chapter 9, would have some difficulty accommodating this type of structure. A phrase structure analysis would have to create two different tree diagrams. Yet, we intuitively recognize that these two sentences must come from a single underlying source.

Let us propose a single tree diagram source which produces a string of elements like: *NP V Particle NP*. Under circumstances like these, let us then propose the optional transformation called 'Particle Movement', which takes that structural description and yields the structural change to: *NP V NP Particle*. By using this simple transformational rule, we have provided the means for explicitly relating the two structures in sentences (i) and (ii) above as 'surface'variations of a single underlying structure. It may not seem much, but this type of transformational analysis solved a number of tricky problems for previous syntactic descriptions.

There is, of course, much more involved in transformational grammar and other methods of syntactic description. (We have barely scratched the surface structures.) However, having explored some of the basic issues in the syntactic description of language, we must move on, as historically the generative grammarians had to do, to come to terms with the place of 'meaning' in linguistic description. This leads us to a consideration of the role of semantics.

Study questions

1. In what ways are these expressions 'structurally ambiguous'?
   - (a) *An American history teacher.*
   - (b) *Flying planes can be dangerous.*
   - (c) *The parents of the bride and the groom were waiting.*
2. Can you provide four, 'superficially distinct' sentences which would each have the same 'underlying' structure as one of the following sentences?
   - (a) *Lara was arrested by the police.*
   - (b) *She took her coat off.*
   - (c) *Someone stole my bicycle.*
   - (d) *I told him to turn down the volume.*
3. Which of the following expressions would be generated by this phrase structure rule: NP→ Art (Adj) N?
   - (a) *a radio*   (c) *a new student*
   - (b) *the rusty car* (d) *the screwdriver*
4. Why are transformational rules considered necessary in syntactic descriptions?
5. Using the phrase structure rules presented in this chapter, you should be able to complete these labeled tree diagrams.

(a)

(b)

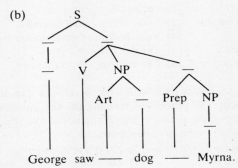

Discussion topics/projects

A. Here are some simple phrase structure rules for Scottish Gaelic:

$$S \rightarrow V\ NP\ NP \qquad NP \rightarrow \begin{Bmatrix} \text{Art N (Adj)} \\ \text{PN} \end{Bmatrix}$$

$$\text{Art} \rightarrow an$$
$$\text{N} \rightarrow \{cu,\ gille\ \}$$
$$\text{PN} \rightarrow \{Tearlach,\ Calum\ \}$$
$$\text{Adj} \rightarrow \{beag,\ mor\}$$
$$\text{V} \rightarrow \{chunnaic,\ bhuail\}$$

Only two of the following sentences would be considered well-formed, according to the rules above. First, identify the ill-formed sentences, using the symbol*, then provide labeled tree diagrams for the two well-formed sentences.

1. *Calum chunnaic an gille*   3. *Bhuail an beag cu*
2. *Bhuail an gille mor an cu*   4. *Chunnaic Tearlach an gille*

B. Here is a simplified set of phrase structure rules for a language called Ewe, spoken in parts of West Africa. Can you use these rules to write out four different well-formed Ewe sentences? (Note that the syntax of Ewe is different from the syntax of English.)

$$S \rightarrow NP\ VP$$
$$NP \rightarrow N\ (Art)$$
$$VP \rightarrow V\ NP$$
$$\text{N} \rightarrow \{oge,\ ika,\ amu\}$$
$$\text{Art} \rightarrow ye$$
$$\text{V} \rightarrow \{xa,\ vo\}$$

C. In the chapter we considered one transformational rule which was used for particle movement. Here is a simple version of the passive transformation rule:

Structural Description: NP_1 V NP_2

Structural Change: $\Rightarrow NP_2$ *be* V-*ed by* NP_1

(Let us add that the tense, past or present, of the verb (V) in the structural description will determine the tense of the verb (*be*) in the structural change. Also, the symbol $\Rightarrow$ is used for transformations.) This transformational rule will produce passive versions of a number of the following sentences. First, identify those sentences for which the rule works, and then try to describe what prevents the rule from working on the other sentences.

(1) *The cats chased the mouse*   (2) *Snow White kissed Grumpy*
(3) *He loves them*   (4) *Betsy borrowed some money from Jim*
(5) *The team played badly*   (6) *The tree fell with a crash*
(7) *The bank manager laughed*   (8) *The duckling became a swan*

D. Each of the following sentences ends with what is called a 'tag question'. For this set of sentences, the process of forming the tag question seems very regular. Can you produce a simple transformational rule which could be used to add tag questions to basic sentence structures?

(1) *She was a dancer, wasn't she?*   (2) *Zee is a good swimmer, isn't he?*
(3) *You are ready, aren't you?*   (4) *They can come, can't they?*
(5) *Diana would help, wouldn't she?*   (6) *You have eaten, haven't you?*

Now, how would you go about making that transformational rule apply for these two sentences?

(7) *He smokes a lot, doesn't he?*   (8) *They arrived early, didn't they?*

Further reading

All introductory textbooks in linguistics have a section on syntax, for example, Chapter 7 of Fromkin & Rodman (1983) or Chapter 5 of Akmajian, Demers & Harnish (1984). For more detailed introductory treatments, try Chapter 6 of Lyons (1968) or Brown & Miller (1980). There are two more advanced texts on syntax, by Culicover (1976) and Matthews (1981), but neither is particularly easy. Perhaps a more useful reference work is Stockwell, Schachter & Partee (1973). The best overview of Chomsky's work is Lyons (1978), or, if you wish to read selections from Chomsky's different publications, try Allen & van Buren (1971). The basic original works are Chomsky (1957; 1965). On matters transformational, try Akmajian & Heny (1975) or Huddleston (1976). For arguments against the Chomskyan approach to linguistic description, try Moore & Carling (1982) or Chapter 6 of Sampson (1980).

Chapter 11

Semantics and pragmatics

There is a perfectly true story of the strip-tease dancer who wrote
to an eminent American linguist asking him to supply a word to replace
'strip-tease' because of its 'wrong connotations'. "I hope", she added,
"that the science of semantics can help the verbally unprivileged
members of my profession." The eminent linguist, knowing his
classical languages, suggested 'ecdysiast'.

Frank Palmer (1981)

ecdysis n. the shedding or casting off of an outer coat or integument
by snakes, crustaceans, etc.

Random House Dictionary (1966)

Semantics and pragmatics are concerned with aspects of meaning in
language. Generally, work in **semantics** deals with the description of
word- and sentence-meaning, and, in **pragmatics**, with the characterization of speaker-meaning.

Neither God nor Humpty Dumpty

Before we investigate these two areas, we should be clear about what
aspects of 'meaning' we are discussing. We cannot assume that there
is some God-given, meaningful connection between a word in a language
and an object in the world. It cannot be the case that we know the
meaning of the word *chair*, for example, because this label has some
natural, 'God-given' connection to the object you are sitting on. In order
to hold that view, you would be forced to claim that God is an English
speaker and that labels such as *chaise* (French), *Stuhl* (German), and
sèdia (Italian) are, in some sense, 'unnatural' ways of referring to the
same object. Instead, a more reasonable approach would lead us to
see the word *chair* as a term which is arbitrary (that is, has no natural
connection to the object), but which is conventionally used by English
speakers when they wish to refer to that type of object that we sit on.

This notion of the meaning of words being based on a convention within the language should also lead us to avoid the view of word-meaning expressed by Humpty Dumpty in Lewis Carroll's *Through the Looking Glass*:

"When I use a word," Humpty Dumpty said in a rather scornful tone, "it means what I choose it to mean – neither more nor less."

If applied generally, this suggestion is surely a recipe for chaos in human language. Could one really say *That melon is blue* and choose it to mean 'That chair is comfortable'? It might work in some rather special, probably humorous, situation, but the notion that we can make words mean whatever we personally choose them to mean cannot be a general feature of linguistic meaning.

Conceptual versus associative meaning

What we set out to describe in semantics, then, are those aspects of conventional meaning which we assume are conveyed by the words and sentences of a language. One further distinction in the description of 'meaning' is also worth noting. When linguists investigate the meaning of words in a language, they are normally interested in characterizing the **conceptual** meaning and less concerned with the **associative** or stylistic meaning of words. Conceptual meaning covers those basic, essential components of meaning which are conveyed by the literal use of a word. Some of the basic components of a word like *needle* in English might include 'thin, sharp, steel, instrument'. These components would be part of the conceptual meaning of *needle*. However, you may have 'associations', or 'connotations', attached to a word like *needle* which lead you to think of 'painful' whenever you encounter the word. This 'association' is not treated as part of the conceptual meaning of *needle*. In a similar way, you may associate the expression *low-calorie*, when used to describe a product, with 'good for you', but we would not want to include this association within the basic conceptual meaning of the expression. Poets and advertisers are, of course, very interested in using terms in such a way that their associative meanings are evoked, and some linguists do investigate this aspect of language use. However, in this chapter we shall be more interested in characterizing what constitutes the conceptual meaning of terms.

Semantic features

So, how would a semantic approach help us to understand something about the nature of language? One way it might be helpful would be as a means of accounting for the 'oddness' we experience when we read 'English' sentences such as the following:

> *The hamburger ate the man*
> *My cat studied linguistics*
> *A table was listening to some music*

Notice that the oddness of these sentences does not derive from their syntactic structure. According to some basic syntactic rules for forming English sentences (such as those presented in Chapter 10), we have well-structured sentences:

The hamburger	*ate*	*the man*
NP	V	NP

This sentence is syntactically good, but semantically odd. Since the sentence *The man ate the hamburger* is perfectly acceptable, what is the source of the oddness we experience? One answer may relate to the components of the conceptual meaning of the noun *hamburger* which differ significantly from those of the noun *man*, especially when those nouns are used as subjects of the verb *ate*. The kinds of nouns which can be subjects of the verb *ate* must denote entities which are capable of 'eating'. The noun *hamburger* does not have this property (and *man* does), hence the oddness of the first sentence above.

We can, in fact, make this observation more generally applicable by trying to determine the crucial component of meaning which a noun must have in order to be used as the subject of the verb *ate*. Such a component may be as general as 'animate being'. We can then take this component and use it to describe part of the meaning of words as either +*animate* (= denotes an animate being) or −*animate* (= does not denote an animate being).

This procedure is a means of analyzing meaning in terms of **semantic features**. Features such as +*animate*, −*animate*; +*human*, −*human*; +*male*, −*male*, for example, can be treated as the basic features involved in differentiating the meanings of each word in the language from every other word. If you were asked to give the crucial distinguishing features of the meanings of this set of English words (*table, cow, girl, woman, boy, man*), you could do so by means of the following diagram:

	table	cow	girl	woman	boy	man
animate	−	+	+	+	+	+
human	−	−	+	+	+	+
male	−	−	−	−	+	+
adult	−	+	−	+	−	+

From a feature analysis like this, you can say that at least part of the basic meaning of the word *boy* in English involves the components (+*human*, +*male*, −*adult*). You can also characterize that feature which is crucially required in a noun in order for it to appear as the subject of a verb, supplementing the syntactic analysis with semantic features:

> The _____ is reading a book.
>   N (+ *human*)

This approach then gives us the ability to predict what nouns would make the above sentence semantically odd. Examples would be *table*, or *tree*, or *dog*, because they all have the feature (−*human*).

Lexical relations

The approach which has just been outlined is not without problems. For many words in a language it may not be so easy to come up with neat components of meaning. If you try to think of which components or features you would use to distinguish the nouns *advice*, *threat* and *warning*, for example, you will have some idea of the scope of the problem. Part of the problem seems to be that the approach involves a view of words in a language as some sort of 'containers', carrying meaning-components. Of course, this is not the only way in which we can think of the meaning of words in our language. If you were asked to give the meaning of the word *conceal*, for example, you might simply reply "it's the same as *hide*", or give the meaning of *shallow* as "the opposite of *deep*", or the meaning of *daffodil* as "it's a kind of *flower*". In doing so, you are not characterizing the meaning of a word in terms of its component features, but in terms of its relationship to other words. This procedure has also been used in the semantic description of languages and is treated as the analysis of **lexical relations**. The types of lexical relations which are usually appealed to are defined and exemplified in the following sections.

Synonymy

Synonyms are two or more forms, with very closely related meanings, which are often, but not always, intersubstitutable in sentences. Examples of synonyms are the pairs *broad – wide, hide – conceal, almost – nearly, cab – taxi, liberty – freedom, answer – reply*.

It should be noted that the idea of 'sameness of meaning' used in discussing synonymy is not necessarily 'total sameness'. There are many occasions when one word is appropriate in a sentence, but its synonym would be odd. For example, whereas the word *answer* fits in this sentence: *Karen had only one answer correct on the test*, its near-synonym, *reply*, would sound odd.

Antonymy

Two forms with opposite meanings are called **antonyms**, and commonly used examples are the pairs *quick – slow, big – small, long – short, old – young, above – below, male – female, alive – dead*.

Antonyms are usually divided into two types, those which are 'gradable', and those which are 'non-gradable'. **Gradable antonyms**, such as the pair *big – small*, can be used in comparative constructions *bigger than – smaller than*, and the negative of one member of the pair does not necessarily imply the other. For example, if you say *that dog is not old*, you do not have to mean *that dog is young*. With **non-gradable antonyms**, also called 'complementary pairs', comparative constructions are not normally used (the expressions *deader* or *more dead* sound strange), and the negative of one member does imply the other. For example, *that person is not dead* does indeed mean *that person is alive*.

Hyponymy

When the meaning of one form is included in the meaning of another, the relationship is described as **hyponymy**, and some typical example pairs are *daffodil – flower, dog – animal, poodle – dog, carrot – vegetable, banyan – tree*. The concept of 'inclusion' involved here is the idea that if any object is a *daffodil*, then it is necessarily a *flower*, so the meaning of *flower* is 'included' in the meaning of *daffodil*. Or, *daffodil* is a hyponym of *flower*.

When we consider hyponymous relations, we are essentially looking at the meaning of words in some type of hierarchical relationship. You could, in fact, represent the relationships between a set of words such as *animal, ant, asp, banyan, carrot, cockroach, creature, daffodil, dog, flower, horse, insect, living things, pine, plant, snake, tree* and *vegetable* as a hierarchical diagram in the following way:

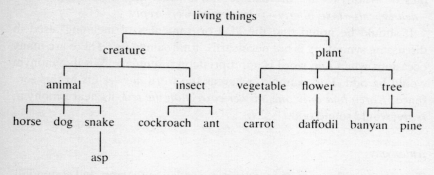

From this diagram, we can say that '*horse* is a hyponym of *animal*' or that '*ant* is a hyponym of *insect*'. We can also say that two or more terms which share the same superordinate (higher up) term are **co-hypo-nyms**. So, *horse* and *dog* are co-hyponyms, and the superordinate term is *animal*.

The relation of hyponymy captures the idea of 'is a kind of', as when you give the meaning of a word by saying "an *asp* is a kind of *snake*". It is often the case that the only thing some people know about the meaning of a word in their language is that it is a hyponym of another term. That is, you may know nothing more about the meaning of *asp* other than that it is a kind of *snake*.

Homophony, homonymy and polysemy

There are three other, less well-known terms which are often used to describe relationships between words in a language. The first of these is **homophony**. When two or more different (written) forms have the same pronunciation, they are described as homophones. Some examples are *bare – bear, meat – meet, flour – flower, pail – pale, sew – so*.

The term **homonymy** is used when one form (written and spoken) has two or more unrelated meanings. Examples of homonyms are the pairs *bank* (of a river) – *bank* (financial institution), *pupil* (at school) – *pupil* (in the eye) and *mole* (on skin) – *mole* (small animal). The temptation is to think that the two types of *bank* must be related in meaning. They are not. Homonyms are words which have quite separate meanings, but which have accidentally come to have exactly the same form.

Relatedness of meaning accompanying identical form is technically known as **polysemy**, which can be defined as one form (written or spoken) having multiple meanings which are all related by extension. Examples are the word *head*, used to refer to the object on top of your body, on top of a glass of beer, on top of a company or department; or *foot* (of person, of bed, of mountain), or *run* (person does, water does, colors do).

The distinction between homonymy and polysemy is not always clear cut. However, one indication of the distinction can be found in the typical dictionary entry for words. If a word has multiple meanings (polysemic), then there will be a single entry, with a numbered list of the different meanings of the word. If two words are treated as homonyms, they will typically have two separate entries. You could check in your dictionary and probably find that the different meanings of words like *head*, *get*, *run*, *face* and *foot* are treated as examples of polysemy, whereas *mail*, *bank*, *sole* and *mole* are treated as examples of homonymy.

These last three lexical relations are, of course, the basis of a lot of word-play, particularly used for humorous effect. The Pillsbury Flour Company once took advantage of homophony to promote a brand of flour with the slogan *Everybody kneads it*. And if you have come across this riddle: *Why are trees often mistaken for dogs?*, then you will have encountered the use of homonymy in the answer: *Because of their bark*.

Interpreting what speakers mean

So far, we have concentrated on meaning in language as a product of the meaning of words. There are, however, other aspects of meaning which are not derived solely from the meanings of the words used in phrases and sentences. When we read or hear pieces of language, we normally try to understand not only what the words mean, but what the writer or speaker of those words intended to convey. The study of 'intended speaker meaning' is called pragmatics.

Driving by a parking lot, you may see a sign like the one in the picture below. Now, you know what each of these words means, and you know what the sign as a whole means. However, you don't normally think that the sign is advertising a place where you can park your 'heated attendant'. (You take an attendant, you heat him up, and this is the place where you can park him.) Alternatively, it may indicate a place

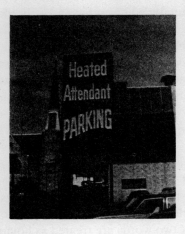

where parking will be carried out by attendants who have been heated. The words may allow these interpretations, but you would normally understand that you can park your car in this place, that it's a heated area, and that there will be an attendant to look after the car. So, how do you decide that the sign means this? (Notice that the sign does not even have the word *car* on it.) Well, you use the meanings of the words, in combination, and the context in which they occur, and you try to arrive at what the writer of the sign intended his message to convey. The notion of the speaker's or writer's intended meaning is a crucial element.

Consider another example, taken from a newspaper advertisement, and think not only about what the words might mean, but also about what the advertiser intended them to mean: *FALL BABY SALE*. In the normal context of our present society, we assume that this store has not gone into the business of selling young children over the counter, but rather that it's advertising clothes for babies. The word *clothes* does not appear, but our normal interpretation would be that the advertiser intended us to understand his message as relating to the sale of baby clothes and not, we trust, of babies.

Context

In our discussion of the two preceding examples, we have emphasized the influence of context. There are, of course, different kinds of context to be considered. One kind is best described as **linguistic context**, or **co-text**. The co-text of a word is the set of other words used in the same phrase or sentence. This surrounding co-text has a strong effect on what we think the word means. We have already noted that the word *bank* is a homonym, a form with more than one meaning. How do we usually know which meaning is intended in a particular sentence? We usually do so on the basis of linguistic context. If the word *bank* is used in a sentence together with words like *steep* or *overgrown*, we have no problem deciding which type of 'bank' is meant. By the same token, when we hear someone say that he has to "get to the bank to cash a check", we know from the linguistic context which type of *bank* is intended. More generally, we know what words mean on the basis of another type of context, best described as **physical context**. If you see the word *BANK* on the wall of a building in a city, the 'physical' location will influence your interpretation. Our understanding of much of what we read and hear is tied to the time and place in which we encounter linguistic expressions.

Deictic expressions

In a more consistent way, some words in the language cannot be interpreted at all unless the physical context, especially the physical context of the speaker, is known. These are words like *here*, *there*, *this*, *that*, *now*, *then*, *yesterday*, as well as most pronouns, such as *I*, *you*, *him*, *her*, *them*. Some sentences of English are virtually impossible to understand if we don't know who is speaking, about whom, where and when. For example: *They'll have to do that tomorrow, because they aren't here now*.

Out of context, this sentence is extremely vague. It contains a large number of **deictic expressions** (*they*, *that*, *here*, *tomorrow*, *now*) which depend for their interpretation on the immediate physical context in which they were uttered. Such expressions are very obvious examples of bits of language which we can only understand in terms of speaker's intended meaning. If someone says, "I like working here", does she mean 'in this office', or 'in this building', or 'in this part of town', or 'in this country', or something else entirely? A word like *here* is a deictic expression (a means of 'pointing' with language), which can only be interpreted in terms of the location that the speaker intends to indicate.

Presupposition

When a speaker uses a deictic expression like *here*, in normal circumstances, she is working with an assumption that the hearer knows which location is intended. In a more general way, speakers continually design their linguistic messages on the basis of assumptions about what their hearers already know. These assumptions may be mistaken, of course, but they underlie much of what we say in the everyday use of language. What a speaker assumes is true or is known by the hearer can be described as a **presupposition**. If someone tells you *Your brother is waiting outside for you*, there is an obvious presupposition that you have a brother. If you are asked *Why did you arrive late?*, there is a presupposition that you did arrive late. And if you are asked the following question, there are at least two presuppositions involved: *When did you stop smoking cigars?* In asking this question, the speaker presupposes that you used to smoke cigars, and that you no longer do so. Questions like this, with built-in presuppositions, are very useful devices for interrogators or trial lawyers. If the defendant is asked by the prosecutor *Okay, Mr Smith, where did you buy the cocaine?*, there is a presupposition that Mr Smith did, in fact, buy the cocaine. If he simply answers the *Where* part of the question, by giving a location, he is behaving as if the presupposition is correct.

One of the tests used to check for the presuppositions underlying sentences involves negating a sentence with a particular presupposition and considering whether the presupposition remains true. Take the sentence *My car is a wreck*. Now take the negative version of this sentence: *My car is not a wreck*. Notice that, although these two sentences have opposite meanings, the underlying presupposition, *I have a car*, remains true in both.

Speech acts

We have been considering some ways in which we interpret the meanings of sentences in terms of what the speaker of those sentences intended to convey. What we have not yet explored is the fact that we also usually know how a speaker intends us to 'take' (or, interpret the function of) what he says. In very general terms, we can usually recognize the type of 'act' performed by a speaker in uttering a sentence. The use of the term **speech act** covers 'actions' such as 'requesting', 'commanding', 'questioning' and 'informing'. It is typically the case that we use the following linguistic 'forms' with the following 'functions'. (The forms would be described in the syntactic analysis of a language, and the functions as what people use language for.)

Forms	Functions
Did you eat the food?	Question
Eat the food (please).	Command (request)
You ate the food.	Statement

When a form such as *Did he ...?*, *Are they ...?* or *Can you ...?* is used to ask a question, it is described as a **direct speech act**. For example, when a speaker doesn't know something and asks the hearer to inform him, he will typically produce a direct speech act of the following type: *Can you ride a bicycle?*

Now compare this utterance with *Can you pass the salt?* In this second example, you would not usually understand the utterance as a question about your ability to do something. In fact, you would not treat this as a question at all. You would treat it as a request and perform the action requested. Yet, this request has been presented in the syntactic form usually associated with a question. Such an example is described as an **indirect speech act**. Whenever one of the forms in the set above is used to perform a function other than the one listed beside it, the result is an indirect speech act. The following utterance has the form normally associated with a statement: *You left the door open*. If you say this sentence to someone who has just come into your room (and it's pretty cold outside), you would probably be understood to have made what speakers intend to 'mean'. Other aspects of this process will be explored in the next chapter.

Study questions

1. What is the lexical relation between the following pairs of words?
   (a) *shallow deep*   (c) *suite sweet*   (e) *single married*
   (b) *mature ripe*   (d) *table furniture*   (f) *move run*
2. What are the deictic expressions in the following statement?
   "I'm busy now so you can't do that here"
3. What is one obvious presupposition of a speaker who says:
   (a) "Where did he buy the beer?"   (b) "Your watch is broken"
4. How would you describe the oddness of the following sentences, using semantic features?
   (a) *The television drank my water*   (b) *Your dog writes poetry*
5. What type of meaning is involved when a person says that the word *summer* means "picnics by the lake"?

Discussion topics/projects

A. A famous example of a sentence which is syntactically 'good', but semantically 'odd', was suggested by Noam Chomsky (1957): *Colorless green ideas sleep furiously.* How many mismatches of meaning are present in this sennot a statement, but a request. You are requesting, indirectly, that the person close the door. Used in this way, it is another example of an indirect speech act.

It is, of course, possible to have humorous effects as a result of one person failing to recognize another person's indirect speech act. Consider the following scene. A visitor to a city, carrying his luggage, looking lost, stops a passer-by:

Visitor: *Excuse me, do you know where the Ambassador Hotel is?*
Passer-by: *Oh sure, I know where it is.* (and walks away)

In this scene, the visitor uses a form which is normally associated with a question (*Do you know . . .?*) and the passer-by answers that question literally (*I know . . .*). Instead of responding to the request, the passer-by replies to the question, treating an indirect speech act as if it were direct.

Perhaps the crucial distinction in the use of these two types of speech acts is based on the fact that indirect commands or requests are simply considered more gentle or more polite in our society than direct commands. Our ability to interpret the function of speech acts is just one more example of the process of interpretation relying on a notion of

tence? Can it be interpreted at all? Having done ... .
of this advertisement from an American store: *Colorful white sale this wee...*

B. One aspect of gradable antonyms is that there is always one member of the pair used more often than the other in certain constructions. It is called the 'unmarked' member. For example, we usually ask *How old is he?* if we want to know someone's age, and not *How young is he?*, unless we intend a special, 'marked' meaning. Can you determine the 'unmarked' member in each of the following pairs?

    (a) *small big*   (c) *short long*   (e) *wild tame*
    (b) *cheap expensive* (d) *near far*   (f) *many few*

C. Here's an example of a newspaper headline which requires the reader to do some work in order to interpret the meaning: *City to get tough on unshoveled walks*. What kinds of interpretations are possible? Is there a most likely interpretation? Does it help to know that the article appeared in the *Minneapolis Star and Tribune*, on January 25, 1984 (i.e. to have some information about time and place)? How about some linguistic context, such as the first sentence of the article – "Minneapolis is intensifying enforcement of its sidewalk snow-shoveling ordinance."?

D. Does the 'constancy under negation' test work as a means of finding the presuppositions of the following sentences? What are the presuppositions?

    (a) *John regrets that he broke your window*
    (b) *The pregnant teacher went on a holiday*
    (c) *The King of France is bald*

Further reading

There are a number of general introductions to the study of semantics. There is a good basic coursebook by Hurford & Heasley (1983), or more general treatments in Palmer (1981) and Leech (1974). The latter has an extended discussion of different types of 'associative' meaning. For specific analyses, using semantic features, try Bever & Rosenbaum (1971) or, using lexical relations, try Lehrer (1969). The most comprehensive work on the subject, and consequently quite difficult, is Lyons (1977). Two other, rather technical treatments of the issues are Kempson (1977), on semantic theory, and Levinson (1983), on pragmatics. More specifically, for a critique of the 'container' view of word-meaning, see Moore & Carling (1982); on the interpretation of language in context, see Brown & Yule (1983a); and for the original ideas behind the concept of speech acts, see Austin (1962).

Chapter 12
Discourse analysis

> The truth is, the modern art of punctuation was not taken from the art of speaking, which certainly ought to have been its archetype, and probably would, had that art been studied and brought to perfection by the moderns; but was in great measure regulated by the rules of grammar, which they had studied; that is, certain parts of speech are kept together, and others divided by stops, according to their grammatical construction, often without reference to the pauses used in discourse.
>
> Thomas Sheridan (1781)

In the study of language, some of the most interesting questions arise in connection with the way language is 'used', rather than what its components are. We have already introduced one of those questions when we discussed pragmatics in the preceding chapter. We were, in effect, asking how it is that language-users interpret what other language-users intend to convey. When we carry this investigation further and ask how it is that we, as language-users, make sense of what we read in texts, understand what speakers mean despite what they say, recognize connected as opposed to jumbled or incoherent discourse, and successfully take part in that complex activity called conversation, we are undertaking what is known as **discourse analysis**.

Interpreting discourse

When we concentrate on the description of a particular language, we are normally concerned with the accurate representation of the forms and structures used in that language. However, as language-users, we are capable of more than simply recognizing correct versus incorrect form and structure. We can cope with fragments such as *Trains collide, two die*, a newspaper headline, and know, for example, that a causal relation exists between the two phrases; and we can make sense of notices like *No shoes, no service*, on shop windows in summer, understanding that a conditional relation exists between the two phrases ('If you are wearing no shoes, you will receive no service'). Moreover, we can encounter examples of texts, written in English, which appear to break a lot of the 'rules' of the English language. The following example, from an essay by a Saudi Arabian student learning English, contains all kinds of 'errors', yet it can be understood.

MY TOWN

My natal was in a small town, very close to Riyadh capital of Saudi Arabia. The distant betweeen my town and Riyadh 7 miles exactly. The name of this Almasani that means in English Factories. It takes this name from the peopl's carrer. In my childhood I remmeber the people live. It was very simple, most the people was farmer.

This example may serve to illustrate an interesting point about the way we react to language which contains ungrammatical forms. Rather than simply rejecting the text as ungrammatical, we try to make sense of it. That is, we attempt to arrive at a reasonable interpretation of what the writer intended to convey. (Most people say they understand the 'My Town' text quite easily.) It is this effort to interpret (and to be interpreted), and how we accomplish it, that are the key elements investigated in the study of discourse. To arrive at an interpretation, and to make our messages interpretable, we certainly rely on what we know about linguistic form and structure. But, as language-users, we have more knowledge than that.

Cohesion

We know, for example, that texts must have a certain structure which depends on factors quite different from those required in the structure of a single sentence. Some of those factors are described in terms of **cohesion**, or the ties and connections which exist within texts. A number of those types of cohesive ties can be identified in the following text:

My father once bought a Lincoln convertible. He did it by saving every penny he could. That car would be worth a fortune nowadays. However,, he sold it to help pay for my college education. Sometimes I think I'd rather have the convertible.

There are connections created here by the use of pronouns, which we assume are used to maintain reference to the same people and things throughout: *father – he – he – he*; *my – my – I*; *Lincoln – it*. There are lexical connections such as *a Lincoln convertible – that car – the convertible*, and the more general connections created by a number of terms which share a common element of meaning (e.g. 'money') *bought – saving – penny – worth a fortune – sold – pay*; (e.g. 'time') *once – nowadays – sometimes*. There is also a connector, *However*, which marks the relationship of what follows to what went before. The verb tenses in the first four sentences are all in the past, creating a connection between those events, and a different time is indicated by the present tense of the final sentence.

Analysis of these cohesive links within a text gives us some insight into how writers structure what they want to say and may be crucial factors in our judgments on whether something is well-written or not. It has also been noted that the conventions of cohesive structure differ from one language to the next and may be one of the sources of difficulty encountered in translating texts.

However, by itself, cohesion would not be sufficient to enable us to make sense of what we read. It is quite easy to create a highly cohesive text which has a lot of connections between the sentences, but which remains difficult to interpret. Note that the following text has connections such as *Lincoln – the car*; *red – that color*; *her – she*; *letters – a letter*; and so on.

My father bought a Lincoln convertible. The car driven by the police was red. That color doesn't suit her. She consists of three letters. However, a letter isn't as fast as a telephone call.

It becomes clear from an example like this that the 'connectedness' which we experience in our interpretation of normal texts is not simply based on connections between the words. There must be some other factor which leads us to distinguish connected texts which make sense from those which do not. This factor is usually described as **coherence**.

Coherence

The key to the concept of coherence is not something which exists in the language, but something which exists in people. It is people who 'make sense' of what they read and hear. They try to arrive at an interpretation which is in line with their experience of the way the world is. Indeed, our ability to make sense of what we read is probably only a small part of that general ability we have to make sense of what we perceive or experience in the world. You may have found, when reading the last example text, that you kept trying to make the text 'fit' some situation or experience which would accommodate all the details. If you work at it long enough, you may indeed find a way to incorporate all those disparate elements into a single coherent interpretation. In doing so, you would necessarily be involved in a process of filling in a lot of 'gaps' which exist in the text. You would have to create meaningful connections which are not actually expressed by the words and sentences. This process is not restricted to trying to understand 'odd' texts. In one way or another, it seems to be involved in our interpretation of all discourse.

It is certainly present in the interpretation of casual conversation. We are continually taking part in conversational interactions where a great deal of what is meant is not actually present in what is said. Perhaps it is the ease with which we ordinarily anticipate each other's intentions that makes this whole complex process seem so unremarkable. Here is a good example, adapted from Widdowson (1978):

> Nancy: *That's the telephone*
> Ron: *I'm in the bath*
> Nancy: *O.K.*

There are certainly no cohesive ties within this fragment of discourse. How do these people manage to make sense of what the other says? They do use the information contained in the sentences expressed, but there must be something else involved in the interpretation. It has been suggested that exchanges of this type are best understood in terms of the conventional actions performed by the speakers in such interactions. Drawing on concepts derived from the study of speech acts (introduced in Chapter 11), we can characterize the brief conversation in the following way:

> Nancy requests Ron to perform action
> Ron states reason why he cannot comply with request
> Nancy undertakes to perform action

If this is a reasonable analysis of what took place in the conversation, then it is clear that language-users must have a lot of knowledge of how conversational interaction works which is not simply 'linguistic' knowledge. Trying to describe aspects of that knowledge has been the focus of research by an increasing number of discourse analysts.

Speech events

In exploring what it is that we know about taking part in conversation, or any other speech event (e.g. debate, interview, various types of discussions), we quickly realize that there is enormous variation in what people say and do in different circumstances. In order to begin to describe the sources of that variation, we would have to take account of a number of criteria. For example, we would have to specify the roles of speaker and hearer, or hearers, and their relationships, whether they were friends, strangers, young, old, of equal or unequal status, and so on. All of these factors will have an influence on what is said and how it is said. We would have to describe what was the topic of the conversation and in what setting or context it took place. Some of the effects of these factors on the way language is used will be explored in greater detail in Chapter 20. Yet, even when we have described all these factors, we will still not have analyzed the actual structure of the conversation itself. As language-users, in a particular culture, we clearly have quite sophisticated knowledge of how conversation works.

Conversational interaction

In simple terms, English conversation can be described as an activity where, for the most part, two or more people take turns at speaking. Typically, only one person speaks at a time and there tends to be an avoidance of silence between speaking turns. (This is not true in other cultures.) If more than one participant tries to talk at the same time, one of them usually stops, as in this example, where A stops until B has finished:

A: *Didn't you* ⌈ *know wh–*
B: ⌊ *But he must've been there by two*
A: *Yes but you knew where he was going*

(The symbol [is conventionally used to indicate where simultaneous talk occurred.)

For the most part, participants wait until one speaker indicates that he or she has finished, usually by signaling a **completion point**. Speakers can mark their turns as 'complete' in a number of ways – by asking a question, for example, or by pausing at the end of a completed syntactic structure like a phrase or a sentence. Other participants can indicate that they want to take the speaking turn, also in a number of ways. They can start to make short sounds, usually repeated, while the speaker is talking, and often use body shifts or facial expressions to signal that they have something to say.

Some of the most interesting research in this area of discourse has revealed different expectations of conversational style and different strategies of participation in **conversational interaction**. Some of these strategies seem to be the source of what is sometimes described by partici- pants as 'rudeness' (if one speaker appears to cut in on another speaker) or 'shyness' (if one speaker keeps waiting for an opportunity to take a turn and none seems to occur). The participants characterized as 'rude' or 'shy' in this way may simply be adhering to slightly different conventions of turn-taking. One strategy which may be overused by 'long-winded' speakers, or those used to 'holding the floor' (like lecturers, politicians), is designed to avoid having normal completion points occur. We all use this strategy to some extent, usually in situations where we have to work out what we are trying to say while actually saying it. If the normal expectation is that completion points are marked by the end of a sentence and a pause, then one way to 'keep the turn' is to avoid having those two indicators occur together. That is, don't pause at the end of sentences, make your sentences run on by using connectors like *and, and then, so, but,* place your pauses at points where the message is clearly incomplete, and preferably 'fill' the pause with hesitation markers such as *er, em, uh, ah*. Note the position of the pauses in this example, placed before and after verbs rather than at the end of sentences:

A: *that's their favorite restaurant because they . . . enjoy French food and when they were . . . in France they couldn't believe it that . . . you know that they had . . . that they had had better meals back home*

And in this next example, Speaker A produces filled pauses after having almost lost the turn at his first brief hesitation:

A: *well that film really was . . .* ⌈ *wasn't what he was good at*
B: ⌊ *when di–*
A: *I mean his other . . . em his later films were much more . . . er really more in the romantic style and that was more what what he was . . . you know . . . em best at doing*
B: *So when did he make that one*

These types of strategies, by themselves, should not be considered undesirable or 'domineering'. They are present in the conversational speech of most people and they are, in a sense, part of what makes conversation work. We recognize these subtle indicators as ways of organizing our turns and negotiating the intricate business of social interaction via language. In fact, one of the most noticeable features of conversational discourse is that it is generally very co-operative. This observation has, in fact, been formulated as a principle of conversation.

The co-operative principle

An underlying assumption in most conversational exchanges seems to be that the participants are, in fact, co-operating with each other. This principle, together with four maxims which we expect will be obeyed, was first set out by Grice (1975). The **co-operative principle** is stated in the following way: "Make your conversational contribution such as is required, at the stage at which it occurs, by the accepted purpose or direction of the talk exchange in which you are engaged." Supporting this principle are the four maxims:

Quantity: Make your contribution as informative as is required, but not more, or less, than is required
Quality: Do not say that which you believe to be false or for which you lack evidence
Relation: Be relevant
Manner: Be clear, brief and orderly

It is certainly true that, on occasion, we can experience conversational exchanges in which the co-operative principle does not seem to be in operation. However, this general description of the normal expectations we have in conversations helps to explain a number of regular features in the way people say things. For example, a number of common expressions like *Well, to make a long story short* and *I won't bore you with all the details* seem to be indicators of an awareness of the Quantity maxim. Some awareness of the importance of the Quality maxim seems to lie behind the way we begin some conversational contributions with expressions like *As far as I know*, *Now, correct me if I'm wrong* and *I'm not absolutely sure but . . .* , and we often take care to indicate that what we report is something we *think* and *feel* (not *know*), is *possible* or *likely* (not *certain*), *may* or *could* (not *must*) happen. Hence the difference between saying *John is ill* and *I think it's possible that John may be ill*; in the first version we will be assumed to have good evidence for the statement.

Given that we operate with the co-operative principle, it also becomes clearer how certain answers to our questions which, on the surface, do not seem to be appropriate, can actually be interpreted. Consider this conversational fragment:

Carol: *Are you coming to the party tonight?*
Laura: *I've got an exam tomorrow*

On the face of it, Laura's statement is not an answer to Carol's question. Laura doesn't say "Yes" or "No." Yet, Carol will immediately interpret the statement as meaning 'No' or 'Probably not.' How can we account for this ability to grasp one meaning from a sentence which, in a literal sense, means something else? It seems to depend, at least partially, on the assumption that Laura is being 'relevant' and 'informative'. (To appreciate this point, try to imagine Carol's reaction if Laura had said something like "Roses are red, you know.") Given that the answers contain relevant information, Carol can work out that 'exam tomorrow' conventionally involves 'study tonight', and 'study tonight' precludes 'party tonight'. Thus, Laura's answer is not simply a statement of tomorrow's activities, it contains an **implicature** (an additional conveyed meaning) concerning tonight's activities.

It is noticeable that in order to describe the conversational implicature involved in Laura's statement, we had to appeal to some background knowledge (about exams, studying and partying) that must be shared by the conversational participants. The ways in which we use our background knowledge to arrive at interpretations of discourse have been the subject of a lot of recent research.

Background knowledge

A particularly good example of the processes involved in using background knowledge has been provided by Sanford & Garrod (1981). Their example begins with these two sentences:

John was on his way to school last Friday.
He was really worried about the math lesson.

Most people who are asked to read these sentences report that they think John is probably a schoolboy. Since this piece of information is not directly stated in the text, it is described as an **inference**. Other inferences, for different readers, are that John is walking or that he is on a bus. These inferences are clearly derived from our conventional knowledge, in our culture, about 'going to school', and no reader has ever suggested that John is swimming or on a boat, though both are physically possible, if unlikely, interpretations.

An interesting aspect of the reported inferences is that they are treated as likely or possible interpretations which readers will easily abandon if they do not fit in with some subsequent information. The next sentence in the text is as follows:

Last week he had been unable to control the class.

On encountering this sentence, most readers decide that John is, in fact, a teacher and that he is not very happy. Many report that he is probably driving a car to school. Then the next sentence is presented:

It was unfair of the math teacher to leave him in charge.

Suddenly, John reverts to his schoolboy status, and the 'teacher' inference is abandoned. The final sentence of this text contains a surprise:

After all, it is not a normal part of a janitor's duties.

This type of text and the manner of presentation, one sentence at a time, is, of course, rather artificial. Yet the exercise involved does provide us with some insight into the ways in which we 'build' interpretations of what we read by using a lot more information than is actually in the words on the page. That is, we actually create what the text is about, based on our expectations of what normally happens. In attempting to describe this phenomenon, many researchers use the concept of **schemata**. Schemata are considered to be conventional knowledge-structures which exist in memory and are activated, under various circumstances, in the interpretation of what we experience. At a very obvious level, we all have versions of a 'Restaurant' schema, which we inevitably use in interpreting a piece of discourse like the following:

Trying not to be out of the office for long, Andrea went into the nearest restaurant, sat down and ordered a sandwich. It was quite crowded, but the service was fast, so she left a good tip when she had to rush back to work.

On the basis of our 'Restaurant' schema, we would be able to say a number of things about the scene and events briefly described in this short text. For example, although the text does not have this information, we would assume that Andrea opened a door to get into the restaurant, that there were tables there, that she ate the sandwich, then she paid for it, and so on. The fact that information of this type can turn up in people's attempts to remember the text is further evidence of the existence of schemata. It is also a good indication of the fact that our understanding of what we read does not directly come from what words and sentences are on the page, but from the interpretation we create, in our minds, of what we read.

This view of the nature of discourse understanding has had a powerful impact on work related to attempts to use computers to process natural language material. Since it has been realized that the way we communicate via language is based on vast amounts of assumed background knowledge, not only of language, but of how the world is, then a fundamental problem is how to give computers this 'knowledge'. Investigations in this area are the subject of the following chapter.

Study questions

1. What is meant by the term 'cohesion' in the study of texts?
2. How would you describe this short exchange in terms of the actions performed by the speakers?

> Motorist: *My car needs a new exhaust system*
> Mechanic: *I'll be busy with this other car all day*

3. What do you think is meant by the term 'turn-taking' in conversation?
4. What are the four maxims of the co-operative principle?
5. Which maxim does this speaker seem to be particularly careful about: *Well, to be quite honest, I don't think she is ill today.*

Discussion topics/projects

A. As an exercise in discovering how our interpretation of what we read can be altered by the expectations we bring to the task, consider the following text (adapted from Anderson *et al.*, 1977):

A prisoner plans his escape
Rocky slowly got up from the mat, planning his escape. He hesitated a moment and thought. Things were not going well. What bothered him most was being held, especially since the charge against him had been weak. He considered his present situation. The lock that held him was strong, but he thought he could break it.

Now answer these questions: (1) Where is Rocky? (2) Is he alone? (3) What has happened to him?

Having done that, remove the title from the text and replace it with this new title: 'A wrestler in a tight corner'. Read the text again and answer the same three questions. Can you come up with different answers? How might you use this evidence to persuade someone that the meaning of the texts we read does not reside solely within the texts themselves?

B. For a few linguists, the analysis of conversational speech is considered to be a poor way of discovering the major properties of language. They point out that conversational speech is full of hesitations, slips, repetitions, lapses of attention, and, as a result, will not provide us with a good representation of the most important elements of a language in a clear way. Consequently, the study of language should be restricted to the analysis of single sentences, constructed by the linguist. Do you agree or disagree? How would you support your opinion?

C. Can you identify the cohesive devices which are present in the following piece of text? In addition to these cohesive elements, what factors can you identify as having an influence on your interpretation?

It was Friday morning. There were two horses out in the field. Susan ran up and caught the nearest one. He seemed quite calm. However, as she turned to take him back, the powerful creature suddenly reared and jumped forward. It was all over in an instant. The animal was running wildly across the field and the girl was left sitting in the mud. Most of the time I love horses, she thought, but sometimes I could just kill one of them.

D. What aspects of this fragment of conversational speech would you use to demonstrate the characteristics of this type of language-in-use?

A: Well it wasn't really a holiday more a ... a ... I don't know ... more an expedition
B: Why? ⌈Did you
A: ⌊Oh I guess because we ed– we ended up carrying so
much ... ⌈equipment and
C: ⌊that sounds like a trip I took ... em two years ago
I think ... yeah in the summer and ... I've never gone again ...
B: So where did you go?
A: Oh we followed the river and the p– the idea you see was to find the source you know ... and ... just to avoid the ... the roads well ...
      ⌈unless th–
C: ⌊and did you?
A: What?
B: ⌈get
C: ⌊find the source ... the river
A: Oh yes sorry ... but we ended up ... em walking on roads quite a bit because ... it ... it just took too long

Further reading

Introductions to discourse analysis with an emphasis on the study of spoken discourse are Coulthard (1977) and Stubbs (1983). A standard textbook is Brown & Yule (1983a). On cohesion, see Halliday & Hasan (1976), on speech events, Hymes (1964), on implicatures, Levinson (1983), and on conversational style, Tannen (1984). Other more specialized approaches can be found in Sinclair & Coulthard (1975), de Beaugrande & Dressler (1981), Sanford & Garrod (1981) and Gumperz (1982).

Chapter 13
Language and machines

> One dark night a policeman comes upon a drunk. The man is on his knees, obviously searching for something under a lamppost. He tells the officer that he is looking for his keys, which he says he lost "over there", pointing out into the darkness. The policeman asks him, "Why, if you lost the keys over there, are you looking for them under the streetlight?" The drunk answers, "Because the light is so much better here." That is the way science proceeds too.
>
> Joseph Weizenbaum (1976)

In 1738, Jacques de Vaucanson produced a fabulous mechanical duck. It could perform the amazing feat of drinking water and eating grain which was digested and then excreted via a mysterious chemical process and some complex tubing in its stomach. This mechanical marvel is simply one example in a long line of 'machines' which humans have created in imitation of living organisms. The interesting thing about Vaucanson's machine is that it simulated digestion without actually containing a replica of the digestive system. It can be seen as an exercise in working with available technology to create a model of some internal processes of a duck. Note that it is a 'model', not a replication. This is an important point, since the aim of many such exercises is not to mimic the details of an internal process, but to have the output of the model be indistinguishable from the output of the real thing. By all accounts, the duck's output passed as genuine.

However, the output which we are more interested in is the result of natural language processing by a machine, or, more specifically, a computer. It is necessary to specify that it is a 'natural' language (e.g. English) rather than an artificial language (e.g. FORTRAN), since it is the human capacity to use language that is being modeled.

Speech synthesis

One of the first aspects of natural language to be modeled was the actual articulation of speech sounds. Early models of talking machines were essentially devices which mechanically simulated the operation of the human vocal tract. More modern attempts to create speech electronically are generally described as **speech synthesis**. From one point of view, it seems remarkably simple. Take the set of phonemes of English, electronically reproduce the acoustic properties of these sounds, then select those phonemes which make up the pronunciation of a word and 'play' the word. While this is not as easy as the brief description suggests, synthetic speech has indeed been produced in this way. It sounds terrible. More tolerable facsimiles of speech have been produced by having machines analyze key acoustic properties of spoken words (not individual sounds) and store the pronouncing information at the word level. In many parts of the United States, when you ask Directory Information for a telephone number, the spoken (seven digit) number which you hear is an example of a synthetically produced set of seven words.

However, in attempting to go further and produce phrases and sentences in synthetic speech, researchers have had to take into account a number of factors other than the pronunciation of individual words. Intonation and pausing, for example, have to be included, as well as syntactic rules for the formation of natural language sentences. Care has also to be taken that the natural processes of assimilation and elision (discussed in Chapter 6) are not ignored. As a result of research in this area, increasingly sophisticated models of speech production have been developed and more 'natural sounding' synthetic speech has been achieved. However, the development of synthetic speech, even if highly successful, would only produce a model of speech articulation. It would not be a model of 'speaking'. The human activity of speaking involves having something to say and not just a means of saying it. Having something to say is an attribute of the human's mental processes and attempting to model that attribute is, in effect, the modeling of intelligence.

Artificial intelligence

The investigation and development of models of intelligent behavior is generally undertaken in the field of **artificial intelligence** (AI), which has been defined as "the science of making machines do things that would require intelligence if done by men" (Minsky, 1968). This field ranges over a large number of topics (e.g. problem-solving, game-playing, visual perception), but has always taken language production and understanding as a major area of investigation. While one ultimate goal may be to produce a computer which can function as a conversational partner, most of the research has been devoted to developing models to cope with language interaction which can take place at a computer terminal. Consequently, descriptions of 'conversations' in this field typically refer to typed rather than spoken dialogs.

Parsers

One of the first developments in the AI approach to the workings of a natural language like English was to produce a means of **parsing** English sentences. This is basically a process of working from left to right along an incoming English sentence, creating an analysis of the syntactic structure and predicting what elements will come next. A number of different types of parsers have been developed, but a brief description of one very elementary version should serve to illustrate the basic processes involved in analyzing a simple sentence like *The boy kicked the ball.*

The parser begins by assigning 'sentence' status to the incoming string of linguistic forms and predicts that the first major constituent will be a 'noun phrase'. The first element encountered is *The*, which is checked in the dictionary to see if it fits the category 'article' (i.e. the predicted first element in a noun phrase). Since it does, it is assigned this description and the parser predicts that the next element may fit the category 'adjective'. The word *boy* is checked and turns out not to be an adjective. This word is then checked against the next predicted category of 'noun' and is identified as such. This should complete the specification of noun phrase (which can be assigned the functional label of 'subject') and the parser goes on to check the next constituent, seeking a word to fit the category 'verb', and so on. As the parser assigns syntactic categories to the elements in the linguistic string, it can also begin to produce a semantic analysis. The subject NP (*The boy*) can be assigned the status 'agent-of-action', the verb (*kicked*) is the 'action', and the following NP (*the ball*) is the 'object-of-action'. This massively oversimplified version of what a parser does may provide an illustration of how a computer, with a limited grammar, a dictionary and a set of procedures, can produce a linguistic description of some simple sentences it receives.

This type of analysis, however, would be an extremely trivial first step in the process of 'understanding' the sentence. In order to go any further, the machine would require 'knowledge' of what words like *boy*, *kicked* and *ball* are used to refer to, and also how an article like *the* indicates something different from the article *a*. If the machine is to function with any resemblance to the intelligent 'understander-system' which operates in the human mind, then it will need some 'knowledge' of how the world is. It would have to know that, for example, the boy used his foot, despite the fact that this information is not present in the sentence. The problems of modeling then cease to be strictly linguistic matters of syntax and basic semantics, and become problems of coping with the colossal amounts of 'world-knowledge' that humans apparently have. The development of computer programs which can access this type of 'knowledge' is the key to the creation of what are generally called **understander-systems**, or machines which really do behave as if they make sense of the linguistic input they receive.

Understander-systems

It would be impossible to document the large number of understander-systems which have been developed in the last two decades. What we can do is explore the workings of two such systems and point out some of their relevant features. First, let us consider an example of how the illusion of 'understanding' can be created.

ELIZA

A program called ELIZA was intended to simulate, or even to 'parody', the psychotherapist's role in a particular type of non-directive psycho-analysis. The 'patient' would sit at a computer terminal, type in one side of the interaction, and receive appropriate responses. The resulting dialog might contain exchanges like this:

Patient: *I'm feeling a bit tired.*
Analyst: *Why do you think you're feeling a bit tired.*

A basic feature of the analyst-program can be discerned in the response illustrated here. The responses are based on a pattern-recognition process whereby the occurrence of a key word or phrase in the patient's turn would activate a particular type of predetermined sentence pattern (generally a question), incorporating the key word or phrase. A limited number of connections between certain key words also gave the program the power to produce more general responses to particular remarks. Note how the connection is made from *mother* to *family* in this exchange:

Patient: *I need some help.*
Analyst: *What would it mean to you if you got some help.*
Patient: *Perhaps I could learn to get along with my mother.*
Analyst: *Tell me more about your family.*

Thus, with a very simple set of linguistic structures, the program could give the impression of considerable thought behind its responses. If a patient-response was difficult to match, then a number of stock expressions such as *I see, That's interesting* or *Go on* could be produced by the analyst. A substantial number of people came to believe that the ELIZA program was a very useful procedure for conducting psychotherapy (much to the chagrin of its original creator; Weizenbaum (1976) provides his reasons). In fact, a number of different versions were actually developed and used.

Although ELIZA provides an interesting view of how one type of psychotherapy may work, it yields very limited insights into the way language interacts with knowledge and understanding. Very simply, ELIZA does not 'interpret' the linguistic material it receives or produces. In essence, it has no understanding of what is taking place in the conversation. This becomes clear when the human really does try to interact more fully with the analyst, as in this discussion of a 'problem' the patient has:

Patient: *At the moment it is a surfeit of children in too small a space.*
Analyst: *Is it.*
Patient: *Yes.*
Analyst: *Can you describe an example.*
Patient: *Of what.*
Analyst: *I see.*
Patient: *No you do not.*
Analyst: *Can you elaborate.*
Patient: *What on.*

Although ELIZA is not a very good example of an understander-system, it does demonstrate the possibility of working, computationally, with a very small subset of a language and a very limited 'world' of reference. By giving the machine an extremely restricted number of things to be talked about, it is possible to carry the illusion of understanding quite far. One of the best known examples of this type of system is called SHRDLU.

SHRDLU

In this program, a limited world of colored boxes, blocks and other shapes on a table, and what happens to them, is all that is discussed. Yet that discussion, between the machine and the human, can be quite thorough and involve clear instances of what would be described as deductive reasoning on the machine's part. The machine can follow commands by a human to move objects around in its world. If the human is unclear in referring to an object, the machine is capable of asking for clarification. In the following example, three pyramids were in the scene:

Human: *Grasp the pyramid.*
Machine: *I don't understand which pyramid you mean.*

The machine also keeps track of what is moved and can answer questions about what has happened (i.e. it has a 'memory') and about where objects are at any point, as in this extract:

Human: *What does the box contain?*
Machine: *The blue pyramid and the blue block.*

The most impressive aspects of SHRDLU are related to its power of working out what the human's linguistic contributions 'mean' in terms of its world. It has the capacity to decipher complex linguistic expressions (via a syntactic parser and a semantics) in a way that ELIZA did not even attempt. Here is a good example of the type of complex sentence which can be converted into action by the program, plus an indication of the strategy the program employs to decide on the reference of pronouns:

Human: *Find a block which is taller than the one you are holding and put it into the box.*
Machine: *By "it", I assume you mean the block which is taller than the one I am holding. OK.*

The simple expression *OK* is used by the program to indicate that it is carrying out the requested action. Within its limited world of reference, SHRDLU also has little trouble with potentially ambiguous directions such as *Put the blue pyramid on the block in the box*. The problem here might be whether the pyramid is on the block to begin with or the block is in the box to begin with. The program can check the 'state of affairs' in its world to decide which meaning makes sense.

The great advantage in terms of comprehensive 'knowledge' of a small world like the one this program enjoys actually turns out to be its greatest limitation as a model of how humans handle linguistic interaction. Humans do operate in 'expert' roles within limited domains analogous to the blocks-world, but they more commonly operate with complex plans and goals, and bring wide-ranging aspects of belief and knowledge to bear on their interpretation of language. Other programs have been developed which try to model many of these other aspects, but the problems created by limited amounts of background knowledge remain. It may be that the development of more sophisticated programs for modeling general human intelligence (as it relates to language) will be created via the integration of numbers of different subsystems, each operating over limited domains of 'expert' knowledge. Thus, the comprehensive understander-system which exists in the mind of a person who works as a travel agent, likes to eat in restaurants, reads news articles and short stories, and can successfully talk about birthday parties may be modeled by integrating all these separate components of specialized knowledge. (Programs do exist separately for each of these specialized areas of language understanding.)

Perhaps more important will be the development of a general computational capacity, not to work from a static store of background knowledge, but to 'learn' via linguistic interaction and to develop a dynamic network of knowledge structures (actually creating the kind of schemata discussed in Chapter 12). It would seem that the limits to this type of development are, at least in part, occasioned by the limits which exist in our own understanding of how we operate as reasonably efficient linguistic machines. By studying the nature of language and trying to create models of what we think may be going on, we may eventually come to understand the workings of our own internal software.

If the metaphor of computer software serves to characterize the mental basis of aspects of language understanding, then we should not lose sight of the fact that a certain amount of hardware is required as well. That hardware, or the human brain, is the subject of the following chapter.

Study questions

1. What is meant by the term 'synthetic speech'?
2. Why would a successful model of speech articulation not be a model of 'speaking'?
3. What is meant by 'artificial intelligence'?
4. Which aspect of linguistic analysis is principally carried out by a parser?
5. Why do machine understander-systems operate within 'limited worlds'?

Discussion topics/projects

A. Consider this traditional recipe for bread sauce:
    Ingredients: *1 small onion   3 oz. fresh breadcrumbs*

> 2 *cloves*   *1 oz. butter or margarine*
> *1 cup of milk*   *Pepper and salt*

Method: *Peel the onion and push cloves into it. Simmer gently with the milk and margarine for at least twenty minutes. Remove the onion, pour the milk over the breadcrumbs. Let this stand to thicken and reheat before serving.*

Now, imagine that you have the latest in labor-saving devices – a robot to do household jobs. You provide your robot with this recipe and point it in the direction of the kitchen. Is that enough? What knowledge is assumed by this recipe which you would have to make explicit in the machine-intelligence program? Will it need kitchen utensils? What else?

B. One obvious application of computer systems using natural language would seem to be in the area of automatic machine translation. Yet efforts to create such systems have not been generally successful. One type of problem is highlighted by Boden (1977: 166) with the example of a sentence being translated from English to Russian, then back again, resulting in *The spirit is willing, but the flesh is weak* being rendered as *The whisky is fine, but the steak's not so good.* What's the basis of the problem in this example? What other problems would have to be overcome in machine translation?

C. Here is an extract from a dialog between a computer system called GUS (Genial Understander System), in the role of travel agent, and a human client:

Client: *I want to go to San Diego on May 28.*
GUS: *What time do you want to leave?*
Client: *I must be in San Diego before 10 a.m.*
GUS: *Would you like PSA flight 102 that arrives at 9.15 a.m.?*
Client: *What is the next flight?*
GUS: *Air California flight 310 that leaves at 8.30 a.m. and arrives at 10 a.m.*
Client: *I'll take the first one.*

The creators of GUS (Bobrow *et al.*, 1977) said that it was "intended to engage a sympathetic and highly cooperative human in an English dialog, directed towards a specific goal within a very restricted domain of discourse". Why do you think these restrictions were necessary? Are there any aspects of the dialog which suggest that GUS has fairly sophisticated knowledge of conversational patterns?

D. One view of artificial intelligence sees that, in the near future, independent machines will evolve and leave humans far behind. Here is an example of the argument:

When we train the chimpanzee to use sign language so that he can speak, we discover that he's interested in talking about bananas and food and being tickled and so on. But if you want to talk to him about global disarmament, the chimp isn't interested and there's no way to get him interested. Well, we'll stand in the same relationship to a super artificial intelligence. They won't have much effect on us because we won't be able to talk to each other. (Edward Fredkin, quoted in McCorduck, 1979)

Do you think this view is correct? How would you support your opinion?

Further reading

There are no easy, non-technical introductions to this subject. Fairly accessible accounts are provided by Hendrix & Sacerdoti (1981) and Winograd (1984), and a relatively accessible survey of the field can be found in Boden (1977). Another good general work is Weizenbaum (1976), which has a description of ELIZA. More specifically, on speech synthesis, see Flanagan (1972), on artificial intelligence, see Winston (1977), on SHRDLU, see Winograd (1972), and on other aspects of understander-systems, see the contributions in Schank & Colby (eds.) (1973). A speculative view of what may be modeled next is provided by Schank (1982). A general work on the history of artificial intelligence is McCorduck (1979).

Chapter 14

Language and the brain

Here is a quite especially instructive slip of the tongue which I should not like to omit. A lady once advanced the following opinion at a social gathering – and the words show that they were uttered with fervour and under the pressure of a host of secret impulses: "Yes, a woman must be pretty if she is to please men. A man is much better off; as long as he has his five straight limbs he needs nothing more."

Sigmund Freud (1910)

In the preceding chapters we have described in some detail the various features of language which people use to produce and understand linguistic messages. Where is this ability to use language located? If the answer is simply 'in the head, or the brain', then how do we explain the case of Phineas Gage?

In September 1848, near Cavendish, Vermont, a construction foreman called Phineas P. Gage was in charge of a construction crew, blasting away rocks to lay a new stretch of railway line. As Phineas pushed an iron tamping rod into the blasting hole in a rock, some gunpowder accidentally exploded, and sent the three and a half foot long tamping rod up through Phineas' upper left cheek and out from the top of his forehead. The rod landed about 50 yards away. Phineas suffered the type of injury from which, it was assumed, no one could recover. However, a month later, Phineas was up and about, with no apparent damage to his senses or his speech.

The medical evidence was clear. A huge metal rod had gone through the front part of Mr Gage's brain, but Mr Gage's language abilities were unaffected. The point of this amazing tale is that, if language ability is located in the brain, it clearly is not situated right at the front.

Parts of the brain

Since Phineas' time, a number of discoveries have been made about the specific areas in the brain which are related to language functions.

In order to talk about this in greater detail, we need to look more closely at some of the grey matter. So, take a head, remove hair, scalp, skull, disconnect the brain stem (which connects the brain to the spinal cord) and cut the corpus callosum (which connects the two hemispheres). If we disregard a certain amount of other material, we will basically be left with two parts, the left hemisphere and the right hemisphere. If we lay the left hemisphere down so that we have a side view, and tilt the right hemisphere up so that the top is next to the top of the left hemisphere, we will have something close to the representation shown in the accompanying illustration (adapted from Penfield & Roberts,

1959). The shaded areas in this illustration indicate the general locations of language functions. We have come to know that these areas exist largely through the examination, in autopsies, of the brains of people who, in life, were known to have specific language disabilities. That is, we have determined where language abilities for normal users must be, because people who had language disabilities also had damage to those specific areas of the brain. The three areas can be described in the following way.

Broca's area

Shown as (1) in the illustration is what is technically described as the anterior speech cortex or, more usually, as **Broca's area**. Paul Broca, a French surgeon, reported in the 1860s that damage to this specific part of the brain was related to extreme difficulty in producing speech. It was noted that damage to the corresponding area on the right hemisphere had no such effect. This finding was first used to argue that language ability must be located in the left hemisphere and since then has been taken as more specifically illustrating that Broca's area is crucially involved in the production of speech.

Wernicke's area

Shown as (2) in the illustration is the posterior speech cortex, or **Wernicke's area**. Carl Wernicke was a German doctor who, in the 1870s, reported that damage to this part of the brain was found among patients who had speech comprehension difficulties. This finding confirmed the left-hemisphere location of language ability and led to the view that Wernicke's area is part of the brain crucially involved in the understanding of speech.

Supplementary motor area

Shown as (3) in the illustration is the superior speech cortex, also known as the **supplementary motor area**. Evidence that this area is involved in the actual physical articulation of speech comes from the work, reported in the 1950s, of two neurosurgeons, Penfield and Roberts. These researchers found that, by applying minute amounts of electrical current to specific areas of the brain, they could identify those areas where the electrical stimulation would interfere with normal speech production. Since the area shown as (3) in the illustration is very close to a fissure along which control of a large number of motor movements (i.e. moving hands, feet, arms, etc.) appeared to be located, it made a lot of sense that the motor movements involved in speech production would also be controlled in this general area.

The localization view

Having identified these three areas, it is tempting, of course, to come to the conclusion that specific aspects of language ability can be accorded specific locations in the brain. It has been proposed that the brain activity involved in hearing a word, understanding it, then saying it, would follow a definite pattern. The word is heard and comprehended via Wernicke's area. This signal is then transferred to Broca's area where preparations are made to produce it. A signal is then sent to the motor area to physically articulate the word.

This is, unfortunately, a massively oversimplified version of what may actually take place. The problem is, essentially, that in attempting to view the complex mechanism of the human brain in terms of a set of language 'locations', we have neglected to mention the intricate interconnections via the central nervous system, the complex role of the brain's blood supply, and the extremely interdependent nature of most brain functions. The **localization view** is one way of saying that our linguistic abilities have identifiable locations in the brain. However, it is invariably argued by others involved in the study of the brain that there is a lot of evidence which does not support the view. Any damage to one area of the brain appears to have repercussions in other areas. Consequently, we should be rather cautious about assigning highly specific connections between particular aspects of linguistic behavior and sites on the wrinkled grey matter inside the head.

Other views

It is probably best to think of any proposal concerning processing pathways in the brain as some form of metaphor which may turn out to be inadequate as a description of what actually takes place. The 'pathway' metaphor may seem very appropriate in an electronic age, since it conjures up the now familiar process of sending signals through electrical circuits. In an earlier age, dominated more by mechanical technology, Freud subtly employed a 'steam engine' metaphor to account for certain aspects of the brain's activity, by talking of the effects of "repression" "building up pressure" to the point of sudden "release". In an even earlier age, Aristotle's metaphor was of the brain as a cold sponge which functioned to keep the blood cool.

In a sense, we are forced to use metaphors mainly because we cannot obtain direct physical evidence of linguistic processes in the brain. Because we have no direct access, we generally have to rely on what we can discover via indirect methods. Some of these methods are considered in the following sections and reflect an attempt, as described by MacKay (1970), "to infer the properties of a complex and unobservable system from its transitory malfunctions".

Tongue tips and slips

Some researchers have noted that, as language-users, we all experience occasional difficulty in getting the brain and speech production to work together smoothly. (Well, some of us more than others, perhaps.) Minor production difficulties of this sort have been investigated as possible clues to the way our linguistic knowledge may be organized within the brain.

There is, for example, the **tip-of-the-tongue** phenomenon in which you feel that some word is just eluding you, that you know the word, but it just won't come to the surface. Studies of this phenomenon have shown that speakers generally have an accurate phonological outline of the word, can get the initial sound correct and mostly know the number of syllables in the word. This experience also mainly occurs with uncommon terms or names. It suggests that our 'word-storage' may be partially organized on the basis of some phonological information and that some words in that 'store' are more easily retrieved than others. When we make mistakes in this retrieval process, there are often strong phonological similarities between the target word and the mistake. For example, speakers produced *secant, sextet* and *sexton*, when asked to name a particular type of navigational instrument (*sextant*). Mistakes of this type are sometimes referred to as **Malapropisms**, after a character called Mrs Malaprop in a play by Sheridan who consistently produced 'near-misses' for words, with great comic effect. The comic use of this type of mistake can still be found, as when the television character Archie Bunker is heard to say *We need a few laughs to break up the monogamy*.

A similar type of speech error is commonly described as a **slip-of-the-tongue**, which often results in tangled expressions such as *a long shory stort* (for 'make a long story short') and *the thine sing* (for 'the sign thing'). This type of slip is also known as a **Spoonerism**, after the Rev. William A. Spooner, an Oxford dean, who was renowned for his tongue-slips. Most of the slips attributed to him involve the interchange of two sounds, as when he addressed a rural group as *Noble tons of soil*, or described God as *a shoving leopard to his flock*, or in this complaint to a student who had been absent from classes: *You have hissed all my mystery lectures*. Using this interchange of forms for comic effect, Oscar Wilde switched the words *work* and *drink* to produce the memorable expression *Work is the curse of the drinking classes*.

Most everyday tongue-slips, however, are not as entertaining. They are often simply the result of a sound being carried over from one word to the next, as in *black bloxes* (for 'black boxes') or a sound used in one word in anticipation of its occurrence in the next word, as in *noman numeral* (for 'roman numeral'). It has been argued that slips of this type are not random, that they never produce a phonologically unacceptable sequence, and that they indicate the existence of different stages in the articulation of linguistic expressions. Although the slips are mostly treated as errors of articulation, it has been suggested that they may result from 'slips of the brain' as it tries to organize linguistic messages.

One other type of slip, less commonly documented, may provide some clues to how the brain tries to make sense of the auditory signal it receives. These have been called **slips-of-the-ear** and can result, for example, in our hearing *great ape*, and wondering why someone should be looking for one in his office. (The speaker actually said 'grey tape'.) A similar type of misunderstanding seems to be behind the child's report that, in Sunday school, everyone was singing about a bear called Gladly who was cross-eyed. The source of this slip turned out to be a line from a religious song which went *Gladly the cross I'd bear*.

Some of these humorous examples of slips may give us a clue to the normal workings of the human brain as it copes with language. However, some problems with language production and comprehension are the result of much more serious disorders in brain function.

Aphasia

If you have experienced any of those 'slips' on occasion, then you will have some hint of the types of experience which some people live with constantly. These people suffer from different types of language disorders, generally described as **aphasia**. Aphasia is defined as an impairment of language function due to localized cerebral damage which leads to difficulty in understanding and/or producing linguistic forms. The most common cause of aphasia is a stroke, though traumatic head injuries suffered through violence or accidents may have similar effects. It is often the case that someone who is aphasic has interrelated language disorders in that difficulties in understanding can lead to difficulties in production. Consequently, the classification of types of aphasia is normally based on the primary symptoms of an aphasic who is having difficulties with language.

Broca's aphasia

The type of serious language disorder known as **Broca's aphasia** (also called 'motor aphasia') is characterized by a substantially reduced amount of speech, distorted articulation and slow, often effortful speech. What is said often consists almost entirely of lexical morphemes (e.g. nouns and verbs). The frequent omission of functional morphemes (e.g. articles, prepositions, inflections) has led to the characterization of this type of aphasia as **agrammatic**. An example of speech produced by someone whose aphasia was not severe is the following answer to a question regarding what the speaker had for breakfast: *I eggs and eat and drink coffee breakfast*. However, this type of disorder can be quite severe and result in speech samples such as *my cheek . . . very annoyance . . . main is my shoulder . . . achin' all round here . . .*, or as in this attempt to say what kind of ship the speaker had been on: *a stail . . . you know what I mean . . . tal . . . stail . . .* (It had been a steamship.)

Wernicke's aphasia

The type of language disorder which results in difficulties in auditory comprehension is sometimes called 'sensory aphasia', but is more commonly known as **Wernicke's aphasia**. Someone suffering from this disorder can actually produce very fluent speech which is, however, often difficult to make sense of. Very general terms are used, even in response to specific requests for information, as in this sample: *I can't talk all of the things I do, and part of the part I can go alright, but I can't tell from the other people*. Difficulty in finding the correct words (sometimes referred to as **anomia**) is also very common and circumlocutions may be used, as in this answer (to the question "What's ink for?"): *to do with a pen*.

However, word-finding difficulties occur in many different types of aphasia. It is also the case that difficulties in speaking will be accompanied by difficulties in writing. Impairment of auditory comprehension tends to be accompanied by reading difficulties. Language disorders of the type we have described are almost always the result of injury to the left hemisphere. This left-hemisphere dominance for language has also been demonstrated by another approach to the investigation of language and the brain.

Dichotic listening

An experimental technique which has demonstrated that, for the majority of subjects tested, the language functions must be located in the left hemisphere is called the **dichotic listening test**. This is a technique which uses the generally established fact that anything experienced on the right-hand side of the body is processed in the left hemisphere of the brain and anything on the left side is processed in the right hemisphere. So a basic assumption would be that a signal coming in the right ear will go to the left hemisphere and a signal coming in the left ear will go to the right hemisphere.

With this information, an experiment is possible in which a subject sits with a set of earphones on and is given two different sound signals simultaneously, one through each earphone. For example, through one earphone comes the sound *ga* or *dog*, and through the other, at exactly the same time, comes the sound *da* or *cat*. When asked to say what was heard, the subject more often correctly identifies the sound which came via the right ear. This has come to be known as the **right ear advantage** for linguistic sounds. The process which is thought to be involved is best explained with the help of the accompanying illustration.

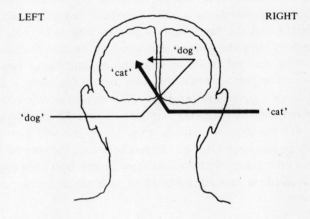

The explanation of this process proposes that a language signal received through the left ear is first sent to the right hemisphere and then has to be sent over to the left hemisphere (language center) for processing. This non-direct route will take longer than a linguistic signal which is received through the right ear and goes directly to the left hemisphere. First signal to get processed wins.

The right hemisphere appears to have primary responsibility for processing a lot of other incoming signals of a non-linguistic nature. In the dichotic listening test, it can be shown that nonverbal sounds (e.g. music, coughs, traffic noises, birds singing) are recognized more often via the left ear (i.e. processed faster via the right hemisphere). So, among the specializations of the human brain, the right hemisphere handles nonverbal sounds (among other things) and the left hemisphere handles language sounds (among other things too).

It should be noted, however, that more recent research in this area has indicated that the specializations of the two hemispheres may have more to do with the type of 'processing' rather than the type of 'material' which is processed. In effect, the real distinction (at least for the majority of right-handed, monolingual, male adults, in the United States) may be between analytic processing, done with the 'left brain', and holistic processing, done with the 'right brain'.

The critical period

The apparent specialization of the left hemisphere for language is often described as lateralization (one-sidedness). Since the human child does not spring from the womb as a fully articulate language-user, it is generally thought that the lateralization process begins in early childhood. It coincides with the period during which language acquisition takes place. The general belief is that during childhood (up until puberty), there is a period when the human brain is most ready to 'receive' and learn a particular language. This period is referred to as the **critical period**. If a child does not acquire language during this period, for any one of a number of reasons, then he or she will have great difficulty learning language later on. In recent years, because of rather unfortunate circumstances, we have had some insight into what happens when the lateralization process takes place without an accompanying linguistic input.

Genie

In 1970 a child called Genie was admitted to a children's hospital in Los Angeles. She was 13 years old and had spent most of her life tied to a chair in a small closed room. Her father was intolerant of any kind of noise and had beaten the child whenever she made a sound. There had been no radio or television, and Genie's only other human contact was with her mother who was forbidden to spend more than a few minutes with the child to feed her. Genie had spent her whole life in a state of physical, sensory, social and emotional deprivation.

As might be expected, Genie was unable to use language when she was first brought into care. However, within a short period of time, she began to respond to the speech of others and to try to imitate sounds. The fact that she went on to develop an ability to speak and understand a certain amount of English provides some evidence against the notion that language cannot be acquired at all after the critical period. One particularly strong view is that the lateralization process is complete by the time of puberty and that language acquisition after that time would present insurmountable difficulties. In this view, it is as if part of the left hemisphere of the brain is open to accept a 'language program' during childhood and, if no program is provided, as in Genie's case, then the facility is closed down.

In Genie's case, tests demonstrated that she had no left-hemisphere language facility. So, how was she able to begin learning language, even in a limited way? Those same tests appeared to indicate the quite remarkable fact that Genie was using the right hemisphere of her brain for language functions. In dichotic listening tests, she had a very strong left-ear advantage for verbal as well as nonverbal signals. Such findings give some indication that there is not necessarily an exclusive brain location for language abilities. It may also help explain the fact that many people who suffer minor brain damage (with temporary loss of language) can recover, in varying degrees, their language-using abilities.

When Genie was developing language, it was noted that she went through many of the same early 'stages' found in normal child language acquisition. In the next chapter, we shall investigate what these normal stages are.

Study questions

1. What are the usual names given to the three areas of the brain generally considered to relate to language function?
2. What is aphasia?
3. What happens in a dichotic listening test?
4. What specializations for the recognition of types of sounds have been found in different parts of the brain (for most people)?
5. Why is Genie's case so remarkable with respect to established notions about areas of language specialization in the human brain?

Discussion topics/projects

A. It is claimed that there is a pattern of similarity in sound between the error and the target in Malapropisms. Below are some examples from Fay & Cutler (1977) used to support that claim. Can you identify the similar features (e.g. initial sound, number of syllables, final sound, etc.) which connect these pairs of errors and targets? Are there any discrepancies?

Error	Target	Error	Target
below	before	technology	terminology
emanate	emulate	equivocal	equivalent
photogenic	photographic	participate	precipitate
conclusion	confusion	area	error
single	signal	radio	radiator
musician	magician	apartment	appointment

B. Below are two pieces of spoken language produced by speakers of English. Identify the 'mistakes' in each sample and suggest what might have caused them.

   (i) "I forget to talker, what, where the name of the police I told where the place there, we wert in on the job"
   (ii) "Well, I was looking for a spoop soon, oh God, a what? A soup spoon, I mean, and what did I say? Isn't that weird?"

C. One aphasia patient was asked to read the written words on the left below and actually said the words which appear on the right. Is there any pattern to be found in these 'errors'? Does this type of phenomenon provide any clues to the way words may be stored in the brain? (You can compare your conclusions with those of Allport & Funnell, 1981, whose paper, listed in the References, provided these examples.)

   commerce – "business"   *binocular* – "telescope"
   apricot – "peach"   *applause* – "audience"
   saddle   – "stirrup"   *element*   – "substance"
   victory – "triumph"   *anecdote* – "narrator"

D. The following samples were produced by speakers suffering from different types of aphasia. Both are describing the same picture. Can you make a reasonable guess at what type of aphasia each has, and explain the reasons for your choice?

   (i) "water ... man, no woman ... child ... no, man ... and girl ... oh dear ... cupboard ... man, falling ... jar ... cakes ... head ... face ... window ... tap"
   (ii) "well, it's a ... it's a place, and it's a ... girl and a boy, and they've got obviously something which is made, some ... some ... made ... it's just beginning"

Further reading

Introductory accounts of the relationship between language and the brain can be found in Bayles (1984) or Geschwind (1972). More technical treatments which are nevertheless quite accessible are Brookshire (1978) or Caramazza & Berndt (1982). For one of the clearest accounts of the localization view, see Geschwind (1979). Penfield & Roberts (1959) provide a detailed account of their investigations. A wealth of interesting case histories involving aphasia can be found in

Weisenberg & McBride (1964). On the tip-of-the-tongue phenomenon, see Brown & McNeill (1966), on Malapropisms, see Fay & Cutler (1977), and on slips-of-the-tongue, see Fromkin (1973) for a brief account, or the more comprehensive contributions in Fromkin (ed.) (1973). Kimura (1973) describes dichotic listening tests and Curtiss (1977) is about Genie.

Chapter 15
First language acquisition

Child: Want other one spoon, Daddy.
Father: You mean, you want the other spoon.
Child: Yes, I want other one spoon, please Daddy.
Father: Can you say "the other spoon"?
Child: Other ... one ... spoon.
Father: Say "other".
Child: Other.
Father: "spoon".
Child: Spoon.
Father: "Other spoon".
Child: Other ... spoon. Now give me other one spoon?

Martin Braine (1971)

First language acquisition is remarkable for the speed with which it takes place. By the time a child enters elementary school, he or she is an extremely sophisticated language-user, operating a communicative system which no other creature, or computer, comes close to matching. The speed of acquisition and the fact that it generally occurs, without overt instruction, for all children, regardless of great differences in a range of social and cultural factors, have led to the belief that there is some 'innate' predisposition in the human infant to acquire language. We can think of this as the 'language-faculty' of the human with which each newborn child is endowed. By itself, however, this faculty is not enough.

Basic requirements

A child growing up in the first two or three years requires interaction with other language-users in order to bring the 'language-faculty' into operation with a particular language, such as English. We have already noted, in the case of Genie (Chapter 14), that a child who does not hear, or is not allowed to use, language will learn no language. We have also stressed the importance of 'cultural transmission' (Chapter

3) whereby the language a child learns is not genetically inherited, but is acquired in a particular language-using environment. The child must also be physically capable of sending and receiving sound signals in a language. All infants make 'cooing' and 'babbling' noises during the first few months, but congenitally deaf infants stop after six months. So, in order to speak a language, a child must be able to hear that language being used. By itself, however, hearing language sounds is not enough. One reported case has demonstrated that, with deaf parents who gave their normal-hearing son ample exposure to T.V. and radio programs, the child did not acquire an ability to speak or understand English. What he did learn very effectively, by the age of three, was the use of American Sign Language – the language he used to interact with his parents. The crucial requirement appears to be the opportunity to interact with others via language.

The acquisition schedule

All normal children, regardless of culture, develop language at roughly the same time, along much the same schedule. Since we could say the same thing for sitting up, standing, walking, using the hands and many other physical activities, it has been suggested that the language acquisition schedule has the same basis as the biologically determined development of motor skills. This biological schedule, it is claimed, is tied very much to the maturation of the infant's brain and the lateralization process. If there is some general biological program underlying language acquisition, it is certainly dependent on an interplay with many social factors in the child's environment. We could think of the child as having the biological capacity to cope with distinguishing certain aspects of linguistic input at different stages during the early years of life. What this acquisition 'capacity' then requires is a sufficiently constant input from which the regularities of the particular language can be worked out. In this view, the child is seen as actively acquiring the language by working out the regularities in what is heard and then applying those regularities in what he or she says.

Some controversies

In our consideration of the basic requirements and the schedule involved in first language acquisition, we have already touched on a number of issues which are the subject of debate among those who study child language. For example, there are studies which show that the early environment of a child differs considerably from one culture to the next. Consequently, the findings of research into the process of acquisition in middle class English-speaking cultures may not be replicated in studies of other cultures. There is also substantial controversy over the issue of 'innateness'. Noam Chomsky (1983) has proposed that language development should be described as "language growth", because the "language organ" simply grows like any other body organ. This view seems to underestimate what others consider the importance of environment and experience in the child's development of language. At issue is the extent to which the process of language acquisition is genetically predetermined in the human species.

Another matter of some debate has arisen over how we should view the linguistic production of young children. The linguist's view tends to concentrate on describing the child's speech in terms of the known units of phonology and syntax, for example. However, the child's view of what is being heard and uttered at different stages may be based on quite different units. For example, a child's utterance of [dùkədæt] may be a single unit for the child, yet may be treated as having three units, *look at that*, by an investigator interested in the child's acquisition of different types of verbs.

It is worth keeping these issues in mind throughout this chapter because some of the standard concepts and analyses which are presented here as basic aspects of child language are likely to be challenged, and possibly amended, as continuing research reveals more about this complex subject.

Caretaker speech

Under normal circumstances, in Western cultures, the human infant is certainly helped in his or her language acquisition by the typical behavior of the adults in the home environment. Adults such as mom, dad, granny and grandpa tend not to address the little gurgler before them as if they are involved in normal adult-to-adult conversation. There is not much of this: *Well, John Junior, shall we invest in blue chip industrials, or would grain futures offer better short term prospects?* However, there does seem to be a lot of this: *Oh, goody, now Daddy push choo-choo?* The characteristically simplified speech style adopted by someone who spends a lot of time interacting with a young child is called **caretaker speech**. Some of the features of this type of speech are frequent questions, often using exaggerated intonation. In the early stages, this type of speech also incorporates a lot of forms associated with 'baby-talk'. These are either simplified words (e.g. *tummy*, *nana*) or alternative forms, with repeated simple sounds, for objects in the child's environment (e.g. *choo-choo*, *poo-poo*, *wawa*).

Built into a lot of caretaker speech is a type of conversational structure which seems to assign an interactive role to the young child even before he or she becomes a speaking participant. If we look at an extract from the speech of one mother to her 2-year-old child as if it were a two-party conversation, then this type of structuring becomes apparent. (This example is from Anderson *et al.*, 1984.)

> Mother: *there's your cup of tea*
> Child: (takes cup)
> Mother: *you drink it nicely*
> Child: (pretends to drink)
> Mother: *oh – is that nice?*
> Child: (assents)
> Mother: *will Mummy drink her tea?*
> Child: (assents)
> Mother: *I'll drink my tea*

Caretaker speech is also characterized by simple sentence structures and a lot of repetition. If the child is indeed in the process of working out a system of putting sounds and words together, then these simplified models produced by the interacting adult may serve as good clues to the basic structural organization involved. Moreover, it has generally been observed that the speech of those regularly interacting with children changes and becomes more elaborate as the child begins using more and more language. Several stages in the acquisition process have been identified.

Pre-language stages

The pre-linguistic sounds of the very early stages of child language acquisition are simply called 'cooing' and 'babbling'. The period from about 3 months to 10 months is usually characterized by three stages of sound production in the infant's developing repertoire. The first recognizable sounds are described as **cooing**, with velar consonants such as [k] and [g] usually present, as well as high vowels such as [i] and [u]. These can normally be heard by the time the child is 3 months old, although many of the child's vocal sounds are very different from those which occur in the speech of mom and dad.

By 6 months, the child is usually able to sit up and can produce a number of different vowels and consonants such as fricatives and nasals. The sound production at this stage is described as **babbling** and may contain syllable-type sounds such as *mu* and *da*. In the later babbling stage, around 9 months, there are recognizable intonation patterns to the consonant and vowel combinations being produced. As children begin to pull themselves into a standing position through the tenth and eleventh months, they are capable of using their vocalizations to express emotions and emphasis. This late babbling stage is characterized by a lot of 'sound-play' and attempted imitations. Some psychologists have suggested that this 'pre-language' vocalization gives children some experience of the social role of speech because parents tend to react to the babbling, however incoherent, as if it is, in fact, their child's contribution to social interaction.

One note of caution should be sounded at this point. Child language researchers certainly report very carefully on the age of any child whose language they study. However, they are also very careful to point out that there is substantial variation among children in terms of the age at which particular features of linguistic development occur. So, we should always treat statements concerning development stages such as "by six months" or "by the age of two" as approximate and subject to variation in individual children. We are, after all, investigating a highly individualized experience while attempting to come up with some general statements about approximate stages of development.

The one-word or holophrastic stage

Between 12 and 18 months, children begin to produce a variety of recognizable single unit utterances. This period, traditionally called the 'one-word stage', is characterized by speech in which single terms are uttered for everyday objects such as 'milk', 'cookie', 'cat' and 'cup'. Other forms such as [ʌsæː] may occur in circumstances which suggest that the child is producing a version of *what's that*, so the label 'one-word' for this stage may be misleading. Terms such as 'single-unit' or 'single-form' may be more accurate, or we could use the term **holophrastic** (a single form functioning as a phrase or sentence), if we believe that the child is actually using these forms as phrases or sentences.

While many of these single forms are used for naming objects, they may also be produced in circumstances that suggest the child is already extending their use. An empty bed may elicit the name of a sister who normally sleeps in the bed, even in the absence of the person named. During this stage, then, the child may be capable of referring to *Karen* and *bed*, but is not yet ready to put the forms together to produce a more complex phrase. Well, it is a lot to expect from someone who can only walk with a stagger and has to come down stairs backwards.

The two-word stage

Depending on what one counts as an occurrence of two separate words, this stage can begin around 18–20 months. By the time the child is 2 years old, a variety of combinations, *baby chair*, *mommy eat*, *cat bad*, will be appearing. The adult interpretation of such combinations is, of course, very much tied to the context of their utterance. The phrase *baby chair* may be taken as an expression of possession (= this is baby's chair), or as a request (= put baby in chair), or as a statement (= baby is in the chair), depending on different contexts. Whatever it is that the child actually intends to communicate via such expressions, the significant functional consequences are that the adult behaves as if communication is taking place. That is, the child not only produces speech, but receives feedback which usually confirms that the utterance 'worked'. By the age of 2, the child will have a vocabulary of more than 50 words and will typically be treated as an entertaining conversational partner by the principal caretaker.

Telegraphic speech

Between 2 and 3 years old, the child will begin producing a large number of utterances which could be classified as multiple-word utterances. The salient feature of these utterances ceases to be the number of words, but the variation in word-forms which begins to appear. Of particular interest is the sequence of inflectional morphemes which occurs. Before we consider this development, however, we should note that there is a stage which is described as **telegraphic speech**. This is characterized by strings of lexical morphemes in phrases such as *Andrew want ball*, *cat drink milk*, and *this shoe all wet*. The child has clearly developed some sentence-building capacity by this stage and can order the forms correctly. While this type of telegram-format speech is being produced, a number of grammatical inflections begin to appear in some of the words, and the simple prepositions (*in*, *on*) also turn up.

By the age of two and a half, the child's vocabulary is expanding rapidly and the child is actually initiating more talk. Of course, increased physical activity such as running and jumping is taking place during this period too. By three, the vocabulary has grown to hundreds of words and pronunciation has become closer to the form of the adult language, so that even visitors have to admit that the little creature really can talk.

The acquisition process

As the linguistic repertoire of the child increases, it is often assumed that the child is, in some sense, being 'taught' the language. This view seems to underestimate what the child actually does. For the vast majority of children, no one provides any instruction on how to speak the language. Nor should we picture a little empty head gradually being filled with words and phrases. A much more realistic view would have children actively constructing, from what is said to them, possible ways of using the language. The child's linguistic production, then, is mostly a matter of trying out constructions and testing whether they work or not. It is extremely unlikely that the child is acquiring the language simply through a process of consistently imitating (parrot-fashion) adult speech. Of course, the child can be heard to repeat versions of what adults say and is in the process of adopting a lot of vocabulary from their speech. However, adults simply do not produce many of the types of expressions which turn up in children's speech.

Nor does adult 'correction' seem to be a very effective determiner of how the child speaks. A lot of very amusing conversational snippets, involving an adult's attempt to correct a child's speech, seem to demonstrate the hopelessness of the task. One typical example was quoted at the beginning of this chapter. Even when the correction is attempted in a more subtle manner, the child will continue to use a personally constructed form, despite the adult's repetition of what the correct form should be. Note that in the following dialog (quoted in Cazden, 1972) the child, a 4-year-old, is neither imitating the adult's speech nor accepting the adult's correction:

> Child: *My teacher holded the baby rabbits and we patted them*
> Mother: *Did you say your teacher held the baby rabbits?*
> Child: *Yes*
> Mother: *What did you say she did?*
> Child: *She holded the baby rabbits and we patted them*
> Mother: *Did you say she held them tightly?*
> Child: *No, she holded them loosely*

One factor which seems to be crucial in the child's acquisition process is the actual use of sound and word combinations, either in interaction with others or in word-play, alone. One 2-year-old, tape-recorded as he lay in bed alone, could be heard playing with words and phrases, *I go dis way ... way bay ... baby do dis bib ... all bib ... bib ... dere* (from Weir, 1966). It is practice of this type which seems to be an important factor in the development of the child's linguistic repertoire. The details of this development beyond the telegraphic stage have been traced, in a number of studies, via the linguistic elements which begin to turn up, on a regular basis, in the steady stream of speech emerging from the little chatterbox.

Morphology

By the time the child is 3 years old, he or she is going beyond telegraphic speech forms and incorporating some of the inflectional morphemes which indicate the grammatical function of the nouns and verbs used. The first to appear is usually the *-ing* form in expressions such as *cat sitting* and *mommy reading book*. Then comes the marking of regular plurals with the *-s* form, as in *boys* and *cats*. The acquisition of this form is often accompanied by a process of **overgeneralization**. The child overgeneralizes the apparent rule of adding *-s* to form plurals and will talk about *foots* and *mans*. When the alternative pronunciation of the plural morpheme used in *houses* (i.e. ending [-əz]) comes into use, it too is given an overgeneralized application and forms such as *boyses* or *footses* can appear. At the same time as this overgeneralization is taking place, some children also begin using irregular plurals such as *men* quite appropriately for a while, but then try out the general rule on the forms, producing expressions like *some mens* and *two feets*, or even *two feetses*.

The use of the possessive inflection *-'s* occurs in expressions such as *girl's dog* and *Mummy's book* and the different forms of the verb 'to be', such as *are* and *was*, turn up. The appearance of forms such as *was* and, at about the same time, *went* and *came* should be noted. These are irregular past tense forms which one would not expect to appear before the more regular forms. However, they do typically precede the appearance of the *-ed* inflection. Once the regular past tense forms begin appearing in the child's speech (e.g. *walked*, *played*), then, interestingly, the irregular forms disappear for a while and are replaced by overgeneralized versions such as *goed* and *comed*. For a period, there is often minor chaos as the -ed inflection is added to everything, producing such oddities as *walkeded* and *wented*. As with the plural forms, however, the child works out, usually after the age of 4, which forms are regular and which are not. Finally, the regular -s marker on third person singular present tense verbs appears. It occurs initially with full verbs (*comes*, *looks*) and then with auxiliaries (*does*, *has*).

Throughout this sequence there is, of course, a great deal of variability. Individual children may produce 'good' forms one day and 'odd' forms the next. It is important to remember that the child is working out how to use the linguistic system while actually using it as a means of communication. For the child, the use of forms such as *goed* and *foots* is simply a means of trying to say what he or she means during a particular stage of development. The embarrassed parents who insist that the child didn't hear such things at home are implicitly recognizing that 'imitation' is not the primary force in child language acquisition.

Syntax

Similar evidence against 'imitation' as the basis of a child's speech production has been found in studies of the syntactic structures used by children. One 2-year-old child, specifically asked to repeat what she heard, would listen to an adult say forms such as *the owl who eats candy runs fast*, and then repeat them in the form *owl eat candy and he run fast*. It is clear that the child understands what the adult is saying. She just has her own way of expressing it.

There have been numerous studies of the development of syntax in children's speech. We shall restrict our consideration to two features which have been well-documented and which seem to be acquired in a regular way. In the formation of questions and the use of negatives, there appear to be three identifiable stages. The ages of children going through these stages can vary quite a lot, but the general pattern seems to be that Stage 1 occurs between 18 and 26 months, Stage 2 between 22 and 30 months, and Stage 3 between 24 and 40 months. (It must be emphasized that no precise ages can ever really be assigned to these developmental stages. Different children proceed at different paces.)

Questions

In forming questions, the first stage has two procedures. Simply add a *wh-* form (*where*, *who*) to the beginning of the expression or utter the expression with a rise in intonation towards the end. Here are some examples:

> *Where kitty?*   *Where horse go?*   *Sit chair?*   *See hole?*

In the second stage, more complex expressions can be formed, but the rising intonation strategy continues to be used. It is noticeable that more *wh-* forms come into use, as in these examples:

> *What book name?*   *Why you smiling?*
> *You want eat?*   *See my doggie?*

In the third stage, the required inversion of subject and verb in English questions has appeared, but the *wh-* forms do not always undergo the required inversion. In fact, children entering school may still prefer to form *wh-* questions (especially in negatives) without the type of inversion found in adult speech. Examples are:

> *Can I have a piece?*   *Did I caught it?*   *Will you help me?*
> *How that opened?*   *What did you do?*   *Why kitty can't stand up?*

Negatives

In the case of negatives, Stage 1 seems to have a simple strategy which says that *no* or *not* should be stuck on the beginning of any expression. Examples are:

> *no mitten*   *not a teddy bear*   *no fall*   *no sit there*

In the second stage, the additional negative forms *don't* and *can't* are used, and with *no* and *not*, begin to be placed in front of the verb rather than at the beginning of the sentence. Some examples are:

> *He no bite you*   *There no squirrels*   *You can't dance*   *I don't know*

The third stage sees the incorporation of other auxiliary forms such as *didn't* and *won't*, and the disappearance of the Stage 1 forms. A very late acquisition is the form *isn't*, so that some Stage 2 forms continue to be used for quite a long time. Examples are:

> *I didn't caught it*   *She won't let go*
> *He not taking it*   *This not ice cream*

The study of the use of negative forms by children has given rise to some delightful examples of children operating their own rules for negative sentences. One famous example (from McNeill, 1966) also shows the futility of overt adult 'correction':

Child: *Nobody don't like me*
Mother: *No, say "nobody likes me"*
Child: *Nobody don't like me*
(Eight repetitions of this dialog)
Mother: *No, now listen carefully; say "nobody likes me"*
Child: *Oh! Nobody don't likes me*

Semantics

Most of those anecdotes which parents retell (to the intense embarrassment of the grown-up child) about their child's early speech center on
examples of the strange use of words. Having been warned that flies
bring germs into the house, one child was asked what "germs" were
and the answer was, "something the flies play with". It is not always
possible to determine so precisely the meanings which children attach
to the words they use.

It seems that during the holophrastic stage many children use their
limited vocabulary to refer to a large number of unrelated objects. One
child first used *bow-wow* to refer to a dog and then to a fur piece with
glass eyes, a set of cufflinks and even a bath thermometer. The word
bow-wow seemed to have a meaning like 'object with shiny bits'. Other
children often extend *bow-wow* to refer to cats, horses and cows. This
process is called **overextension** and the most common pattern is for the
child to overextend the meaning of a word on the basis of similarities
of shape, sound and size, and, to a lesser extent, of movement and
texture. Thus, a *tick-tock* is initially a watch, but can also be used for
a bathroom scale with a round dial. On the basis of size, presumably,
the word *fly* was first used for the insect, and then came to be used
for specks of dirt and even crumbs of bread. Apparently due to similarities of texture, the expression *sizo* was first used by one child for scissors,
and then came to be used for all metal objects. The semantic development in a child's use of words is usually a process of overextension
initially, followed by a gradual process of narrowing down the application
of each term as more words are learned.

Although overextension has been well-documented in children's
speech production, it isn't necessarily used in speech comprehension.
One 2-year-old child, in speaking, used *apple* to refer to a number of
other round objects like tomatoes and balls, but had no difficulty picking
out *the apple*, when asked, from a set of such round objects.

One interesting feature of the young child's semantics is the way
certain lexical relations are treated. In terms of hyponymy, the child

will almost always use the 'middle' level term in a hyponymous set such as *animal*:*dog*:*poodle*. It would seem more logical to learn the most general term (*animal*), but all evidence suggests that children first use *dog* with an overextended meaning close to the meaning of *animal*. This may be connected with a similar tendency in adults, when talking to young children, to refer to *flowers* (not the general *plants*, or the specific *tulips*). It also seems that antonymous relations are acquired fairly late (after the age of 5). A large number of kindergarten children in one study pointed to the same heavily laden apple tree when asked *Which tree has more apples?*, and also when asked *Which tree has less?* The conclusion seems to be that *more* and *less* were not treated as antonyms, but as synonyms. The distinctions between a number of other pairs such as *before* and *after*, *buy* and *sell*, also seem to be later acquisitions.

Despite the fact that the child is still acquiring aspects of his or her native language through the later years of childhood, it is normally assumed that, by the age of 5, with an operating vocabulary of more than 2,000 words, the child has completed the greater part of the basic language acquisition process. According to some, the child is then in a good position to start learning a second (or foreign) language. However, most educational systems do not introduce foreign language instruction until much later. The question which always arises is: if first language acquisition was so straightforward, why is learning a second language so difficult? We shall consider this question in the next chapter.

Study questions

1. Can you describe two noticeable features of caretaker speech?
2. What size of vocabulary would you expect an average 24-month-old child to have and which 'stage' would that child already have reached?
3. In a normal child acquisition schedule, what would be the order of regular appearance of the following inflections: *-ed*; *-ing*; *-'s*; *-s* (plural)?
4. The following two sentences were produced by children of different ages. Which would you expect from the older child and on which features did you base your answer?
   (a) *I not hurt him*   (b) *No the sun shining*
5. What is the term used to describe the process whereby a child uses one word like *ball* to refer to an apple, an egg, a grape and a ball?

Discussion topics/projects

A. Consider this point of view, expressed by Chomsky (1983):

All through an organism's existence, from birth to death, it passes through a series of genetically programmed changes. Plainly language growth is simply one of these predetermined changes. Language depends upon a genetic endowment that's on a par with the ones that specify the structure of our visual or circulatory systems, or determine that we have arms instead of wings.

Do you agree or disagree with this view? What kind of evidence would you use to support your opinion? (Chapter 2 of Elliot, 1981, may provide some ideas.)

B. Below are samples of speech from children at three different stages in the acquisition process. Identify the most likely order (from least to most advanced) of these three samples. Describe the features in each child's utterances which you would use as evidence to support your ordering.

Child *X*	Child *Y*	Child *Z*
You want eat?	*Where those dogs goed?*	*No picture in there*
I can't see my book	*You didn't eat supper*	*Where momma boot?*
Why you waking me up?	*Does lions walk?*	*Have some?*

C. Young children do not always use the words they acquire in exactly the same way as adults. In the following examples of situation and utterance, can you discern any patterns in the use of verbs by these 2- and 3-year-olds?

(You can compare your conclusions with those of Clark, 1982, from whose data these examples were selected.)

Situation	Utterance
(wanting to have some cheese weighed)	– *you have to scale it*
(talking about getting dressed)	– *Mummy trousers me*
(not wanting his mother to sweep his room)	– *Don't broom my mess*
(putting crackers in her soup)	– *I'm crackering my soup*
(wanting a bell to be rung)	– *Make it bell*
(to mother preparing to brush his hair)	– *Don't hair me*

D. The following two transcriptions are from conversations between the same mother and child, the first (1) when the child was 24 months, and the second (2) three months later. Can you describe some of the changes which appear to have taken place in the child's ability to use language during that period? (These extracts are from Bellugi, 1970.)

(1) Eve: *Have that?*
    M: *No, you may not have it.*
    Eve: *Mom, where my tapioca?*
    M: *It's getting cool. You'll have it in just a minute*
    Eve: *Let me have it.*
    M: *Would you like to have your lunch right now?*
    Eve: *Yeah. My tapioca cool?*
    M: *Yes, it's cool.*
    Eve: *You gonna watch me eat my lunch?*

(2) M: *Come and sit over here.*
    Eve: *You can sit down by me. That will make me happy. Ready to turn it.*
    M: *We're not quite ready to turn the page.*
    Eve: *Yep, we are.*
    M: *Shut the door, we won't hear her then.*
    Eve: *Then Fraser won't hear her too. Where he's going? Did you make a great big hole there?*

M: *Yeah, I'm gonna watch you*
     eat your lunch.
Eve: *I eating it*
M: *I know you are.*

M: *Yes, we made a great big*
     hole in here; we have to get
     a new one.
Eve: *Could I get some other*
     piece of paper?

Further reading

Good introductory treatments of language acquisition can be found in Moskowitz (1978), Chapter 4 of Aitchison (1976), or part 4 of Clark & Clark (1977). Standard textbooks are Brown (1973), de Villiers & de Villiers (1978) and Elliot (1981). A recent approach which attempts to explore the child's view of the acquisition process is Peters (1983). The original research on questions and negatives in children's speech can be found in Klima & Bellugi (1966), and some criticisms of the methodology are raised by Campbell & Wales (1970). A recent volume on the 'state of the art' in child language acquisition is edited by Wanner & Gleitman (1983).

Chapter 16

Second language acquisition/learning

---

for no Tongue can be acquired without Grammatical rules; since then all other Tongues, and Languages are taught by Grammar, why ought not the English Tongue to be taught so too. Imitation will never do it, under twenty years; I have known some Foreigners who have been longer in learning to speak English and yet are far from it: the not learning by Grammar, is the true cause.

Joseph Aickin (1693)

While it is true that many young children whose parents speak different languages can acquire a second language in circumstances similar to those of first language acquisition, the vast majority of people are not exposed to a second language until much later. Moreover, for most people, the ability to use their first language is rarely matched, even after years of study, by a comparable ability in the second language. There is something of an enigma here, since there is apparently no other system of 'knowledge' which one can 'learn' better at 2 or 3 years old than at 15 or 25. A number of reasons have been put forward to account for this enigma, and a number of proposals have been made which might enable learners to become as proficient in a second language (**L2**) as they are in their first language (**L1**).

Acquisition barriers

Some obvious reasons for the problems experienced in L2 acquisition are related to the fact that most people attempt to learn another language during their teenage or adult years, in a few hours each week of school time (rather than via the constant interaction experienced by a child), with a lot of other occupations (the child has little else to do), and with an already known language available for most of their daily communicative requirements. Some less likely reasons include the suggestion that adults' tongues 'get stiff' from pronouncing one type of language (e.g. English) and just cannot cope with the new sounds of another language (e.g. French or Japanese). It's a cute idea, but there is no physical evidence to support it.

Perhaps the primary difficulty for most people can be captured in terms of a distinction between **acquisition** and **learning**. The term 'acquisition', when used of language, refers to the gradual development of ability in a language by using it naturally in communicative situations. The term 'learning', however, applies to a conscious process of accumulating knowledge of the vocabulary and grammar of a language. (Mathematics, for example, is learned, not acquired.) Activities associated with learning have traditionally been used in language-teaching in schools, and tend, when successful, to result in knowledge 'about' the language studied. Activities associated with acquisition are those experienced by the young child and, analogously, by those who 'pick up' another language from long periods spent in social interaction (daily use of the language) in another country. Those whose L2 experience is primarily a learning one tend not to develop the proficiency of those who have had an acquiring experience.

However, even in ideal acquisition situations, very few adults seem to reach native-like proficiency in using a second language. There are individuals who can achieve great expertise in writing, but not in speaking. One example is the author Joseph Conrad, whose novels have become classics of English literature, but whose English speech is reported to have retained the strong Polish accent of his first language. This might suggest that some features (e.g. vocabulary, grammar) of a second language are easier to acquire than others (e.g. phonology). Although it continues to be a matter of some debate, this type of observation is sometimes taken as evidence that, after the critical period has passed (around puberty), it becomes very difficult to acquire another language fully. In support of this view, the process of lateralization of the brain (discussed in Chapter 14) is cited as a crucial factor. We might think of this process in terms of the 'language-faculty' being strongly taken over by the features of the L1, with a resulting loss of flexibility or openness to receive the features of another language.

Against this view, it has been demonstrated that students in their early teens are quicker and more effective L2 learners than, for example, 7-year-olds. It may be, of course, that the acquisition of an L2 requires a combination of factors. The optimum age may be during the years 11–16 when the 'flexibility' of the language acquisition faculty has not been completely lost, and the maturation of cognitive skills allows a more effective 'working out' of the regular features of the L2 encountered.

Yet even during this 'optimum age', there may exist an acquisition barrier of quite a different sort. Teenagers are typically much more self-conscious than young children. If there is a strong element of unwillingness or embarrassment in attempting to produce the 'different' sounds of other languages, then it may override whatever physical and cognitive abilities there are. If this self-consciousness is combined with a lack of empathy with the foreign culture (e.g. no identification with its speakers or their customs), then the subtle effects of not wanting to sound like a Russian or an American may strongly inhibit the acquisition process. The literature on child L2 acquisition is full of instances where such inhibitions have been overcome by young children acquiring a second language. In one intriguing study, a group of adult L2 learners had their 'self-consciousness' levels reduced by having their alcohol levels gradually increased. Up to a certain point, the pronunciation of the L2 noticeably improved, but after a number of drinks, as you might expect, pronunciations deteriorated rapidly. Courses on "French-with-cognac" or "Russian-with-vodka" may provide a partial solution, but the inhibitions are likely to return with sobriety.

Acquisition aids

Despite all these barriers, the need for instruction in other languages has led to a variety of educational approaches which are aimed at fostering L2 acquisition. In 1483, William Caxton used his newly established printing press to produce a book of *Right good lernyng for to lerne shortly frenssh and englyssh*. He was not the first to compile 'course material' for L2 learners, and his phrase-book format (e.g. customary greetings: *Syre, god you kepe. I haue not seen you in longe tyme.*) has many modern counterparts. Approaches designed to promote L2 acquisition which have been used in this century, however, have tended to reflect different views on how a foreign language is best learned.

Grammar–translation method

The most traditional approach is to treat second, or foreign, language learning on a par with any other academic subject. Long lists of words and a set of grammatical rules have to be memorized, and the written language rather than the spoken language is emphasized. This method has its roots in the traditional approach to the teaching of Latin and is generally described as the **grammar–translation method**. This label has actually been applied to the approach by its detractors who have pointed out that its emphasis on learning about the L2 leaves students quite ignorant of how the language is used. Learners leaving school, having achieved high grades in French class via this method, typically find themselves at a loss when confronted by the way the French in France actually use their language.

Direct method

As a reaction to that approach, an attempt was made via what was called the **direct method** to recreate the exposure which young children have in language acquisition. Everything said in the classroom, for example, had to be expressed in the L2. Emphasis was placed on the spoken language, while vocabulary lists and explanations of grammatical rules were avoided. The assumption was that the correct way of using the language would be 'picked up' in passing. Unfortunately, as we have already noted, the experience of the young child at home and the experience of the student in a language classroom are quite different. Some students claim to have benefited from this approach, particularly in the version used by the Berlitz language schools, but many others seem to have had extremely frustrating experiences.

Audiolingual method

An attempt was made to improve on the shortcomings of the direct method by devising more structured material for the student. This involved a systematic presentation of grammatical constructions of the L2, moving from the simple to the more complex, often in the form of drills which the student had to repeat. This approach, called the **audio-lingual method**, was strongly influenced by a belief that the fluent use of a language was essentially a set of 'habits' which could be developed with a lot of practice. Much of this practice involved hours spent in a language laboratory repeating oral drills. During the 1950s, this approach was justified by claims that "foreign-language learning is basically a mechanical process of habit formation" (quoted in Rivers, 1964). Only thirty years later, it would be hard to find a psychologist or a linguist who would agree with the statement, yet versions of the audiolingual method are still very common in language-teaching. Its critics point out that individual practice in drilling language patterns bears no resemblance to the interactional nature of actual language use. Moreover, it can be incredibly boring.

The communicative approach

The most recent approach to L2 teaching which is widely used is generally described as the **communicative approach**. It is partially a reaction against the artificiality of 'pattern-practice' and also against the belief that consciously learning the grammar of a language will result in an ability to use the language. Although there are different versions of how to create 'communicative' experiences in the L2 classroom, they are all based on a view that the functions of language (i.e. what it is used for) should be emphasized rather than the forms of the language (i.e. correct grammatical or phonological structure). This approach is characterized by lessons organized around concepts such as "asking for things" in different social contexts, rather than "the forms of the past tense" in different sentences. It has also coincided with attempts to provide more appropriate materials for L2 learning which has a specific purpose (e.g. English for medical personnel or Japanese for business people).

Acquisition processes

One of the features of most versions of the communicative approach which sets it apart from the others we have considered is the toleration of 'mistakes' or 'errors' produced by learners. Traditionally, 'errors' were regarded negatively and had to be eradicated. The more recent acceptance of such errors in learners' language is based on a fundamental shift in perspective from the more traditional view of how second languages are acquired. Rather than consider a Spanish speaker's production of *In the room there are three womens* as simply a failure to learn correct English (which could be remedied by extra practice of the correct form), we could look upon it as an indication of the actual acquisition process in action. An 'error', then, is not something which hinders a student's progress, but is probably a clue to the active learning progress being made by a student as he or she tries out strategies of communication in the new language. Just as children acquiring their L1 produce certain ungrammatical forms in the acquisition process, so we might expect the L2 learner to produce overgeneralizations at certain stages. The example of *womens* might be seen as a type of **creative construction**, used by the learner in accordance with the most general way of making plural forms in English.

Of course, some 'errors' may be due to the **interference** of expressions or structures from the L1. An L1 Spanish speaker who produces *take it from the side inferior* may be trying to use the Spanish adjective *inferior* (=English *lower*) and placing it after the noun, as in Spanish constructions. However, on close inspection, the language produced by learners contains a large number of 'errors' which seem to have no connection to the forms of either L1 or L2. For example, the Spanish speaker who says in English *She name is Maria*, is producing a form which is not used by adult speakers of English, does not occur in English L1 acquisition by children, and is not found in Spanish. Evidence of this sort suggests that there may be some in-between system used in L2 acquisition which certainly contains aspects of L1 and L2, but which is an inherently variable system with rules of its own. The term **interlanguage** is sometimes used in descriptions of this phenomenon and has become the focus of some debate and a lot of research in recent years. The study of the interlanguage phenomenon has led to a reassessment of the way L2 acquisition should be perceived. Instead of treating the language of an L2 learner as the product of someone who is, in some way, competent in one language and incompetent in another, we should consider it as a type of language in its own right, which may, as it varies and develops, provide us with crucial insights into the very nature of that more general phenomenon called human language.

Study questions

1. What are four obvious barriers to adult L2 acquisition?
2. What do you think the term 'the Joseph Conrad phenomenon' refers to in terms of L2 learning?
3. What is likely to be the 'optimum age' for L2 learning?
4. Why would self-consciousness interfere with learning a second language?
5. In which L2 teaching approach would you most likely find a lesson entitled "How to ask for permission"?

Discussion topics/projects

A. Here are some principles proposed by Krashen & Terrell (1983) which they argue are necessary for successful L2 acquisition:
   (1) *the instructor always uses the target language*
   (2) *speech errors which do not interfere with communication are not corrected*

(3) *each classroom activity is organized by topic, not grammatical structure; practice of specific grammatical structures is not focused on in these activities*

(4) *an environment which is conducive to acquisition must be created by the instructor – low anxiety level, good rapport with the teacher, friendly relationship with other students*

Is this a description of a second language learning environment which you have experienced? What, if any, are the differences? Do you think the approach described here would be successful, or might there be drawbacks?

B. Here is a transcription of a native Spanish speaker's account of a classroom scene. What would you identify as 'errors' in this sample of English? Can you classify those errors in terms of overgeneralization, interference from L1, or resulting from some other process?

In a room there are three womens ... one is blond ... blond hair ... there are three womens ... one woman is the teacher ... and the other two womans are seat in the chair ... one of them are ... are blond hair ... and the other woman ... is black hair ... the teacher is made an explanation about shapes ... triangle circle

C. A common difficulty experienced in trying to communicate in a second language (and occasionally in the L1) is lack of knowledge of the precise term to describe something. In these circumstances, speakers use different types of 'communication strategies' to get their description across. Can you you identify the different strategies used by the following speakers (whose L1s are in parentheses) as they attempted to describe a riding crop? (You can compare your conclusions with those of Tarone & Yule, 1985, from whose data these examples are taken.)

1. (Japanese) *it's a long stick and eh ... on top of it eh there is a ... a ring*
2. (Italian) *it's like a rope ... but it's rigid ... at one end has like of ring but it's not rigid ... you can use to stimulate the horse to ... go faster*
3. (Chinese) *a tick or bar and I think we use to ... play or to ... attack someone*
4. (Spanish) *is no common piece ... it consist of ... a main piece of dark color*
5. (Korean) *plastic stick ... one end side ... like a round*
6. (Spanish) *it's a ... using for jocking ... for to hit the horse*
7. (Chinese) *I don't know what's this*

D. If you have tried to learn a second or foreign language, what did you find caused the greatest difficulty – pronunciation, vocabulary, grammar, or something else? Did you have an opinion on why there were difficulties? Do you believe there is a 'best age' for beginning to learn a second language? How about a 'best personality'? Do you think some languages are easier to learn than others, and why might that be?

Further reading

General treatments of the issues in L2 acquisition can be found in Oller & Richards (eds.) (1973), Richards (1978), Hatch (ed.) (1978) or Scarcella & Krashen (eds.) (1980). McLaughlin (1978) is more specifically about childhood L2 acquisition. On the teaching of English, there is an excellent historical review by Howatt (1984); examples of more general works are Mackey (1965), Corder (1973), Paulston & Bruder (1976), Stevick (1982) and McArthur (1983). Works on more specific issues of current interest are Widdowson (1978; 1983), Brown & Yule (1983b) and Krashen & Terrell (1983). On pronunciation with martinis, see Guiora *et al.* (1972), and on learners' errors and interlanguage, see Richards (ed.) (1974) or Corder (1981).

Chapter 17

Sign language

In our consideration of the acquisition of language, we concentrated, for the most part, on the fact that what is naturally acquired by most children is speech. It would be a mistake to think that this is the only form a first language can take. Just as most children of English-speaking or French-speaking parents naturally acquire English or French at an early age, so the deaf children of deaf parents naturally acquire **sign language**. If those deaf children grow up in American homes, they will typically acquire American Sign Language, also known as Ameslan or ASL. With a signing population of almost 500,000, ASL is the third most commonly used non-English language (after Spanish and Italian) in the United States. The size of this number is quite remarkable since, until very recently, the use of ASL was discouraged in most educational institutions for the deaf. In fact, historically, very few teachers of the deaf knew anything about ASL, or even considered it to be a 'real' language at all.

Oralism

To be fair to those generations of teachers in deaf education, we must acknowledge that it is only in the last two decades that any serious consideration has been given to the status of ASL as a natural language. It was genuinely believed by many well-intentioned teachers that the use of sign language by deaf children, perhaps because it was 'easy', actually inhibited the acquisition of speech. Since speech was what these children really required, a teaching method generally known as **oralism** was rigorously pursued. This method, which dominated deaf education for a century, required that the students practice English speech sounds and develop lipreading skills. Despite its resounding lack of success, the method was never seriously challenged, perhaps because of a belief among many during this period that, in educational terms, most deaf children could not achieve very much anyway.

Whatever the reasons, the method produced few students who could speak intelligible English (reckoned to be less than 10 percent) and even fewer who could lipread (around 4 percent). While oralism was failing, the use of ASL was surreptitiously flourishing. Many deaf children of hearing parents actually acquired the banned language at schools for the deaf – from other children. Since only one in ten deaf children had deaf parents from whom they acquired sign language, it would seem that ASL is a rather unique language in that its major cultural transmission has been carried out from child to child.

Signed English

Substantial changes in deaf education have taken place in recent years. There remains an emphasis on the acquisition of English, written rather than spoken, and as a result, many institutions promote the learning of what is called **Signed English** (sometimes described as Manually Coded English). This is essentially a means of producing signs which correspond to the words in an English sentence, in English word order. In many ways, Signed English is designed to facilitate interaction between the deaf and the hearing community. Its greatest advantage is that it seems to present a much less formidable learning task for the hearing parent of a deaf child and provides that parent with a 'language' to use with the child.

For similar reasons, hearing teachers in deaf education can make use of Signed English when they sign at the same time as they speak (known as the 'simultaneous method'). It is also easier to use for those hearing interpreters who produce a simultaneous translation of public speeches or lectures for deaf audiences. Many deaf people actually prefer interpreters to use Signed English because they say there is a better chance of understanding the message. When most interpreters try to use ASL, the message seems to suffer, for the simple reason that few hearing people who didn't learn ASL in childhood are very proficient at it.

However, Signed English is neither English nor is it ASL. When used to produce an exact version of a spoken English sentence, Signed English takes twice as long as the production of the sentence in either English or ASL. Consequently, in practice, exact versions are rarely produced and a hybrid format emerges, using some word-signs and incomplete English word order. (In many cases, even the word-signs are 'anglified' with, for example, a G letter-shape used to represent the English word *glad*, rather than the actual ASL sign for this concept.) It's sort of like producing messages with German word order, but containing French nouns, adjectives, verbs, and so on. The product is neither French nor German, but, it could be argued, it is one way of getting French speakers to learn how German sentences are constructed. The type of argument we have just noted is what has been used in support of teaching Signed English in deaf schools, since one of the major aims is to prepare students to be able to read and write English. Underlying that aim is the principle that deaf education should be geared towards enabling the deaf, for obvious economic reasons, to take part in the hearing world. The net effect is to make ASL a kind of underground language, used only in deaf–deaf interaction. As such, it continues to be poorly understood and subject to many of the myths which have existed throughout its history.

Origins of ASL

It would indeed be surprising if ASL really was, as some would have it, 'a sort of gestured version of English'. Historically, it developed from the French Sign Language used in a Paris school founded in the eighteenth century. Early in the nineteenth century, a teacher from this school, named Laurent Clerc, was brought to the United States by an American Congregational minister called Thomas Gallaudet. Clerc not only taught deaf children, he trained other teachers. During the nineteenth century, this imported version of Sign Language, incorporating features of indigenous natural sign languages used by the American deaf, evolved into what became ASL. Such origins help explain why users of ASL and users of British Sign Language (BSL) do not, in fact, share a common sign language. ASL and BSL are separate languages and neither should be treated as versions of spoken English which happen to involve the use of the hands.

The structure of signs

The idea that natural sign languages involve simple gestures with the hands is a persistent fallacy. In producing linguistic forms in ASL, signers will help themselves to four key aspects of visual information. These are usually classified as shape, orientation, location and movement. In analogies with natural spoken languages, these four elements are sometimes called the **articulatory parameters** of ASL. These parameters can be illustrated by referring to the following representation of a clear, isolated use of the sign for THANK-YOU. To describe the articulation

of THANK-YOU in ASL, we would start with the **shape**, or configuration of the hand(s) used in forming the sign. In forming THANK-YOU, a 'flat hand' is used and not a 'fist hand' or 'cupped hand' or other permissible shape. The **orientation** of the hand describes the fact that the hand is 'palm-up' rather than 'palm-down'. In other signs the hand can be oriented in a number of other ways, such as the 'flat hand', 'palm towards signer' form used to indicate MINE. The **location** of the sign captures the fact that, in THANK-YOU, it is first at the chin, then at waist level, and the **movement** (in this case, out and downward) involved in the formation of the sign is the fourth parameter. These four general parameters can be analyzed into a set of **primes** (e.g. 'flat hand' and 'palm-up' are primes in shape and orientation respectively) in order to produce a full feature-analysis of each sign.

In addition to these parameters, there are very important functions served by nonmanual components such as head-movement, eye-movement and a number of specific facial expressions. For example, if a sentence is functioning as a question, it is typically accompanied by a raising of the eyebrows, widened eyes, and a slight leaning forward of the head.

If a new term or name is encountered, there is the possibility of **finger-spelling** via a system of hand configurations conventionally used to represent the letters of the alphabet.

It should be obvious from this very brief description of some of the basic features of ASL that it is a linguistic system designed for the visual medium. Signing is done in face-to-face interaction. The majority of signs are located around the neck and head, and if a sign is made near the chest or waist, it tends to be two-handed. One of the key differences between a system using the visual as opposed to the vocal–auditory channel is that visual messages can incorporate a number of elements simultaneously. Spoken language is produced with a structure determined by the linear sequence of sound signals. It is extremely difficult to produce or to perceive more than one sound signal at a time. In the visual medium, multiple components can be produced all at the same time. Thus, from a structural point of view, a spoken word is a linear sequence of sound segments, while a sign is a combination of components within spatial dimensions which occur simultaneously.

The meaning of signs

The signs of ASL are often, erroneously, thought to be clear visual representations or 'pictures' of the objects or actions they refer to. Indeed, the language of the deaf is still considered by many to be some type of pantomime or mime in which EATING is represented by mimicking the act of eating or TREE is represented by 'forming' a tree with the hands. This misconception is usually accompanied by the myth that a sign language like ASL consists of a fairly primitive set of gestures which can only really be used to refer to 'concrete' entities and actions, but not to anything 'abstract'. Such misconceptions may persist because the hearing world rarely witnesses conversations or discussions in ASL, which range over every imaginable topic, concrete and abstract, and which bear little resemblance to any form of pantomime.

However, a visual communication system can avail itself of forms of representation which have an iconic basis. **Icons** are symbolic representations which are physically similar to the objects represented. (Pictograms and ideograms, discussed in Chapter 2, are types of iconic representation.) So, in using ASL, a signer can indeed produce an iconic representation to refer to something encountered for the first time, or something rarely talked about. A good example is provided by Klima & Bellugi (1979), in which several different signers produced a range of different forms to refer to a straitjacket. Interestingly, when you are told that a sign is used for referring to a particular object or action, you can often create some iconic connection. You may have seen the sign for THANK-YOU as some appropriately symbolic version of the action involved. However, most of the time, it does not work in the opposite direction – you may find it difficult to get the 'meaning' of a sign simply on the basis of what it looks like. Indeed, you may not even be able to identify individual signs in fluent signing. In this sense, most everyday use of ASL signs is not based on the use and interpretation of icons, but on conventional linguistic symbols. Even if some signs have traceable iconic sources, their actual use in ASL does not depend on the signer thinking of the iconic source in order to interpret the sign. Here is an example of a common sign. This sign

consists of rotating both hands with the fingers interlocked. Two quite different iconic sources have been suggested: that it represents the stripes which occur on a country's flag or that it derives from the union of a number of separate states together. To suggest that either of these images comes into the mind of a signer who, in conversation, uses this sign to refer to AMERICA is as absurd as saying that in hearing the word *America*, an English speaker must be thinking about Amerigo Vespucci, the sixteenth century Italian whose name is reputed to be the source of the modern word.

Writing in ASL

The fact that a sign language exploits the visual medium in quite subtle ways makes it difficult to represent accurately on the page. As Lou Fant (1977) has observed, "strictly speaking, the only way to write Ameslan is to use motion pictures". One of the major problems is finding a way to incorporate those aspects of facial expression which contribute to the message. One partial solution is to produce one line of the manually signed 'words' and over this line to indicate the extent and nature of the conventional facial expression which accompanies those words. Thus, the *q* in the following transcription shows that the facial expression indicated a question function and lasted throughout the word-signing of what would be translated as *Can I borrow the book*?

q
_____

ME BORROW BOOK

Other subtle aspects of meaning which can be conveyed by facial expression are still the subject of investigation. In one study, it was noted that a signer, in the middle of telling a story, produced a signed message such as MAN FISH CONTINUOUS, which we would translate as *the man was fishing*. However, other ASL users, watching the signer, would translate the message as *the man was fishing with relaxation and enjoyment*. The source of this extra information was a particular facial expression in which the lips were together and pushed out a little, with the head slightly tilted. This nonmanual signal was clearly capable of functioning as the equivalent of an adverb in English and was an integral part of the message. The notation *mm* was chosen as a way of incorporating this element and so a more accurate transcription of the message might look like this:

mm
_____

MAN FISH CONTINUOUS

A number of other such notations have been devised to capture major nonmanual elements in ASL communication. No doubt others will have to be introduced as other aspects of this subtle and rich communication system become better known.

ASL as a linguistic system

Investigations of ASL, from a linguistic point of view, are a relatively recent phenomenon. Yet it has become very clear that any feature which is characteristically found in spoken languages has a counterpart in ASL. All the defining properties of human language which we considered in Chapter 3 are present in ASL; there are equivalent levels of phonology, morphology and syntax; children acquiring ASL go through many of the recognized stages of children learning spoken language, though the production of signs seems to begin earlier than the production of spoken words; in the hands of witty individuals, ASL is used for a wide range of jokes and 'sign-play'; there are different ASL dialects in different regions and historical changes in the form of signs can be traced since the beginning of the century (older versions are preserved on old films). In short, ASL is a natural language which is quite remarkable for its endurance in the face of decades of prejudice and misunderstanding. There is a very old joke among the deaf which begins with the question *What is the greatest problem facing deaf people*? Perhaps increased knowledge and appreciation of their language among the world at large will bring about a change in the old response to that question. The traditional answer was *Hearing people*.

Study questions

1. What are the four most commonly used languages in the United States?
2. What was the main aim of oralism?
3. What is the major difference between Signed English and ASL?
4. What are the four articulatory parameters of ASL?
5. What would be the most likely English translation of:

(i)   q

—————————————————————

HAPPEN YESTERDAY NIGHT

(ii)   mm

—————————————————————

BOY NOT WALK CONTINUOUS

Discussion topics/projects

A. If the signs of ASL really were primarily iconic, it should be possible to look at the signs and 'see' their meaning in some transparent way. Here are three common ASL signs. Do you have any ideas on their likely meaning?

Can you describe which features are the basis of your ideas? (Compare your suggestions with the translations of these signs found in Chapter 4 of Baker & Cokely, 1980, from which these illustrations were adapted.)

B. Consider this description of the attitude of Alexander Graham Bell (the inventor of the telephone) to the use of ASL, around the end of the nineteenth century. How would you try to convince Bell that he was mistaken?

> Bell was opposed to the use of sign language at any time or place; it was easier for the deaf to master and more reliable in use, hence it would supplant or preempt speech. It was not only unsuited for integrating the deaf into society, but was a prison intellectually as well as socially, he believed, because it was ideographic rather than phonetic, limited in precision, flexibility, subtlety, and power of abstraction. (Lane, 1980:149)

(If you would like to do some research into other aspects of Bell's views on the deaf, try to locate Bell (1883).)

C. Consider this statement from Woodward (1980:105):

> Not all hearing impaired individuals belong to the deaf community; in fact, audiometric deafness, the actual degree of hearing loss, often has very little to do with how a person relates to the deaf community. Attitudinal deafness, self-identification as a member of the deaf community, and identification by other members as a member appear to be the most basic factors determining membership in the deaf community.

> Why do you think it is "attitudinal deafness" that is the key to membership in the deaf community? What social, psychological or linguistic factors might lie behind this phenomenon? Do you know of any other minority groups where this type of phenomenon has been noted?

D. Here is one view of reasons why oralism flourished in deaf education:

> Oralism was a nineteenth-century idea, with its enthusiasm for apparatus, its confidence in the future of technology. It was reinforced by the Protestant ethic of hard work, unremitting practice, and strength of character to overcome all of life's afflictions. It flourished in the framework of Victorian manners (and Victorian science), and reflected a deep Anglo-Saxon antagonism toward all languages other than English. (Neisser, 1983:29)

> Is this view of things still present today? Can it be justified? What kind of general repercussions follow from this view in terms of language-study, the teaching of minority languages, or education in general?

Further reading

A good up-to-date introduction to ASL is provided by Baker & Cokely (1980). For a well-illustrated presentation of signing, see Fant (1977), or on the form of conversational ASL, Madsen (1982). The original descriptions of ASL which really stimulated modern research are in Stokoe (1960) and Stokoe, Casterline & Croneberg (1965). For examples of recent research, see Klima & Bellugi (1979), Friedman (ed.) (1977), Lane & Grosjean (eds.) (1980) or Liddell (1980). Swisher (1984) is a good recent paper, somewhat technical, on the study of how hearing mothers cope with using Signed English to communicate with their deaf children. One of the best general works on sign language and the deaf community is Neisser (1983).

Chapter 18

Language history and change

Fæder ure þu þe eart on heofonum,
si þin nama gehalgod.
Tobecume þin rice.
Gewurþe þin willa on eorðan swa swa on heofonum.
Urne gedæghwamlican hlaf syle us to dæg.
And forgyf us ure gyltas,
swa swa we forgyfað urum gyltendum.
And ne gelæd þu us on costnunge,
ac alys us of yfele.

The Lord's Prayer (circa A.D. 1000)

In 1786, a British government official called Sir William Jones, who was working as a judge of the high court in India, made the following observation about the ancient language of Indian law which he had been studying:

The Sanskrit language, whatever be its antiquity, is of a wonderful structure; more perfect than the Greek, more copious than the Latin, and more exquisitely refined than either, yet bearing to both of them a stronger affinity, both in the roots of verbs and in the forms of grammar, than could possibly have been produced by accident.

Sir William went on to suggest, in a way that was quite revolutionary for its time, that a number of languages from very different geographical areas must have some common ancestor. It was clear, however, that this common ancestor could not be described from any existing records, but had to be hypothesized on the basis of similar features existing in records of languages which were believed to be descendants. Linguistic investigation of this type, still carried on two centuries after Sir William's original insight, focuses on the historical development of languages and attempts to characterize the regular processes which are involved in language change.

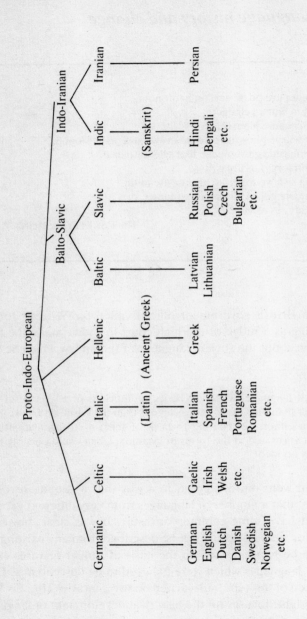

Family trees

During the nineteenth century, when the historical study of languages (more generally described as philology) was the major preoccupation of linguists, a term came into use to describe that common ancestor. It incorporated the notion that this was the original form (*proto*) of a language which was the source of modern languages in the Indian sub-continent (*Indo*), and in Europe (*European*). With **Proto-Indo-European** established as the 'great-grandmother', scholars set out to trace the branches of her family tree, showing the lineage of many modern languages, as illustrated in the accompanying diagram.

Of course, this diagram shows only one family tree covering a small number of the languages of the world. There are considered to be about thirty such language families which have produced the more than 4,000 languages in the world. Some of these languages are much more widely spoken than others. In terms of numbers of speakers, Mandarin Chinese has the most native speakers (more than 400 million), while English (about 300 million) is more widely used in different parts of the world. Russian and Spanish (with close to 200 million native speakers each) come next.

Family relationships

Looking at the Indo-European family tree, one might ask how it can be determined that these language groups are 'related'. On the face of it, two languages such as Italian and Hindi would seem to have nothing in common. One way to see the relationships more clearly is by looking at records of an older generation, like Latin and Sanskrit, from which the modern languages developed. For example, if we use familiar letters to write out the words for *father* and *brother* in Sanskrit, Latin and Ancient Greek, some common features become apparent:

Sanskrit	Latin	Greek	
pitar	*pater*	*patēr*	('father')
bhrātar	*frāter*	*phrāter*	('brother')

It is, however, extremely unlikely that exactly the same forms will regularly turn up, but the fact that close similarities occur (especially in the probable pronunciations of the forms) is good evidence for proposing a family connection.

Cognates

The process we have just employed in establishing some possible family connection between different languages involved looking at what are called **cognates**. Within groups of related languages, we often find close similarities in particular sets of terms. A cognate of a word in one language (e.g. in English) is a word in another language (e.g. in German) which has a similar form and is, or was, used with a similar meaning. Thus, the English forms *mother*, *father* and *friend* are cognates of the German forms *Mutter*, *Vater* and *Freund*. On the basis of these cognate sets, we would propose that such sets in modern English and modern German probably have a common ancestor in what has been labeled the Germanic branch of Indo-European. By the same process, we can look at similar sets, one from Spanish, *madre*, *padre* and *amigo*, and one from Italian, *madre*, *padre* and *amico*, and conclude that these close cognates also must be a clue to a common ancestor in the Italic branch.

Comparative reconstruction

Using information from these cognate sets, we can then embark on a procedure called **comparative reconstruction**. The aim of this procedure is to reconstruct what must have been the original, or 'proto' form in the common ancestral language. It's a bit like trying to work out what the great-grandmother must have been like on the basis of common features possessed by the set of granddaughters. In carrying out this procedure, those working on the history of languages operate on the basis of some general principles, two of which are presented here.

The **majority principle** is very straightforward. If, in a cognate set, three forms begin with a [p] sound and one form begins with a [b] sound, then our best guess is that the majority have retained the original sound (i.e. [p]), and the minority has changed a little through time.

The **most natural development principle** is based on the fact that certain types of sound-change are very common, whereas others are extremely unlikely. Here are some well-documented types of sound-change:

(1) final vowels often disappear
(2) voiceless sounds become voiced between vowels
(3) stops become fricatives (under certain conditions)
(4) consonants become voiceless at the end of words

If you were faced with some examples from three languages, as shown here, could you make a start on comparative reconstruction by deciding what was the most likely form of the initial sound in the original language source of the three?

Languages			
A	B	C	
cavallo	*caballo*	*cheval*	('horse')
cantare	*cantar*	*chanter*	('sing')
catena	*cadena*	*chaîne*	('chain')
caro	*caro*	*cher*	('dear')

Since the written forms can often be misleading, you would find out that the initial sounds of the words in languages A and B are all [k] sounds, while in language C the initial sounds are pronounced [š]. So, no doubt you immediately conclude that, in the original language, the words began with [k] sounds. What is the evidence?

Well, first, there is the 'majority principle' in evidence, since two sets of forms have [k] and only one has [š]. Moreover, one could argue, the [k] sound is a stop consonant and the [š] sound is a fricative. According to the 'most natural development principle', changes tend to occur in the direction of stops becoming fricatives, so the [k] is more likely to have been the original. By this type of procedure we have started on the comparative reconstruction of the common origins of some words in Italian (set A), Spanish (set B) and French (set C). In this particular case, you have some way of checking your findings because the generally proposed common origin for all three of these languages is Latin. Checking the Latin cognates for the forms under consideration, we will come up with *caballus*, *cantare*, *catena* and *carus*. So, our initial consonant reconstruction appears to be accurate.

Taking a more exotic example, imagine that the following fragment of data from three related (but otherwise unknown) languages is handed to you by a delirious linguist just rescued from the depths of the Amazon jungle. You realize that these examples represent a set of cognates and that it should be possible, via comparative reconstruction, to arrive at the proto-forms.

Languages				
1	2	3	Protoforms	
mube	*mupe*	*mup*	_____	('stream')
abadi	*apati*	*apat*	_____	('rock')
agana	*akana*	*akan*	_____	('knife')
enugu	*enuku*	*enuk*	_____	('diamond')

A quick glance at the data might suggest that you can begin with the majority principle, and say that the most likely basic forms are those found in language 2 or in language 3. If this is indeed the case, then the consonant changes must have been of the type: [p]→[b]; [k]→[g]; [t]→[d], in order to produce the forms in language 1. There is a definite pattern here which is in accord with one type of 'most natural development', i.e. that voiceless consonants become voiced between vowels. So, the forms in lists 2 and 3 must have preceded those in list 1. Which of the two lists, 2 or 3, contains the older forms? Remembering one other 'natural development' feature (i.e. that final vowels often disappear), we can propose that the forms in list 3 have consistently lost the final vowels which still exist in list 2. Our best guess, then, is that the forms in list 2 come closest to what must have been the original proto-forms. One of our delirious linguist's problems has been solved.

Language change

The reconstruction of proto-forms is an attempt to determine what a language must have been like before written records began. However, even when we have written records from an older period of a language such as English, they may not bear any resemblance to the written English to be found in your daily newspaper. The version of the Lord's Prayer quoted at the beginning of the chapter provides a good illustration of this point. To see how one language has undergone substantial changes through time, let us take a brief look at the history of English.

The historical development of English is usually divided into three major periods. The Old English period is considered to last from the time of the earliest written records, the seventh century, to the end of the eleventh century. The Middle English period is from 1100 to 1500, and Modern English from 1500 to the present.

Old English

The primary sources for what developed as the English language were the Germanic languages spoken by a group of tribes from northern Europe which invaded the British Isles in the fifth century A.D. In one early account, these tribes of Angles, Saxons and Jutes were described as "God's wrath toward Britain". It is from the names of the first two that we have the term 'Anglo-Saxons' to describe these people and, from the name of the first tribe, the Angles, that we get the word for their language, *Englisc*, and for their new home, *Engla-land*.

From this early variety of *Englisc*, we have many of the most basic terms in our language: *mann* ('man'), *wīf* ('woman'), *cild* ('child'), *hūs* ('house'), *mete* ('food'), *etan* ('eat'), *drincan* ('drink') and *feohtan* ('fight'). By all accounts, these pagan settlers certainly liked *feohtan*. However, they did not remain pagan for long. From the sixth to the eighth century, there was an extended period in which these Anglo-Saxons were converted to Christianity and a number of terms from the language of religion, Latin, came into English at that time. The origins of the modern words *angel*, *bishop*, *candle*, *church*, *martyr*, *priest* and *school* all date from this period.

From the eighth century through the ninth and tenth centuries, another group of northern Europeans came first to plunder, and eventually to settle in, parts of the coastal regions of Britain. They were the Vikings and it is from their language, Old Norse, that we derived the forms which gave us a number of common modern terms such as *give*, *law*, *leg*, *skin*, *sky*, *take* and *they*.

Middle English

The event which more than anything marks the end of the Old English period, and the beginning of the Middle English period, is the arrival of the Norman French in England, following their victory at Hastings under William the Conqueror in 1066. These French-speaking invaders proceeded to take over the whole of England. They became the ruling class, so that the language of the nobility, the government, the law and civilized behavior in England for the next two hundred years was French. It is the source of such modern terms as *army*, *court*, *defense*, *faith*, *prison* and *tax*.

Yet the language of the peasants remained English. The peasants worked on the land and reared *sheep*, *cows* and *swine* (words from Old English), while the French-speaking upper classes ate *mutton*, *beef* and *pork* (words of French origin). Hence the different words in modern English to refer to these creatures 'on the hoof' as opposed to 'on the plate'.

Throughout this period, French (or, more accurately, an English version of French) was the prestige language and Chaucer tells us that one of his Canterbury pilgrims could speak it.

> She was cleped Madame Eglentyne
> Ful wel she song the service dyvyne,
> Entuned in hir nose ful semely,
> And Frenshe she spak ful faire and fetisly.

This is an example of Middle English, written in the late fourteenth century. It has changed substantially from Old English, but several changes were yet to take place before the language took on its modern form. Most significantly, the vowel sounds of Chaucer's time were very different from those we hear in similar words today. Chaucer lived in what would have sounded like a 'hoos', with his 'weef', and 'hay' would romance 'heer' with a bottle of 'weena', drunk by the light of the 'moan'. In the two hundred years, from 1400 to 1600, which separated Chaucer and Shakespeare, the sounds of English underwent a substantial change to form the basis of Modern English pronunciation. Whereas the types of borrowed words we have already noted are examples of external change in a language, many of the following examples can be seen as internal changes within the historical development of English.

Sound changes

One of the most obvious differences between Modern English and the English spoken in earlier periods is in the quality of the vowel sounds. Here are some examples of words, in phonetic transcription, whose general form has remained the same, but whose vowel sounds have changed considerably. (Note the use of the colon which indicates that the vowel sound is long.)

Old English	Modern English	
hu:s	*haws*	('house')
wi:f	*wayf*	('wife')
spo:n	*spu:n*	('spoon')
brɛ:k	*bre:k*	('break')
hɔ:m	*hom*	('home')

Not only did types of sounds change, but some sounds simply disappeared from the general pronunciation of English. One notable example is a voiceless velar fricative /x/ which was used in the Old English pronunciation of *nicht*, as [nɪxt], (close to the modern German pronunciation), but is absent in the present-day form *night*, as [nayt]. A number of other changes have been documented.

The change known as **metathesis** involves a reversal in position of two adjoining sounds. Examples are (from Old English to Modern English):

bridd→*bird*   *hros*→*horse*

Indeed, the cowboy who pronounces the expression *pretty good* as something close to *purty good* is producing a similar example of metathesis as a dialect variant within Modern English.

Another change involves the addition of a sound to the middle of a word, which is known as **epenthesis**. Examples are:

> *spinel→spindle*   *aemtig→empty*

If you sometimes pronounce the word *film* as if it were *filum*, then you are producing an example of epenthesis in Modern English.

One other type of change worth noting, though not found in English, occurs in the development of other languages. It involves the addition of a sound to the beginning of a word and is called **prothesis**. It is very common in the change of pronunciation of some forms from Latin to Spanish, as in these examples:

> *schola→escuela* ('school')
> *spiritus→espíritu* ('spirit')

Syntactic changes

Some noticeable differences between the structure of sentences in Old and Modern English involve word order. In Old English texts, we find the subject–verb–object ordering most common in Modern English, but we can also find a number of different orders which are no longer possible. For example, the subject can follow the verb, as in *fērde he* ('he traveled'), and the object can be placed before the verb, as in *hē hine geseah* ('he saw him'), or at the beginning of the sentence *him man ne sealde* ('no man gave (any) to him'). In this last example, the use of the negative also differs from Modern English, since the sequence **not gave* is no longer grammatical. A 'double-negative' construction was also possible, as in this example, with both 'not' and 'never':

and	ne	sealdest	þū	mē	næfre	ān	ticcen
(and)	(not)	(gave)	(you)	(me)	(never)	(a)	(kid)

'and you never gave me a kid'

Perhaps the most sweeping change in the form of English sentences was the loss of a large number of inflectional affixes from many parts of speech. Notice that, in our examples, the verb forms *sealde* ('he gave') and *sealdest* ('you gave') are differentiated by inflectional suffixes which are no longer found in Modern English. Nouns, adjectives, articles and pronouns all took different inflectional forms according to their grammatical function in the sentence.

Lexical changes

The most obvious way in which Modern English differs lexically from Old English is in the number of borrowed words, particularly words of Latin and Greek origin, which have come into the language since the Old English period. Less obviously, many words have ceased to be used. Since we no longer carry swords (most of us, at least), the word *foin*, meaning 'the thrust of a sword', is no longer common usage. A common Old English term for 'man' was *were*. This is no longer in general use, but within the domain of horror films, it has survived in the compound form, *werewolf*. A number of expressions, such as *lo*, *verily*, *egad*, are immediately recognized as belonging to a much earlier period of the language and, as has been pointed out by Langacker (1973), there is a certain medieval ring to some names – *Egbert*, *Percival* or *Bertha* – which makes them quite unfashionable in Modern English.

Perhaps more interesting are the two processes of broadening and narrowing of meaning. An example of **broadening** of meaning is the modern use of the word *dog*. We use it very generally, to refer to all breeds, but in its older form (Old English *docga*), it was only used for one particular breed. The reverse process, called **narrowing**, has overtaken the Old English word *hund*, once used for any kind of dog, but now, as *hound*, used only for a specific breed. Another example is *mete*, once used for any kind of food, which has in its modern form, *meat*, become restricted to only some specific types. The Old English version of the word *wife* could be used of any woman, but has narrowed in its application to only married women.

The process of change

None of the changes described here happened overnight. They were gradual and probably difficult to discern while they were in progress. Although some changes can be linked to major social changes caused by wars, invasions and other upheavals, the most pervasive source of change in language seems to be in the continual process of cultural transmission. Each new generation has to find a way of using the language of the previous generation. In this unending process whereby each new language-user has to 'recreate' for him- or herself the language of the community, there is an unavoidable propensity to pick up some elements exactly and others only approximately. There is also the occasional desire to be different. Given this tenuous transmission process, it should be expected that languages will not remain stable, but that change and variation are inevitable.

In this chapter we have concentrated on variation in language viewed **diachronically**, that is, from the historical perspective of change through time. The type of variation which can be viewed **synchronically**, that is, in terms of differences within one language in different places and among different groups at the same time, is the subject of the final two chapters.

Study questions

1. How would you group the following languages into pairs which are closely related from a historical point of view: Romanian, Czech, Dutch, French, Gaelic, German, Russian, Welsh?
2. What are 'cognates'?
3. If you had the following data to work from, could you make a first guess at the probable proto-forms?

Languages

1	2	3	
cosa	*chose*	*cosa*	('thing')
capo	*chef*	*cabo*	('head')
capra	*chèvre*	*cabra*	('goat')

4. What are the dates roughly associated with the three historical periods in the development of the English language?
5. From what you know of the influence of Norman French in the Middle English period, which member of the following pairs would you guess was from Old English, and which from Old French: *calf veal*; *venison deer*?

Discussion topics/projects

A. Consider the following data:

Languages

1	2	3	4	5	6	7	
fem	*pyat*	*cinco*	*piec*	*itsutsu*	*fünf*	*cinque*	('five')
fire	*chetyre*	*cuatro*	*cztery*	*yottsu*	*vier*	*quattro*	('four')

(i)   There are six sets of examples from Indo-European languages here. Which one sample is most likely to be non-Indo-European?

(ii) The remaining six sets can be divided into three pairs of closely related languages. Which examples go together as pairs?

(iii) With which pair would you associate the English language?

(iv) With which pair would you associate another language which has the cognates *quinque* and *quattuor*?

B. With the following data to work from, complete the list of proto-forms, and describe three different processes of change which must have taken place in the development of this language set.

Languages

1	2	3	4	Proto-forms	
lik	*ligu*	*ligu*	*liku*	_____	('insect')
hip	*hiba*	*hiba*	*hipa*	_____	('path')
rad	*radi*	*rathi*	*radi*	_____	('cloud')
nam	*namu*	*namu*	*namu*	_____	('dwelling')

C. Some people maintain that English cannot be a Germanic language. They usually argue that English is derived from Latin. How would you present an argument, and what evidence would you use, to convince such a person that English is best considered as a member of the Germanic branch of Indo-European? (You could consult any one of the following texts: Baugh & Cable, 1978; Gordon, 1972; Williams, 1975.)

D. Here are four versions of the same biblical event described in Matthew, Chapter 2. Can you provide an account of the different forms, structures and probable pronunciations to be found in these different versions?

> *Contemporary English*
> After they had gone, an angel of the Lord appeared to Joseph in a dream
>
> *Early Modern English* (*early seventeenth century*)
> And when they were departed, behold, the Angel of the Lord appear-eth to Joseph in a dreame
>
> *Middle English* (*fourteenth century*)
> And whanne thei weren goon, lo, the aungel of the Lord apperide to Joseph in sleep
>
> *Old English* (*tenth century*)
> þā hī þā ferdon, þa ætȳwde Drihtnes engel Iosepe on swefnum

Further reading

Introductory treatments of the historical study of language can be found in Chapter 7 of Langacker (1973), Chapter 9 of Fromkin & Rodman (1983) or in the textbooks by Arlotto (1972) and Lehmann (1973). More advanced texts are Anttila (1972) and Bynon (1977). For more information on the different language families of the world, consult Ruhlen (1976). For a readable account of the language and culture of the original Indo-Europeans, see Thieme (1958).

A standard textbook on the history of English is Baugh & Cable (1978), with Bolton (1982) or Myers & Hoffman (1979) as other accessible treatments. If you would like to hear how English was spoken during different historical periods, listen to the recordings which accompany Finnie (1972).

Chapter 19

Language varieties

It seems to me a matter of observable fact that some young children growing up with, for example, an East London dialect offshoot pronouncing 'station' as 'stition' and 'shouldn't have' as 'shoodenov' are lacking entire sounds and words in their vocal repertoire.

John Ezard (1975)

In many of the preceding chapters, we have treated languages, such as English, as if all speakers of the particular language used that language in a uniform way. That is, we have largely ignored the fact that every language will have more than one variety, especially in the way in which it is spoken. Yet this variation in speech is an important and well-recognized aspect of our daily lives as language-users in different regional and social communities. In this chapter we shall consider the type of variation which has been investigated via a form of 'linguistic geography', concentrating on regional varieties, and, in the following chapter, we shall consider the factors involved in social variation in language use. First, we should identify that particular variety which is normally meant when the general terms English, French, German, and so on are used.

The Standard Language

When we described the sounds, words and sentences of English, we were, in fact, concentrating on the features of only one variety, usually labeled **Standard English**. This is the variety which forms the basis of printed English in newspapers and books, which is used in the mass media and which is taught in schools. It is the variety we normally try to teach to those who want to learn English as a second language. It is also the variety which some people consider to be the only type of 'correct' English and, as such, should be kept 'pure'. An extreme version of this point of view has been institutionalized in France where a body of scholars, known as the French Academy, regularly meets and decides whether a particular word, for example, is part of Standard French or not. In their attempts to keep the French language 'pure', the Academy mostly decides against words which have been borrowed from other languages. Despite these decisions, terms such as *le whisky* and *le weekend* have become commonly used expressions in what we would normally think of as Standard French.

Accent and dialect

Whether or not you think you speak Standard English, you will certainly speak with an **accent**. It is a myth that some speakers have accents while others do not. Some speakers may have particularly strong or easily recognized types of accent while others do not, but every language-user speaks with an accent. The term accent, when used technically, is restricted to the description of aspects of pronunciation which identify where an individual speaker is from, regionally or socially. It is to be distinguished from the term **dialect** which describes features of grammar and vocabulary, as well as aspects of pronunciation. For example, the sentence *You don't know what you're talking about* will generally 'look' the same whether spoken with an American or a Scottish accent. Both speakers will be using Standard English forms, but have different pronunciations. However, this next sentence – *Ye dinnae ken whit yer haverin' aboot* – has the same meaning as the first, but has been written out in an approximation of what a person who speaks one dialect of Scottish English might say. There are, of course, differences in pronunciation (e.g. *whit, aboot*), but there are also examples of different vocabulary (*ken, haverin'*) and a different grammatical form (*dinnae*).

While differences in vocabulary are often easily recognized, dialect variations in the meaning of grammatical constructions are less frequently documented. Here is an example, quoted in Trudgill (1983), of an exchange between two British English speakers (B and C), and a speaker from Ireland (A), which took place in Donegal, Ireland:

> A: *How long are youse here?*
> B: *Till after Easter.*
> (Speaker A looks puzzled)
> C: *We came on Sunday.*
> A: *Ah. Youse're here a while then.*

It is clear that the construction *How long are youse here*, in speaker A's dialect, is used with a meaning close to the structure *How long have you been here*, used in other dialects, rather than with the future reference interpretation made by speaker B.

Despite occasional difficulties of this sort, there is a general impression of mutual intelligibility among speakers of different dialects, or varieties, of English. The important point to remember is that, from a linguistic point of view, no one variety is 'better' than another. They are simply different. From a social point of view, some varieties do, of course, become more prestigious. In fact, the variety which develops as the Standard Language has usually been one socially prestigious dialect, originally connected with a political or cultural center (e.g. London for British English, and Paris for French). Yet, there always continue to be other varieties of a language, spoken in different regions.

Regional dialects

The existence of different regional dialects is widely recognized and often the source of some humor for those living in different regions. Thus, in the United States, someone from Brooklyn may joke about the Southerner's definition of *sex* by telling you that *sex is fo' less than tin*, in his best imitation of someone from the Southern states. The Southerner can, in return, wonder what a *tree guy* is in Brooklyn, since he has heard Brooklyn speakers refer to *doze tree guys*. Some regional dialects clearly have stereotyped pronunciations associated with them.

Those involved in the serious investigation of regional dialects are fairly uninterested in such stereotypes, however, and have devoted a lot of research to the identification of consistent features of speech found in one geographical area rather than another. These dialect surveys often involved painstaking attention to detail and tended to operate with very specific criteria in identifying acceptable informants. After all, it is important to know if the person whose speech you are tape-recording really is a typical representative of the region's dialect. Consequently, the informants in many dialect surveys tended to be NORMS, or non-mobile, older, rural, male speakers. Such speakers were selected because it was believed that they were less likely to have influences from outside the region in their speech. One unfortunate consequence of using such criteria is that the dialect description which results is probably more true of a period well before the time of investigation. Nevertheless, the detailed information obtained has provided the basis for a number of Linguistic Atlases of whole countries (e.g. England) or of regions (e.g. the New England area of the United States).

Isoglosses and dialect boundaries

Let us take a look at some examples of regional variation found in one survey, that which resulted in the Linguistic Atlas of the Upper Midwest of the United States. One of the aims of such a survey is to find a number of significant differences in the speech of those living in different areas and to be able to chart where the boundaries are, in dialect terms, between those areas. If it is found, for example, that the vast majority of informants in one area say they take their groceries home in a *paper bag* while the majority in another area say they use a *paper sack*, then it is usually possible to draw a line across a map separating the two areas, as shown on the accompanying illustration. This line is called an **isogloss** and represents a boundary between the areas with regard to that one particular linguistic item. If a very similar distribution is found for another two items, such as a preference for *pail* to the north and for *bucket* to the south, then another isogloss, probably overlapping, can be drawn in. When a number of isoglosses come together in this way, a more solid line, indicating a dialect boundary, can be drawn.

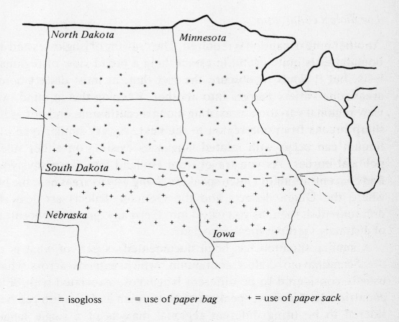

– – – – = isogloss   ⋅ = use of *paper bag*   + = use of *paper sack*

Using this dialect boundary information, we find that in the Upper Midwest there is a Northern dialect area which includes Minnesota,

North Dakota, most of South Dakota, and Northern Iowa. The rest of Iowa and Nebraska show characteristics of the Midland dialect. Some of the noticeable pronunciation differences, and some vocabulary differences, are illustrated here:

	('*taught*')	('*roof*')	('*creek*')	('*greasy*')
Northern:	[ɔ]	[ʊ]	[ɪ]	[s]
Midland:	[a]	[u]	[i]	[z]

Northern:	*paper bag*	*pail*	*kerosene*	*slippery*	*get sick*
Midland:	*paper sack*	*bucket*	*coal oil*	*slick*	*take sick*

So, if an American English speaker pronounces the word *greasy* as [grizi] and takes groceries home in a *paper sack*, then he is not likely to have grown up and lived most of his life in Minnesota. It is worth noting that the characteristic forms listed here are not used by everyone living in the region. They are used by a significantly large percentage of the people interviewed in the dialect survey.

The dialect continuum

Another note of caution is required. The drawing of isoglosses and dialect boundaries is quite useful in establishing a broad view of regional dialects, but it tends to obscure the fact that, at most dialect boundary areas, one variety merges into another. Keeping this in mind, we can view regional variation as existing along a **continuum**, and not as having sharp breaks from one region to the next. A very similar type of continuum can occur with related languages existing on either side of a political border. As you travel from Holland into Germany, you will find concentrations of Dutch speakers giving way to areas near the border where the Dutch dialects and the German dialects are less clearly differentiated; then, as you travel into Germany, greater concentrations of distinctly German speakers occur.

A similar situation has been documented as part of what is called the Scandinavian dialect continuum, which extends across what are usually considered to be different languages, associated with different countries. In this view, speakers of Norwegian and Swedish can be considered to be using different regional dialects of a single language. Someone who is at ease speaking both Swedish and Norwegian might then be described as **bidialectal** ('speaking two dialects'). However, because we are talking about what are normally taken to be two languages, that speaker would more commonly be described as **bilingual** ('speaking two languages').

Bilingualism

In many countries, regional variation is not simply a matter of two dialects of a single language, but a matter of two quite distinct and different languages. Canada, for example, is an officially bilingual country, with both French and English as official languages. This recognition of the linguistic status of the country's French speakers, largely in Quebec, did not come about without a lot of political upheaval. For most of its history, Canada was essentially an English-speaking country, with a French-speaking minority group. In such a situation, bilingualism, at the individual level, tends to be a feature of the minority group. In this form of bilingualism, a member of a minority group grows up in one linguistic community, primarily speaking one language, such as Gaelic (as was the case for many years in parts of Scotland), but learns another language, such as English, in order to take part in the larger, dominant, linguistic community.

Individual bilingualism, however, can simply be the result of having two parents who speak different languages. If a child simultaneously acquires the French spoken by her mother and the English spoken by her father, then the distinction between the two languages may not even be noticed. There will simply be two ways of talking according to the person being talked to. However, even in this type of bilingualism, one language tends eventually to become the dominant one, with the other in a subordinate role.

Language planning

Perhaps because bilingualism in Europe and North America tends to be found only among minority groups, a country like the United States is often assumed to be a single homogeneous speech community where everyone speaks English and all radio and T.V. broadcasts and all newspapers use Standard English. This is a mistaken view. It ignores the existence of large communities for whom English is not the first language of the home. As one example, the majority of the population in San Antonio, Texas, are more likely to listen to radio broadcasts in Spanish than in English. This simple fact has quite large repercussions in terms of the organization of local representative government and the educational system. Should elementary school teaching take place in English or Spanish?

Consider a similar question in the context of Guatemala where, in addition to Spanish, there are 26 Mayan languages spoken. If, in this situation, Spanish is selected as the language of education, are all those Mayan speakers put at an early educational disadvantage within the society? Questions of this type require answers on the basis of some type of **language planning**. Government, legal and educational bodies in many countries have to actively plan which varieties of the languages spoken in the country are to be used for official business. In Israel, despite the fact that Hebrew was not the most widely used language among the population, it was chosen as the official government language. In India, the choice was Hindi, yet, in many non-Hindi-speaking regions, there were riots against this decision.

The process of language planning may be seen in a better light when the full series of stages is implemented over a number of years. A good modern example has been provided by the adoption of Swahili as the national language of Tanzania in East Africa. There still exist a large number of tribal languages as well as the colonial vestiges of English, but the educational, legal and government systems have gradually introduced Swahili as the official language. The process of 'selection' (choosing an official language) is followed by 'codification' in which basic grammars, dictionaries and written models are used to establish the Standard variety. The process of 'elaboration' follows, with the Standard variety being developed for use in all aspects of social life and the appearance of a body of literary work written in the Standard. The process of 'implementation' is largely a matter of government attempts to encourage use of the Standard, and 'acceptance' is the final stage when a substantial majority of the population have come to use the Standard and to think of it as the national language, playing a part in not only social, but also national, identity.

Pidgins and creoles

In some areas, the Standard chosen may be a variety which originally had no native speakers. For example, in New Guinea, most official business is conducted in Tok Pisin, a language sometimes described as Melanesian Pidgin. A **Pidgin** is a variety of a language (e.g. English) which developed for some practical purpose, such as trading, among groups of people who did not know each other's languages. As such, it would have no native speakers. The origin of the term 'Pidgin' is thought to be from a Chinese Pidgin version of the English word 'business'. There are several English Pidgins still used today. They are characterized by an absence of any complex grammatical morphology and a limited vocabulary. Functional morphemes often take the place of inflectional morphemes found in the source language. For example, instead of changing the form of *you* to *your*, as in the English phrase *your book*, English-based Pidgins use a form like *bilong*, and change the word order to produce phrases like *buk bilong yu*.

The origin of many words in Pidgins can be phrases from other languages, such as one word used for 'ruin, destroy' which is *bagarimap* (derived from the English phrase "bugger him up"), or for 'lift' which is *haisimap* (from "hoist him up"), or for 'us' which is *yumi* (from "you" plus "me"). Original borrowings can be used creatively to take on new meanings such as the word *ars* which is used for 'cause' or 'source', as well as 'bottom', and originated in the English word *arse*.

The syntax of Pidgins can be quite unlike the languages from which terms were borrowed and modified, as can be seen in this example from Tok Pisin:

Bimeby	*hed*	*bilongyu*	*i-arrait*	*gain*
(by and by)	(head)	(belong you)	(he-alright)	(again)

'Your head will soon get well again'

There are considered to be between 6 and 12 million people still using Pidgin languages and between 10 and 17 million using descendants from Pidgins called **Creoles**. When a Pidgin develops beyond its role as a trade language and becomes the first language of a social community, it is described as a Creole. Tok Pisin, for example, would more accurately be described nowadays as a Creole. Unlike Pidgins, Creole languages have large numbers of native speakers. They often develop and become established among former slave populations in ex-colonial areas. Thus, there are French Creoles spoken in Haiti and in Louisiana, and English Creoles in Jamaica and Sierra Leone.

In the course of discussing language varieties in terms of regional differences, we have excluded, in a rather artificial way, the complex social factors which are also at work in determining language variation. In the final chapter, we shall go on to consider the influence of a number of these social variables.

Study questions

1. What is the difference between a dialect and an accent?
2. What does an isogloss represent?
3. What are the five stages in the complete language planning process?
4. What are the official languages of India, Israel, Tanzania and Canada?
5. What is the major difference between a Pidgin and a Creole?

Discussion topics/projects

A. In studies of language variation, a large geographical barrier is often seen as a factor in the development of different varieties of a language. Since the Atlantic Ocean is a fairly large barrier, we should not be surprised to find some variation between British and American English, particularly in their vocabularies. Can you identify the meanings of the following words in each variety? Are there other terms which belong to only one variety and not the other? Why do you think the variation is in fact not substantial even though the barrier is?

> *biscuits   braces   bonnet (of car)   boot (of car)   bum   chips*
> *dustman   first floor   flat (n.)   lift (n.)   lorry   mean (adj.)*
> *paraffin   pavement   petrol   spanner   surgery   sweets*

B. The following statistics regarding the population of Montreal in 1961 were published by the Royal Commission on Bilingualism and Biculturalism. You should be able to work out the percentage size of each group in terms of origin, whether bilingual or not, and whether monolingual or not. Is bilingualism or monolingualism more prevalent in any one group? Then, consider which of the two official languages was more frequently learned by those in the group labeled 'Other'. Why do you think this happened in a Canadian city?

	British	French	Other
Population by ethnic origin	377,625	1,353,480	378,404
Number of bilinguals by ethnic origin	101,767	554,929	119,907
Number of individuals monolingual in each official language	462,260	826,333	—

C. Here are some examples of Hawaiian Creole English (from Bickerton, 1983b) and their Standard English translations. What are the linguistic differences between these two varieties? (You might start with the ways in which past time and plurals are indicated.)

Us two bin get hard time raising dog	"The two of us had a hard time raising dogs"
John-them stay cockroach the kaukau	"John and his friends are stealing the food"
He lazy, 'a'swhy he no like play	"He doesn't want to play because he's lazy"
More better I bin go Honolulu for buy om	"It would have been better if I'd gone to Honolulu to buy it"
The guy gon' lay the vinyl bin quote me price	"The man who was going to lay the vinyl had quoted me a price"
Bin get one wahine she get three daughter	"There was a woman who had three daughters"
She no can go, she no more money, 'a'swhy	"She can't go because she hasn't any money"

D. In the opinion of some (one representative is quoted at the beginning of this chapter), some regional dialect speakers suffer from a form of 'linguistic deficit'. In its strongest form, this view states that something is actually 'missing' from the linguistic repertoire of some children (speaking a non-Standard dialect) who enter the school system. It is then argued that it is the duty of the school system to discourage the use of the non-Standard dialects and to provide these children with what they have been 'missing' in their language. Do you agree or disagree with this point of view? How does this argument relate to those children whose first language is Spanish, Hindi, Urdu or a Creole when they enter the English-speaking school system?

Further reading

A number of good introductory texts on this subject are available, for example, Trudgill (1974) or Downes (1984). A standard textbook is Chambers & Trudgill (1980). On regional dialect surveys, see Kurath (1972) for methods used, and Kurath *et al.* (1939–43) for a detailed example of the results. For more data on the Upper Midwest, see Allen (1973–6). On American dialects in general, see Williamson & Burke (eds.) (1971), and on British English varieties, see Wakelin (1972) or Hughes & Trudgill (1979). On the Scandinavian situation, good background is provided by Haugen (1972). On Pidgins and Creoles, see Hall (1959), Bickerton (1983b), or the more technical papers in Hymes (ed.) (1971) or Valdman (ed.) (1977).

Chapter 20
Language, society and culture

Professor Linton first brought the ritual of the Nacirema to the attention of anthropologists twenty years ago, but the culture of this people is still very poorly understood. Little is known of their origin, although tradition states that they came from the east. According to Nacirema mythology, their nation was originated by a culture hero, Notgnihsaw, who is otherwise known for two great feats of strength – the throwing of a piece of wampum across the river Pa-To-Mac and the chopping down of a cherry tree in which the Spirit of Truth resided.

Horace Miner (1956)

We have already noted that the way you speak may provide clues, in terms of regional accent or dialect, to where you spent most of your early life. However, your speech may also contain a number of features which are unrelated to regional variation. Two people growing up in the same geographical area, at the same time, may speak differently because of a number of social factors. It is important not to overlook this social aspect of language because, in many ways, speech is a form of social identity and is used, consciously or unconsciously, to indicate membership of different social groups or different speech communities.

Social dialects

In modern studies of language variation, a great deal of care is taken to document, usually via questionnaires, certain details of the social backgrounds of speakers. It is as a result of taking such details into account that we have been able to make a study of **social dialects**, which are varieties of language used by groups defined according to class, education, occupation, age, sex, and a number of other social parameters.

Education, occupation, social class

It is important to know, for example, whether a group of speakers share similar educational backgrounds. In some dialect surveys, it has been found that, among those leaving the educational system at an early age, there is a greater tendency to use forms which are relatively infrequent in the speech of those who go on to college. Expressions such as those contained in *Them boys throwed somethin'* are much more common in the speech of the former group than the latter. It seems to be the case that a person who spends a long time going through college or university will tend to have spoken language features which derive from a lot of time spent working with the written language. The complaint that some professor "talks like a book" is possibly a recognition of an extreme form of this influence.

Related to education are differences in occupation and social class which have some effect on the speech of individuals. Every job has a certain amount of 'jargon' which those not involved in a similar occupation find difficult to understand. An extreme example of speech determined by occupation could be the waiter's call of *Bucket of mud, draw one, hold the cow* at a lunch counter – a variation on the customer's order for "a chocolate ice cream and a coffee without cream".

A famous study by Labov (1972) combined elements from place of occupation and socio-economic status by looking at pronunciation differences among salespeople in three New York City department stores, Saks (high status), Macy's (middle status) and Klein's (low status). Measurable differences were indeed found to exist. In British English, where social class differences in speech may be more widely recognized than in the United States, the use of [n] as opposed to [ŋ] for the sound of *-ing* at the end of words like *walking* and *going* has been found to be much more common among working class speakers, in several regional varieties, than among middle class speakers.

Age, sex

Even within groups of the same social class, however, other differences can be found which seem to correlate with factors such as the age or sex of speakers. Many younger speakers living in a particular region often look at the results of a dialect survey of their area (conducted mainly with older informants) and claim that their grandparents may use those terms, but they do not. Variation according to age is most noticeable across the grandparent–grandchild time span. While grandfather still talks about the *icebox* or the *wireless*, he may be confused by some of the speech of a teenage granddaughter who likes to *pig out* on whatever's in the *fridge* while listening to her *boombox*.

Variation according to the sex of the speaker has been the subject of a lot of recent research. One general conclusion from dialect surveys is that female speakers tend to use more prestigious forms than male speakers with the same general social background. That is, forms such as *I done it* and *he ain't* can be found more often in the speech of males, and *I did it* and *he isn't* in the speech of females. In some cultures, there are much more marked differences between male and female speech. Quite different pronunciations of certain words in male and female speech have been documented in some North American Indian languages such as Gros Ventre and Koasati. Indeed, when Europeans first encountered the different vocabularies of male and female speech among the Carib Indians, they reported that the different sexes used different languages. What had, in fact, been found was an extreme version of variation according to the sex of the speaker.

Ethnic background

Within a society, other differences in speech may come about because of different ethnic backgrounds. In very obvious ways, the speech of recent immigrants, and often of their children, will contain identifying features. In some areas, where there is strong language loyalty to the original language of the group, a large number of features are carried over into the new language. More generally, the speech of American blacks, also called **Black English**, is a widespread social dialect, often cutting across regional differences. When a group within a society under-goes some form of social isolation, such as the discrimination or segregation experienced historically by American blacks, then social dialect differences become more marked. The accompanying problem, from a social point of view, is that the resulting variety of speech may be stigmatized as "bad speech". One example is the frequent absence of the copula (forms of the verb 'to be') in Black English, as in expressions like *They mine* or *You crazy*. Standard English requires that the verb form *are* be used in such expressions. However, many other English dialects do not use the copula in such structures and a very large number of languages (e.g. Arabic, Russian) have similar structures without the copula. Black English, in this respect, cannot be "bad" any more than Russian is "bad" or Arabic is "bad". As a dialect, it simply has features which are consistently different from the Standard.

Another aspect of Black English which has been criticized, sometimes by educators, is the use of double negative constructions, as in *He don't know nothing* or *I ain't afraid of no ghosts*. The criticism is usually that such structures are 'illogical'. If that is so, then French which typically employs a two-part negative form, as exemplified by *il NE sait RIEN* ('he doesn't know anything'), and Old English, also with a double negative, as in *Ic NAHT singan NE cuðe* ('I didn't know how to sing'), must be viewed as equally 'illogical'. In fact, far from being illogical, this type of structure provides a very effective means of emphasizing the negative part of a message in this dialect. It is basically a dialect feature, present in one social dialect of English, sometimes found in other dialects, but not in the Standard Language.

Idiolect

Of course, aspects of all these elements of social and regional dialect variation are combined, in one form or another, in the speech of each individual. The term **idiolect** is used for the personal dialect of each individual speaker of a language. There are other factors, such as voice quality and physical state, which contribute to the identifying features in an individual's speech, but many of the social factors we have described determine each person's idiolect. From the perspective of the social study of language, you are, in many respects, what you say.

Style and register

All of the social factors we have considered so far are related to variation according to the user of the language. Another source of variation in an individual's speech is occasioned by the situation of use. There is a gradation of style of speech, from the very formal to the very informal. Going for a job interview, you may say to a secretary *Excuse me, is the manager in his office? I have an appointment.* Alternatively, speaking to a friend about another friend, you may produce a much less formal version of the message: *Hey, is that lazy dog still in bed? I gotta see him about something.*

This type of variation is more formally encoded in some languages than others. In Japanese, for example, there are different terms used for the person you are speaking to, depending on the amount of respect or deference you wish to show. French has two pronouns (*tu* and *vous*), corresponding to singular *you*, with the first reserved for close friends and family. Similar distinctions are seen in the *you* forms in German (*du* and *Sie*) and in Spanish (*tu* and *usted*).

Although English no longer has such pronoun distinctions, there are definite options available for indicating the relevant status of the person you address. We all have a variety of names or 'titles' which are used by different people, at different times, to get our attention. To illustrate this aspect of what is sometimes called **style-shifting**, according to role-relation, imagine yourself in each of the social 'roles' shown in the list on the left below, and consider which form (or forms) of address you would most likely use to that person whose various 'names' are listed on the right:

1. a tailor calling up to say his new suit is ready	*Ron*
2. a good friend for a number of years	*Mr Reagan*
3. his young grandchild	*Ronald*
4. his drill sergeant in the army	*Gramps*
5. his former elementary school teacher	*Reagan*
6. a store-detective who thinks he's a shoplifter	*Ronnie, baby*
7. his former Hollywood agent	*Hey, you*

Differences in style carry over into the written language, with letters to businesses (e.g. *I am writing to inform you . . .*) versus letters to friends (*Just wanted to let you know ...*) as good illustrations. The general pattern, however, is that a written form of a message will inevitably be more formal in style than its spoken equivalent. If you see someone on the local bus, eating, drinking and playing a radio, you can say that what he's doing isn't allowed and that he should wait until he gets off the bus. Alternatively, you can draw his attention to the more formal language of the printed notice which reads:

The city has recently passed an ordinance that expressly prohibits the following while aboard public conveyances. Eating or Drinking. The Playing of Electronic Devices.

The formality of expressions such as *expressly prohibit* and *electronic devices* is more extreme than is likely to occur in the spoken language.

Variation according to use in specific situations is also studied in terms of **register**. There is a religious register in which we expect to find expressions not found elsewhere, as in *Ye shall be blessed by Him in times of tribulation*. In another register you will encounter sentences such as *The plaintiff is ready to take the witness stand*. The legal register, however, is unlikely to incorporate some of the expressions you are becoming familiar with from the linguistics register, such as *The morphology of* *this dialect contains inflectional suffixes*. In general, the choice of register, when you speak, will have a direct effect on the style of what you say.

Diglossia

Taking all the preceding social factors into account, we might imagine that managing to say the right thing to the right person at the right time is a monumental social accomplishment. In some respects, it is. It is a skill which language-users must acquire over and above the other linguistic skills of pronunciation and grammar. In some societies, however, the choice of appropriate linguistic forms is made a little more straightforward because of **diglossia**. This term is used to describe a situation in which two very different varieties of language co-exist in a speech community, each with a distinct range of social function. There is normally a 'High' variety, for formal or serious matters, and a 'Low' variety, for conversation and other informal uses.

A form of diglossia exists in most Arabic-speaking countries where the high, or classical, variety is used in lectures, religious speech and formal political speech, while the low variety is the local dialect of colloquial Arabic. In Greek, there is also a high and a low (or 'demotic') variety. In some situations, the high variety may be a quite separate language. Through long periods of Western European history, a diglossic situation existed with Latin as the high variety and local languages such as French and English as the low variety. In present-day Paraguay, a form of diglossia exists with Spanish as the high variety and Guaraní (an Indian language) as the low variety.

Language and culture

Many of the factors which give rise to linguistic variation are sometimes discussed in terms of cultural differences. It is not unusual to find linguistic features quoted as identifiable aspects of 'working class culture' or 'Black culture', for example. In many respects, this view has been influenced by the work of anthropologists who tend to treat language as one element among others, such as beliefs, within the definition of culture as 'socially acquired knowledge'. Given the process of cultural transmission by which languages are acquired, it makes a lot of sense to emphasize the fact that linguistic variation is tied very much to the existence of different cultures. In the study of the world's cultures, it has become clear that different tribes not only have different languages, they have different world views which are reflected in their languages. In very simple terms, the Aztecs not only did not have a figure in their culture like Santa Claus, they did not have a word for this figure either. In the sense that language reflects culture, this is a very important observation and the existence of different world views should not be ignored when different languages or language varieties are studied. However, one quite influential theory of the connection between language and world view proposes a much more deterministic relationship.

Linguistic determinism

If two languages appear to have very different ways of describing the way the world is, then it may be that, as you learn one of those languages, the way your language is organized will determine how you perceive the world being organized. That is, your language will give you a ready-made system of categorizing what you perceive and, as a consequence, you will be led to perceive the world around you only in those categories. Stated in this way, you have a theory of language which has been called **linguistic determinism** and which, in its strongest version, holds that "language determines thought". In short, you can only think in the categories which your language allows you to think in.

A much quoted example used to support this view is the number of words the Eskimos have for what, in English, is described as *snow*. When you, as an English speaker, look at wintry scenes, you may see a single white entity called *snow*. The Eskimo, viewing similar scenes, may see a large number of different entities, and he does so, it is claimed, because his language allows him to categorize what he sees differently from the English speaker. We shall return to this example.

The Sapir–Whorf hypothesis

The general idea we are considering is part of what has become known as **the Sapir–Whorf hypothesis**. Edward Sapir and Benjamin Whorf produced arguments, in the 1930s, that the language of American Indians, for example, led them to view the world differently from those who spoke European languages. Let us look at an example of this reasoning. Whorf claimed that the Hopi Indians of Arizona perceived the world differently from other tribes (e.g. the English-speaking tribe) because their language led them to do so. In the grammar of Hopi, there is a distinction between 'animate' and 'inanimate', and among the set of entities categorized as 'animate' were clouds and stones. Whorf concluded that the Hopi believe that clouds and stones are animate (living) entities and that it is their language which leads them to believe this. Now, English does not mark in its grammar that clouds and stones are animate, so English speakers do not see the world in the same way as the Hopi. In Whorf's words, "We dissect nature along lines laid down by our native languages."

A number of arguments have been presented against this view. Here is one from Sampson (1980). Imagine a tribe which has a language in which differences in sex are marked grammatically, so that the terms used for females have special markings in the language. Now, you find that these 'female markings' are also used with the terms for *stone* and *door*. We may then conclude that this tribe believes that stones and doors are female entities in the same way as girls and women. This tribe is probably not unfamiliar to you. They use the terms *la femme* ('woman'), *la pierre* ('stone') and *la porte* ('door'). It is the tribe which lives in France. Do you think that the French believe that stones and doors are 'female' in the same way as women?

The problem with the conclusions in both these examples is that there is a confusion between linguistic categories ('animate', 'feminine') and biological categories ('living', 'female'). Of course, there is frequently a correspondence in languages between these categories, but there does not have to be. Moreover, the linguistic categories do not force you to ignore biological categories. While the Hopi language has a particular linguistic category for 'stone', it does not mean that the Hopi thinks he has killed a living creature when he runs over a stone with his car.

Returning to the Eskimos and 'snow', we realize that English does not have a large number of single terms for different kinds of snow. However, the English speaker can create expressions, by manipulating his language, to refer to *wet snow*, *powdery snow*, *spring snow*, and so on. The average English speaker probably does have a very different view of 'snow' from the average Eskimo speaker. That is a reflection of their different experiences in different cultural environments. The languages they have learned reflect the different cultures. The notion that language determines thought may be partially correct, in some extremely limited way, but it fails to take into account the fact that users of a language do not inherit a fixed set of patterns to use. They inherit the ability to manipulate and create with a language, in order to express their perceptions.

If thinking and perception were totally determined by language, then the concept of language change would be impossible. If the Hopi had no word in his language for the object known to us as a *bus*, would he fail to perceive the object? Would he be unable to think about it? What the Hopi does when he encounters a new entity is to change his language to accommodate the need to refer to the new entity. The human manipulates the language, not the other way around.

Language universals

While many linguists have recognized the extent to which languages are subject to variation, they have also noted the extent to which all languages have certain common properties. Those common properties, called **language universals**, can be described, from one point of view, as those definitive features of language which we investigated in Chapter 3. Specifically, every human language can be learned by children, employs an arbitrary symbol system, and can be used to send and receive messages by its users. From another point of view, every language has nounlike and verblike components which are organized within a limited set of patterns to produce complex utterances. At the moment, much of what is known about the general character of languages is in the form of certain established relationships. For example, if a language uses fricative sounds, it invariably also uses stops. If a language places objects after verbs, it will also use prepositions. By discovering universal patterns of this type, it may be possible one day to describe, not just the grammars of all languages, but the single grammar of human language.

Study questions

1. How would you describe the constructions used in these two examples from one English dialect: (a) *We ain't got none.* (b) *He going now.*
2. What is meant by the term 'idiolect'?
3. What is diglossia?
4. What is the strong version of 'linguistic determinism'?
5. What are language universals?

Discussion topics/projects

A. Below is a graphic representation of some findings of Labov (1972) concerning the use of [n] (e.g. *walkin'*) as opposed to [ŋ] (*walking*) in different speech styles by different social groups. How would you interpret these findings? For example, which group uses [n] most frequently and in which speech style? Which group uses it least often, and when? Say you wanted to investigate the occurrence of this feature in the population of your city, how would you go about it?

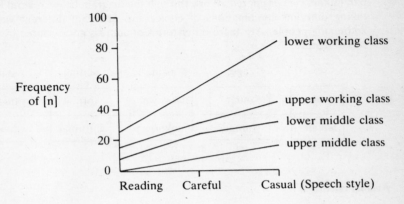

B. Here are some percentages of the use of certain expressions by male and female informants in the Upper Midwest (U.S.A.) dialect survey, conducted around 1950. (Professor Harold B. Allen reported these results to the annual meeting of the American Dialect Society in 1984.) Can you make any generalizations about the way different forms are used by men and women? Why might this type of variation exist?

	Male (%)	Female (%)
vomit	38	40
puke	22	11
bastard	57	20
illegitimate child	29	63
grew	74	95
growed	26	5
he isn't	35	48
he ain't	44	27
those apples	59	76
them apples	41	24
[dɛf]('deaf')	60	86
[dif]('deaf')	40	13

C. To which 'registers' do the following samples belong? Can you provide clear examples of language used in other registers?
  (1) "a review of the weekly consolidated condition report of the large commercial banks and their subsidiaries"
  (2) "Services will be held at Olinger's mortuary with burial at Mt. Lindo cemetery"

    (3) "the Hurricanes are no slouches on offense with their pro-style passing attack"

    (4) "cloudy with a chance of light snow or freezing drizzle"

    (5) "fine quality classic apparel, and accessories, all from our regular stock"

D. Forms of address in English seem to differ according to a number of the parameters we considered. Work through the diagram below several times, taking different combinations of choices, to arrive at different ways of addressing people. Are there other forms of address not captured by these sets of features?

sex	age	name	setting	status
male	older	known	formal	higher
female	younger	unknown	informal	lower

Further reading

Any introductory text on language will have a section on social factors in variation, often called 'sociolinguistics'. Trudgill (1974) and Downes (1984) are general texts, Hudson (1980) is a standard textbook. More technical treatments can be found in Labov (1972), Pride & Holmes (eds.) (1972), or Scherer & Giles (eds.) (1979). More specifically, on modern Black English, see Baugh (1983), on style and register, Gregory & Carroll (1978), on diglossia, Ferguson (1959) or Fishman (1971), on Whorf, see Carroll (ed.) (1956) and on universals, see Greenberg (1966).

Appendix

Suggested answers to Study questions

Chapter 1. The origins of language
1. The "bow-wow theory".
2. The sounds produced by humans when exerting physical effort (grunts) may be the origins of speech sounds ("yo-heave-ho").
3. The patterns of movement in articulation (of tongue, lips) would be the same as gestural movement (of hands), hence waving tongue from waving hand.
4. Human teeth are upright and roughly even in height; human lips are very flexible because of their intricate muscle interlacing.
5. "Interactional" – mainly a social function of language, and "transactional" – mainly a function involving the communication of knowledge and information.

Chapter 2. The development of writing
1. The Cyrillic alphabet.
2. Japanese.
3. An extremely large number of separate symbols are involved, so there are problems of learning all the symbols and also in remembering them.
4. Rebus writing involves a process whereby the symbol used for an entity comes to be used for the sound of the spoken word used for that entity.
5. (a) syllabic   (b) pictographic   (c) alphabetic   (d) logographic.

Chapter 3. The properties of language
1. Cultural transmission.
2. Linguistic forms are described as arbitrary because there is generally no natural connection between the form and its meaning.
3. Displacement.
4. No, since many animal communication systems use the vocal–auditory channel for signaling and for no other purpose.
5. Duality.

Chapter 4. Animals and human language
1. It's debatable – Viki produced versions of three English words, but it is not clear that she actually produced human speech sounds; the problem is that no other creature is physiologically equipped to produce human speech sounds.
2. Yes; for example, she produced a new sign, *water bird*, for swan.
3. Arbitrariness.
4. After careful examination of the filmed record, Terrace concluded that chimpanzees were performing tricks to get food rewards.
5. They designed an experiment in which no humans could provide cues and Washoe still produced correct signs.

Chapter 5. The sounds of language
1. (a) voiced   (b) voiceless.
2. (a) labiodental   (b) alveolar   (c) bilabial   (d) alveo-palatal   (e) dental   (f) velar.
3. (a) voiceless   (b) voiced   (c) voiced   (d) voiceless   (e) voiced   (f) voiceless.
4. (a) [bi]   (b) [tep]   (c) [fɛl]   (d) [dop]   (e) [wɔk]   (f) [say].
5. (a) face   (b) sheep   (c) the   (d) who   (e) eighth   (f) back   (g) bought   (h) how   (i) joy   (j) chef.

Chapter 6. The sound patterns of language
1. Phonology is the study of systems or patterns of sounds, at an abstract level, while phonetics is concerned with the actual physical properties of sounds.
2. If we substitute one sound for another in a word and we get a change of meaning, then the two sounds must be phonemes.
3. Pat – fat; pat – pit; heat – heel; tape – tale; bun – ban; fat – far; bell – bet; meal – heel.
4. Substituting phonemes changes meaning and sound; substituting allophones only changes sound.
5. (a) elision of [d], assimilation of [n] to [m] before bilabial [p] (b) elision of [t].

Chapter 7. Words and word-formation processes
1. (a) is 'calque', because the elements are directly translated; (b) and (c) are 'borrowings'.
2. Coinage.
3. Un-, re-, dis- are prefixes; -ful, -less, -ness, -able are suffixes.
4. (a) conversion   (b) acronym   (c) blending   (d) infixing.
5. (a) clipping from 'telephone' to 'phone', then compounding; (b) compounding of 'foot' and 'ball', then derivation with '-er'; (c) compounding of 'blue' and 'print', then conversion to a verb; (d) blending of 'sky' and 'hijack', then derivation with '-ing'.

Chapter 8. Morphology
1. (a) mis-, -s, pre-, -er, -en, -ed, un-, -er, -less, -ly (b) atypical.
2. The, on, a, and, them, of.
3. (a) -'s, -s   (b) -ing   (c) -est   (d) -ed.
4. -s, -en, ∅, -es, -a.
5. bibili; kəji; sal; abaloŋgo; táwa; tiap; kumain.

Chapter 9. Phrases and sentences: grammar
1. 'The' (article); 'boy' (noun); 'rubbed' (verb); 'the' (article); 'magic' (adjective); 'lamp' (noun); 'and' (conjunction); 'suddenly' (adverb); 'a' (article); 'genie' (noun); 'appeared' (verb); 'beside' (preposition); 'him' (pronoun).
2. (a) You must not end a sentence with a preposition. (b) You must not split an infinitive.
3. The descriptive approach has, as a general principle, a procedure which

involves describing the regular structures actually found in the particular language being analyzed.

4.

[[[The]   [policeman]] [[chased] [[a]   [robber]]]]
      Art   N   V   Art   N
  NP   VP   NP
S

5. (a) The small boy hit the black dog. (b) The dog saw the big man.

Chapter 10. Syntax

1. (a) "a teacher of American history" or "an American who teaches history"
   (b) "planes which are flying" or "when a person flies in a plane" (c) "parents of the bride, plus the groom" or "the parents of both the bride and the groom".
2. (a) The police arrested Lara. (b) She took off her coat. (c) My bicycle was stolen. (d) I told him to turn the volume down.
3. All of them.
4. The phrase structure rules will generate sentences with a fixed order, so transformational rules are needed to move or change constituents.

5. (a)

(b)

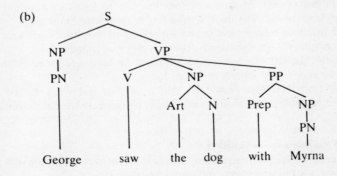

Chapter 11. Semantics and pragmatics

1. (a) antonymy   (b) synonymy   (c) homophony   (d) hyponymy
   (e) antonymy   (f) hyponymy.
2. "I", "now", "you", "that", "here".
3. (a) He bought the beer. (b) You have a watch.
4. (a) The verb "drink" requires a subject with the feature '+animate', but "television" has the feature '−animate'. (b) The verb "write" requires a subject with the feature '+human', and the noun "dog" has the feature '−human'.
5. Associative meaning.

Chapter 12. Discourse analysis

1. The ties and connections which exist across sentences in texts.
2. Motorist requests mechanic to perform action; mechanic states reason why he cannot comply with request.
3. It describes the observed fact that people take turns at speaking, one at a time, in conversation.
4. Quantity, Quality, Relation, Manner.
5. Quality – since the speaker is stressing the 'honesty' of what he says.

Chapter 13. Language and machines

1. Spoken language produced electronically.
2. Speaking involves having something to say (a mental process) whereas articulation is simply the activity of saying (a physical process).
3. Modeling human intelligence via machines or the science of making machines do what would require intelligence if done by humans.
4. Syntactic analysis, primarily.
5. It is computationally impossible to give the machine all world-knowledge, but the machine can be very knowledgeable within a small, limited world.

Chapter 14. Language and the brain

1. Broca's area, Wernicke's area and the supplementary motor area.
2. Aphasia is an impairment of language function due to localized cerebral damage which leads to difficulty in understanding or producing language.
3. In a dichotic listening test, a person sits with a set of earphones on, and through each earphone, simultaneously, comes a different sound.
4. For most people, the left hemisphere is specialized for language sounds and the right hemisphere for environmental sounds.
5. Genie did not learn language during the critical period, and when she did begin using language, she appeared to have a right-hemisphere specialization.

Chapter 15. First language acquisition

1. Caretaker speech has frequent questions, exaggerated intonation, simple sentence structures, a lot of repetition, and simple vocabulary.

2. By the age of 2, the average child has a vocabulary of more than 50 words and will have reached the 'two-word' stage.
3. The order would be: *-ing*; *-s* (plural); *-'s*; *-ed*.
4. The more advanced form is (a) since the negative element is no longer stuck on the front of the sentence, as in (b).
5. Overextension.

Chapter 16. Second language acquisition/learning
1. An L2 is mostly learned in teenage or adult years, in brief periods at school, while the learners are busy with other things, and already have an L1 to use for communicative purposes.
2. The ability of adults to master aspects of the written language, but still speaking with a foreign accent.
3. 11–16 years old.
4. Someone who is self-conscious may be unwilling to try to produce unfamiliar sounds in another language and may not want to sound like a speaker of another language.
5. The communicative approach.

Chapter 17. Sign language
1. English, Spanish, Italian, ASL.
2. To have deaf students produce English speech and to lipread, in order to make them members of the hearing community.
3. Signed English is essentially the English language, in a shorthand version, employing signs for vocabulary; ASL is a separate language, with a quite different structural organization from English.
4. Shape, orientation, location and movement.
5. (i) Did it happen last night? (ii) The boy isn't/wasn't walking with pleasure/enjoyment.

Chapter 18. Language history and change
1. Romanian & French; Czech & Russian; Dutch & German; Gaelic & Welsh.
2. Cognates are two words in different languages which are similar in form and meaning.
3. Proto-forms: *cosa – capo – capra*.
4. Old English (600–1100); Middle English (1100–1500); Modern English (1500–present).
5. 'Calf' and 'deer' are from Old English; 'veal' and 'venison' are from Old French.

Chapter 19. Language varieties
1. The term 'accent' is used only to describe pronunciation, whereas 'dialect' covers grammar, vocabulary and pronunciation.
2. It represents the limit of an area in which a particular linguistic feature is used.

3. Selection, codification, elaboration, implementation and acceptance.
4. Hindi, Hebrew, Swahili, English/French.
5. A Creole has native speakers, a Pidgin has none.

Chapter 20. Language, society and culture

1. (a) double-negative construction (b) absence of copula.
2. The personal dialect of an individual speaker.
3. Diglossia describes a situation in which two distinct varieties of a language, a 'high' and a 'low', are used, each with separate social functions.
4. Briefly, that your language determines the way you think.
5. Common properties shared by all languages.

References

Abercrombie, D. (1967) *Elements of General Phonetics* Edinburgh University Press

Adams, V. (1973) *An Introduction to Modern English Word-Formation* Longman

Aickin, J. (1693) *The English Grammar* (facsimile edition, 1967) Scolar Press

Aitchison, J. (1976) *The Articulate Mammal* Hutchinson

Akmajian, A., Demers, R. A. & Harnish, R. M. (1984) *Linguistics: An Introduction to Language and Communication* (2nd edition) M.I.T. Press

Akmajian, A. & Heny, F. (1975) *An Introduction to the Principles of Transformational Syntax* M.I.T. Press

Allen, H. B. (1973–6) *The Linguistic Atlas of the Upper Midwest* (3 volumes) University of Minnesota Press

Allen, J. P. B. & van Buren, P. (1971) *Chomsky: Selected Readings* Oxford University Press

Allport, D. A. & Funnell, E. (1981) Components of the mental lexicon. In *The Psychological Mechanisms of Language* The Royal Society and the British Academy

Anderson, A. H., Yule, G., Brown, G. & Shillcock, R. (1984) *Teaching Talk: Strategies for Production and Assessment* Cambridge University Press

Anderson, R. C., Reynolds, R. E., Schallert, D. L. & Goetz, E. T. (1977) Frameworks for comprehending stories. *American Educational Research Journal* 14: 367–81

Anttila, R. (1972) *An Introduction to Historical and Comparative Linguistics* Macmillan

Arlotto, A. (1972) *Introduction to Historical Linguistics* Houghton Mifflin

Aronoff, M. (1976) *Word Formation in Generative Grammar* M.I.T. Press

Austin, J. L. (1962) *How to do Things with Words* Clarendon Press

Baker, C. & Cokely, D. (1980) *American Sign Language* T. J. Publishers

Bauer, L. (1983) *English Word-Formation* Cambridge University Press

Baugh, A. C. & Cable, T. (1978) *A History of the English Language* (3rd edition) Prentice-Hall

Baugh, J. (1983) *Black Street Speech* University of Texas Press

Baxter, R. (1673) *A Christian Directory* Publisher unknown

Bayles, K. (1984) Language and the brain. Chapter 12 in Akmajian, Demers & Harnish

Bell, A. G. (1883) *Memoir upon the Formation of a Deaf Variety of the Human Race* (reprinted 1969) Alexander Graham Bell Association

Bellugi, U. (1970) Learning the language. *Psychology Today* 4: 32–5

Bever, T. G. & Rosenbaum, P. S. (1971) Some lexical structures and their empirical validity. In D. D. Steinberg & L. A. Jakobovits (eds.) *Semantics* Cambridge University Press

Bickerton, D. (1983a) *The Roots of Language* Karoma
  (1983b) Creole Languages. *Scientific American* 249: 116–23
Bloomfield, L. (1933) *Language* Holt, Rinehart & Winston
Bloomfield, M. (1895) On assimilation and adaptation in congeneric classes of
  words. *American Journal of Philology* 16: 409–34
Boas, F. (1911) *Handbook of American Indian Languages* Smithsonian
  Institution
Bobrow, D. G., Kaplan, R. M., Kay, M., Norman, D. A., Thompson, H.
  & Winograd, T. (1977) GUS, a frame-driven dialog system. *Artificial
  Intelligence* 8: 155–73
Boden, M. A. (1977) *Artificial Intelligence and Natural Man* Basic Books
Bolinger, D. (1975) *Aspects of Language* Harcourt, Brace, Jovanovich
Bolton, W. F. (1982) *A Living Language* Random House
Borden, G. J. & Harris, K. S. (1980) *Speech Science Primer* Williams & Wilkins
Braine, M. D. S. (1971) The acquisition of language in infant and child. In
  C. E. Reed (ed.) *The Learning of Language* Appleton-Century-Crofts
Brookshire, R. H. (1978) *An Introduction to Aphasia* BRK
Brown, E. K. & Miller, J. E. (1980) *Syntax: A Linguistic Introduction to
  Sentence Structure* Hutchinson
Brown, G. (1977) *Listening to Spoken English* Longman
Brown, G. & Yule, G. (1983a) *Discourse Analysis* Cambridge University Press
  (1983b) *Teaching the Spoken Language* Cambridge University Press
Brown, R. (1973) *A First Language: The Early Stages* Harvard University Press
Brown, R. & McNeill, D. (1966) The 'tip of the tongue' phenomenon. *Journal
  of Verbal Learning and Verbal Behavior* 5: 325–37
Buchanan, C. D. (1963) *A Programmed Introduction to Linguistics: Phonetics
  and Phonemics* Heath
Budge, W. (1913) *The Book of the Dead* (2 volumes) The Medici Society
Bynon, T. (1977) *Historical Linguistics* Cambridge University Press
Callary, R. E. (1981) Phonology. In V. P. Clark, P. A. Eschholz & A. F. Rosa
  (eds.) *Language: Introductory Readings* (3rd edition) St Martin's Press
Campbell, J. (1982) *Grammatical Man* Simon & Schuster
Campbell, R. & Wales, R. (1970) The study of language acquisition. In Lyons
  (ed.)
Caramazza, A. & Berndt, R. S. (1982) A psycholinguistic assessment of adult
  aphasia. In S. Rosenberg (ed.) *Handbook of Applied Psycholinguistics*
  Lawrence Erlbaum
Carroll, J. B. (ed.) (1956) *Language, Thought and Reality; Selected Writings
  of Benjamin Lee Whorf* M.I.T. Press
Cazden, C. (1972) *Child Language and Education* Holt
Celce-Murcia, M. & Larsen-Freeman, D. (1983) *The Grammar Book* Newbury
  House
Chambers, J. K. & Trudgill, P. (1980) *Dialectology* Cambridge University Press
Chomsky, N. (1957) *Syntactic Structures* Mouton
  (1965) *Aspects of the Theory of Syntax* M.I.T. Press
  (1972) *Language and Mind* Harcourt, Brace, Jovanovich
  (1983) An interview (by John Gliedman) *Omni* 6: 112–18

Chomsky, N. & Halle, M. (1968) *The Sound Pattern of English* Harper & Row

Clark, E. V. (1983) The young word-maker. In Wanner & Gleitman (eds.)

Clark, E. V. & Clark, H. H. (1979) When nouns surface as verbs. *Language* 55: 767–811

Clark, H. H. & Clark, E. V. (1977) *Psychology and Language* Harcourt, Brace, Jovanovich

Corder, S. P. (1973) *Introducing Applied Linguistics* Penguin Books (1981) *Error Analysis and Interlanguage* Oxford University Press

Coulthard, M. (1977) *An Introduction to Discourse Analysis* Longman

Culicover, P. W. (1976) *Syntax* Academic Press

Curtiss, S. (1977) *Genie. A Psycholinguistic Study of a Modern-day Wild Child* Academic Press

de Beaugrande, R. & Dressler, W. U. (1981) *Introduction to Text Linguistics* Longman

Denes, P. & Pinson, E. N. (1973) *The Speech Chain* Anchor Books

Descartes, R. (1637) *Discourse on Method* (trans. F. E. Sutcliffe) Penguin Books

de Villiers, P. & de Villiers, J. (1978) *Language Acquisition* Harvard University Press

Diamond, A. S. (1965) *The History and the Origin of Language* Citadel Press

Diringer, D. (1968) *The Alphabet* (2 volumes) (3rd edition) Hutchinson

Downes, W. (1984) *Language and Society* Fontana Paperbacks

Elliot, A. J. (1981) *Child Language* Cambridge University Press

Elyot, Sir T. (1531) *The Boke named the Governour* (facsimile edition, 1970) Scolar Press

Evans, W. E. & Bastain, J. (1969) Marine mammal communication: social and ecological factors. In H. T. Anderson (ed.) *The Biology of Marine Mammals* Academic Press

Ezard, J. (1975) Article in the *Guardian* newspaper, August 12, 1975, quoted in Trudgill (1983: 199)

Fant, L. (1977) *Sign Language* Joyce Media

Fay, D. & Cutler, A. (1977) Malapropisms and the structure of the mental lexicon. *Linguistic Inquiry* 8: 505–20

Ferguson, C. A. (1959) Diglossia. *Word* 15: 325–40

Finnegan, E. (1980) *Attitudes toward English Usage* Teachers College Press

Finnie, W. B. (1972) *The Stages of English* Houghton Mifflin

Fishman, J. A. (1971) *Sociolinguistics: A Brief Introduction* Newbury House

Flanagan, J. L. (1972) The synthesis of speech. *Scientific American* 226: 48–58

Freud, S. (1910) *Psychopathology of Everyday Life* (trans. A. A. Brill, 1958) New American Library

Friedman, L. A. (ed.) (1977) *On the Other Hand* Academic Press

Fromkin, V. (1973) Slips of the tongue. *Scientific American* 229: 110–17 (ed.) (1973) *Speech Errors as Linguistic Evidence* Mouton

Fromkin, V. & Rodman, R. (1983) *An Introduction to Language* (3rd edition) Holt, Rinehart & Winston

Fry, D. B. (1979) *The Physics of Speech* Cambridge University Press

Gardner, B. T. (1981) Project Nim: who taught whom? *Contemporary Psychology* 26: 425–6

Gardner, R. A. & Gardner, B. T. (1969) Teaching sign language to a chimpanzee. *Science* 165: 664–72

(1978) Comparative psychology and language acquisition. *Annals of the New York Academy of Sciences* 309: 37–76

Gelb, I. J. (1963) *A Study of Writing* University of Chicago Press

Geschwind, N. (1972) Language and the brain. *Scientific American* 226: 76–83

(1979) Specializations of the human brain. *Scientific American* 241: 180–99

Gleason, H. A. (1955) *Workbook in Descriptive Linguistics* Holt, Rinehart & Winston

(1961) *An Introduction to Descriptive Linguistics* Holt, Rinehart & Winston

Gordon, J. D. (1972) *The English Language: An Historical Introduction* Crowell

Greenberg, J. H. (1966) *Language Universals* Mouton

Gregory, M. & Carroll, S. (1978) *Language and Situation: Language Varieties and their Social Contexts* Routledge & Kegan Paul

Grice, H. P. (1975) Logic and conversation. In P. Cole & J. Morgan (eds.) *Syntax and Semantics 3: Speech Acts* Academic Press

Guiora, A. Z., Beit-Hallahmi, B., Brannon, R. C. L., Dull, C. Y. & Scovel, T. (1972) The effects of experimentally induced change in ego states on pronunciation ability in a second language: an exploratory study. *Comprehensive Psychiatry* 13: 5–23

Gumperz, J. J. (1982) *Discourse Strategies* Cambridge University Press

Hall, R. A. (1959) Pidgin languages. *Scientific American* 200: 124–34

Halliday, M. A. K. & Hasan, R. (1976) *Cohesion in English* Longman

Hatch, E. M. (ed.) (1978) *Second Language Acquisition* Newbury House

Haugen, E. (1972) *The Ecology of Language* Stanford University Press

Hayes, C. (1951) *The Ape in our House* Harper

Hendrix, G. G. & Sacerdoti, E. D. (1981) Natural-language processing. *Byte* 6: 304–52

Hinnebusch, T. J. (1979) Swahili. In T. Shopen (ed.) *Languages and their Status* Winthrop

Hockett, C. F. (1954) Two models of grammatical description. *Word* 10: 210–31

(1958) *A Course in Modern Linguistics* Macmillan

(1960) The origin of speech. *Scientific American* 203: 89–96

(1963) The problem of universals in language. In J. H. Greenberg (ed.) *Universals of Language* M.I.T. Press

Howatt, A. P. R. (1984) *A History of English Language Teaching* Oxford University Press

Huddleston, R. (1976) *An Introduction to English Transformational Syntax* Longman

(1984) *Introduction to the Grammar of English* Cambridge University Press

Hudson, R. A. (1980) *Sociolinguistics* Cambridge University Press

Hughes, A. & Trudgill, P. (1979) *English Accents and Dialects* Edward Arnold

Hughes, J. P. (1962) *The Science of Language* Random House

Hurford, J. R. & Heasley, B. (1983) *Semantics: A Coursebook* Cambridge University Press

Hyman, L. M. (1975) *Phonology: Theory and Analysis* Holt, Rinehart & Winston

Hymes, D. (1964) Toward ethnographies of communicative events. In P. P. Giglioli (ed.) *Language and Social Context* (1972) Penguin Books

(ed.) (1971) *Pidginisation and Creolisation of Languages* Cambridge University Press

Jensen, H. (1970) *Sign, Symbol and Script* Allen & Unwin

Jespersen, O. (1921) *Language; Its Nature, Development and Origin* Macmillan (1924) *The Philosophy of Grammar* Allen & Unwin

Johnson, S. (1747) *The Plan of a Dictionary of the English Language* (facsimile edition, 1970) Scolar Press

Kellogg, W. N. & Kellogg, L. A. (1933) *The Ape and the Child* McGraw-Hill

Kempson, R. (1977) *Semantic Theory* Cambridge University Press

Kimura, D. (1973) The asymmetry of the human brain. *Scientific American* 228: 70–8

Klima, E. S. & Bellugi, U. (1966) Syntactic regularities in the speech of children. In J. Lyons & R. J. Wales (eds.) *Psycholinguistic Papers* Edinburgh University Press

(1979) *The Signs of Language* Harvard University Press

Krashen, S. D. & Terrell, T. D. (1983) *The Natural Approach* Pergamon Press

Kurath, H. (1972) *Studies in Area Linguistics* Indiana University Press

Kurath, H., Hanley, M., Bloch, B. & Lowman, G. S. (1939–43) *Linguistic Atlas of New England* (3 volumes) Brown University Press

Labov, W. (1972) *Sociolinguistic Patterns* University of Pennsylvania Press

Ladd, D. R. (1982) Review article *Language* 58: 890–6

Ladefoged, P. (1982) *A Course in Phonetics* (2nd edition) Harcourt, Brace, Jovanovich

Lane, H. (1980) A chronology of the oppression of Sign Language in France and the United States. In Lane & Grosjean (eds.)

Lane, H. & Grosjean, F. (eds.) (1980) *Recent Perspectives on American Sign Language* Lawrence Erlbaum

Langacker, R. W. (1973) *Language and its Structure* (2nd edition) Harcourt, Brace, Jovanovich

Leech, G. N. (1974) *Semantics* Penguin Books

Lehmann, W. P. (1973) *Historical Linguistics: An Introduction* (2nd edition) Holt, Rinehart & Winston

(1983) *Language: An Introduction* Random House

Lehrer, A. (1969) Semantic cuisine. *Journal of Linguistics* 5: 39–55

Lenneberg, E. H. (1967) *Biological Foundations of Language* Wiley

Levinson, S. (1983) *Pragmatics* Cambridge University Press

Liddell, S. K. (1980) *American Sign Language Syntax* Mouton

Lieberman, P. (1975) *On the Origins of Language* Macmillan

Linden, E. (1976) *Apes, Men and Language* Penguin Books

Lyons, J. (1968) *Introduction to Theoretical Linguistics* Cambridge University Press

(ed.) (1970) *New Horizons in Linguistics* Penguin Books

(1977) *Semantics* (2 volumes) Cambridge University Press

(1978) *Noam Chomsky* (revised edition) Penguin Books/Viking Press

MacKay, D. G. (1970) Spoonerisms: the structure of errors in the serial order of speech. *Neuropsychologia* 8: 323–50

Mackey, W. F. (1965) *Language Teaching Analysis* Longman

Madsen, W. J. (1982) *Intermediate Conversational Sign Language* Gallaudet Press

Marchand, H. (1969) *The Categories and Types of Present-Day English Word-Formation* (2nd edition) Beck

Martinet, A. (1964) *Elements of General Linguistics* University of Chicago Press

Matthews, P. H. (1974) *Morphology* Cambridge University Press
  (1981) *Syntax* Cambridge University Press

McArthur, T. (1983) *A Foundation Course for Language Teachers* Cambridge University Press

McCorduck, P. (1979) *Machines Who Think* Freeman

McLaughlin, B. (1978) *Second-Language Acquisition in Childhood* Lawrence Erlbaum

McMillan, J. B. (1980) Infixing and interposing in English. *American Speech* 55: 163–83

McNeill, D. (1966) Developmental psycholinguistics. In Smith & Miller (eds.)

Merrifield, W. R., Naish, C. M., Rensch, C. R. & Story, G. (1962) *Laboratory Manual for Morphology and Syntax* Summer Institute of Linguistics

Miner, H. (1956) Body ritual among the Nacirema. *American Anthropologist* 58: 503–7

Minsky, M. L. (1968) *Semantic Information Processing* M.I.T. Press

Moore, T. & Carling, C. (1982) *Language Understanding* St Martin's Press

Moskowitz, B. A. (1978) The acquisition of language. *Scientific American* 239: 92–108

Myers, L. M. & Hoffman, R. L. (1979) *The Roots of Modern English* Little, Brown

Neisser, A. (1983) *The Other Side of Silence* Alfred Knopf

O'Connor, J. D. (1973) *Phonetics* Penguin Books

Oller, J. W. & Richards, J. C. (eds.) (1973) *Focus on the Learner* Newbury House

Paget, R. (1930) *Human Speech* Harcourt, Brace

Palmer, F. R. (1971) *Grammar* Penguin Books
  (1981) *Semantics* Cambridge University Press

Paulston, C. B. & Bruder, M. N. (1976) *Teaching English as a Second Language* Little, Brown

Pedersen, H. (1972) *The Discovery of Language* Indiana University Press

Penfield, W. & Roberts, L. (1959) *Speech and Brain Mechanisms* Princeton University Press

Peters, A. M. (1983) *The Units of Language Acquisition* Cambridge University Press

Pfungst, O. (1911) *Clever Hans, the Horse of Mr. Von Osten* Holt

Prator, C. H. & Robinett, B. W. (1985) *Manual of American English Pronunciation* (4th edition) Holt, Rinehart & Winston

Premack, A. J. & Premack, D. (1972) Teaching language to an ape. *Scientific American* 227: 92–9

Pride, J. B. & Holmes, J. (eds.) (1972) *Sociolinguistics* Penguin Books

Quirk, R. & Greenbaum, S. (1973) *A Concise Grammar of Contemporary English* Harcourt, Brace, Jovanovich

Quirk, R., Greenbaum, S., Leech, G. & Svartvik, J. (1972) *A Grammar of Contemporary English* Longman

Richards, J. C. (ed.) (1974) *Error Analysis* Longman
  (1978) *Understanding Second and Foreign Language Learning* Newbury House

Rivers, W. (1964) *The Psychologist and the Foreign-Language Teacher* University of Chicago Press

Roach, P. (1983) *English Phonetics and Phonology: A Practical Course* Cambridge University Press

Robertson, S. & Cassidy, F. G. (1954) *The Development of Modern English* Prentice-Hall

Robins, R. H. (1964) *General Linguistics* Longman

Ross, J. R. (1967) *Constraints on Variables in Syntax* Indiana University Linguistics Club

Ruhlen, M. (1976) *A Guide to the Languages of the World* Stanford University Language Universal Project

Rumbaugh, D. M. (1977) *Acquisition of Linguistic Skills by a Chimpanzee* Academic Press

Salus, P. H. (ed.) (1969) *On Language: Plato to von Humboldt* Holt, Rinehart & Winston

Sampson, G. (1980) *Schools of Linguistics* Hutchinson/Stanford University Press

Sanford, A. J. & Garrod, S. C. (1981) *Understanding Written Language* Wiley

Scarcella, R. C. & Krashen, S. D. (eds.) (1980) *Research in Second Language Acquisition* Newbury House

Schank, R. C. (1982) *Dynamic Memory* Cambridge University Press

Schank, R. C. & Colby, K. M. (eds.) (1973) *Computer Models of Thought and Language* Freeman

Scherer, K. R. & Giles, H. (eds.) (1979) *Social Markers in Speech* Cambridge University Press

Schmandt-Besserat, D. (1978) The earliest precursor of writing. *Scientific American* 238: 50–9

Sebeok, T. A. & Sebeok, J. U. (eds.) (1980) *Speaking of Apes: A Critical Anthology of Two-Way Communication with Man* Plenum Press

Sheridan, T. (1781) *A Rhetorical Grammar of the English Language* (facsimile edition, 1969) Scolar Press

Sinclair, J. McH. & Coulthard, R. M. (1975) *Towards an Analysis of Discourse* Oxford University Press

Smith, F. & Miller, G. A. (eds.) (1966) *The Genesis of Language* M.I.T. Press

Stein, G. (1973) *English Word-Formation over Two Centuries: A Bibliography* Tübinger Beiträge zur Linguistik

Stevick, E. W. (1982) *Teaching and Learning Languages* Cambridge University Press

Stockwell, R. P., Schachter, P. & Partee, B. H. (1973) *The Major Syntactic Structures of English* Holt, Rinehart & Winston

Stokoe, W. C. (1960) *Sign Language Structure* Studies in Linguistics: Occasional Papers 8, University of Buffalo Press

Stokoe, W. C., Casterline, D. & Croneberg, C. (1965) *A Dictionary of American Sign Language on Linguistic Principles* Gallaudet College Press

Stubbs, M. (1983) *Discourse Analysis* Basil Blackwell

Swisher, M. V. (1984) Signed input of hearing mothers to deaf children. *Language Learning* 34: 69–85

Tannen, D. (1984)) *Conversational Style* Ablex

Tarone, E. & Yule, G. (1985) Communication strategies in East–West interactions. In L. E. Smith (ed.) *Discourse across Cultures* Pergamon Press

Terrace, H. S. (1979) *Nim: A Chimpanzee Who Learned Sign Language* Alfred Knopf

Thieme, P. (1958) The Indo-European Language. *Scientific American* 199: 63–74

Trudgill, P. (1974) *Sociolinguistics: An Introduction* Penguin Books
    (1983) *On Dialect* New York University Press

Ullman, B. L. (1969) *Ancient Writing and its Influence* M.I.T. Press

Valdman, A. (ed.) (1977) *Pidgin and Creole Linguistics* Indiana University Press

von Frisch, K. (1962) Dialects in the language of the bees. *Scientific American* 207: 79–87
    (1967) *The Dance Language and Orientation of Bees* Belknap Press

Wakelin, M. F. (1972) *English Dialects: An Introduction* Athlone Press

Wanner, E. & Gleitman, L. R. (eds.) (1983) *Language Acquisition: The State of the Art* Cambridge University Press

Weir, R. H. (1966) Questions on the learning of phonology. Γ.ı Smith & Miller (eds.)

Weisenberg, T. & McBride, K. E. (1964) *Aphasia* Hafner

Weizenbaum, J. (1976) *Computer Power and Human Reason* Freeman

Widdowson, H. G. (1978) *Teaching Language as Communication* Oxford University Press
    (1983) *Learning Purpose and Language Use* Oxford University Press

Williams, J. M. (1975) *Origins of the English Language: A Social and Linguistic History* The Free Press

Williamson, J. V. & Burke, V. M. (eds.) (1971) *A Various Language: Perspectives on American Dialects* Holt, Rinehart & Winston

Winograd, T. (1972) *Understanding Natural Language* Academic Press
    (1984) Computer software for working with language. *Scientific American* 251: 130–45

Winston, P. H. (1977) *Artificial Intelligence* Addison-Wesley

Woodward, J. (1980) Some sociolinguistic aspects of French and American Sign Languages. In Lane & Grosjean (eds.)

Index

Technical terms and page references where definitions can be found are indicated by bold type.